Ordnance Survey

STREET ATLAS Merseyside

Contents

PHILIP'S

First edition published 1997 by

Ordnance Survey®
Romsey Road
Maybush
Southampton SO16 4GU

and

George Philip Ltd.
an imprint of Reed Books
Michelin House, 81 Fulham Road, London SW3 6RB
and Auckland, Melbourne, Singapore and Toronto

ISBN 0-540-06480-7 (hardback)
ISBN 0-540-06481-5 (wire-o)

Printed and bound in Spain by Cayfosa

The representation in this atlas of a road, track or path is no evidence of the existence of a right of way.

The mapping between pages 1 and 89 (inclusive) in this atlas is derived from Ordnance Survey® OSCAR® and Land-Line® data, and Landranger® mapping.

Key to map symbols

22a	**Motorway** (with junction number)
	Primary Routes (Dual carriageway and single)
	A Roads (Dual carriageway and single)
	B Roads (Dual carriageway and single)
	C Roads (Dual carriageway and single)
	Minor Roads
	Roads under construction
	County boundaries
	All Railways
	Miniature Railways
	Track or private road
	Gate or obstruction to traffic (restrictions may not apply at all times or to all vehicles)
	All paths, bridleways, BOATs, RUPPs etc.
	The representation in this atlas of a road, track or path is no evidence of the existence of a right of way
174	**Adjoining page indicator**

	British Rail station
	Private Railway station
	Bus, coach station
	Ambulance station
	Coastguard station
	Fire station
	Police station
	Casualty entrance to hospital
	Churches, Place of worship
H	**Hospital**
i	**Information Centre**
P	**Parking**
PO	**Post Office**
All Saints RC Jun Sch	**Important buildings, schools, colleges, universities and hospitals**
River Soar	**Water Name**
	Stream
	River or canal (minor and major)
	Water Fill
	Tidal Water
	Woods
	Houses

Acad	**Academy**	Mon	**Monument**
Cemy	**Cemetery**	Mus	**Museum**
C Ctr	**Civic Centre**	Obsy	**Observatory**
CH	**Club House**	Pal	**Royal Palace**
Coll	**College**	PH	**Public House**
Ex H	**Exhibition Hall**	Resr	**Reservoir**
Ind Est	**Industrial Estate**	Ret Pk	**Retail Park**
Inst	**Institute**	Sch	**School**
Ct	**Law Court**	Sh Ctr	**Shopping Centre**
L Ctr	**Leisure Centre**	Sta	**Station**
LC	**Level Crossing**	TH	**Town Hall/House**
Liby	**Library**	Trad Est	**Trading Estate**
Mkt	**Market**	Univ	**University**
Meml	**Memorial**	YH	**Youth Hostel**

0 — ¼ — ½ — ¾ — **1 mile**

0 — **250** m — **500** m — **750** m — **1 Kilometre**

The scale of the maps is 5.52 cm to 1 km ($3^1/_2$ inches to 1 mile)

The small numbers around the edges of the maps identify the 1 kilometre National Grid lines

Key to map pages

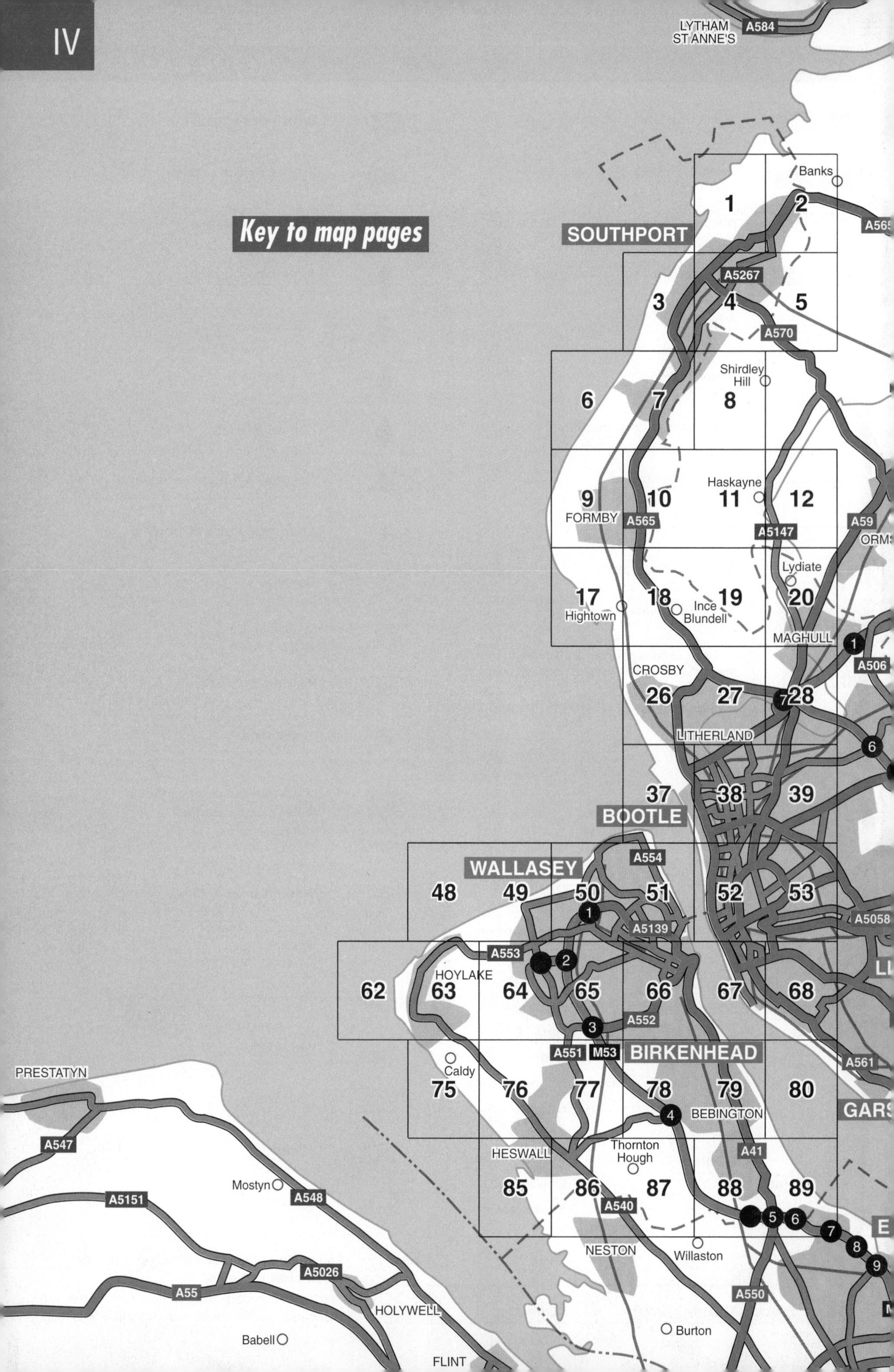

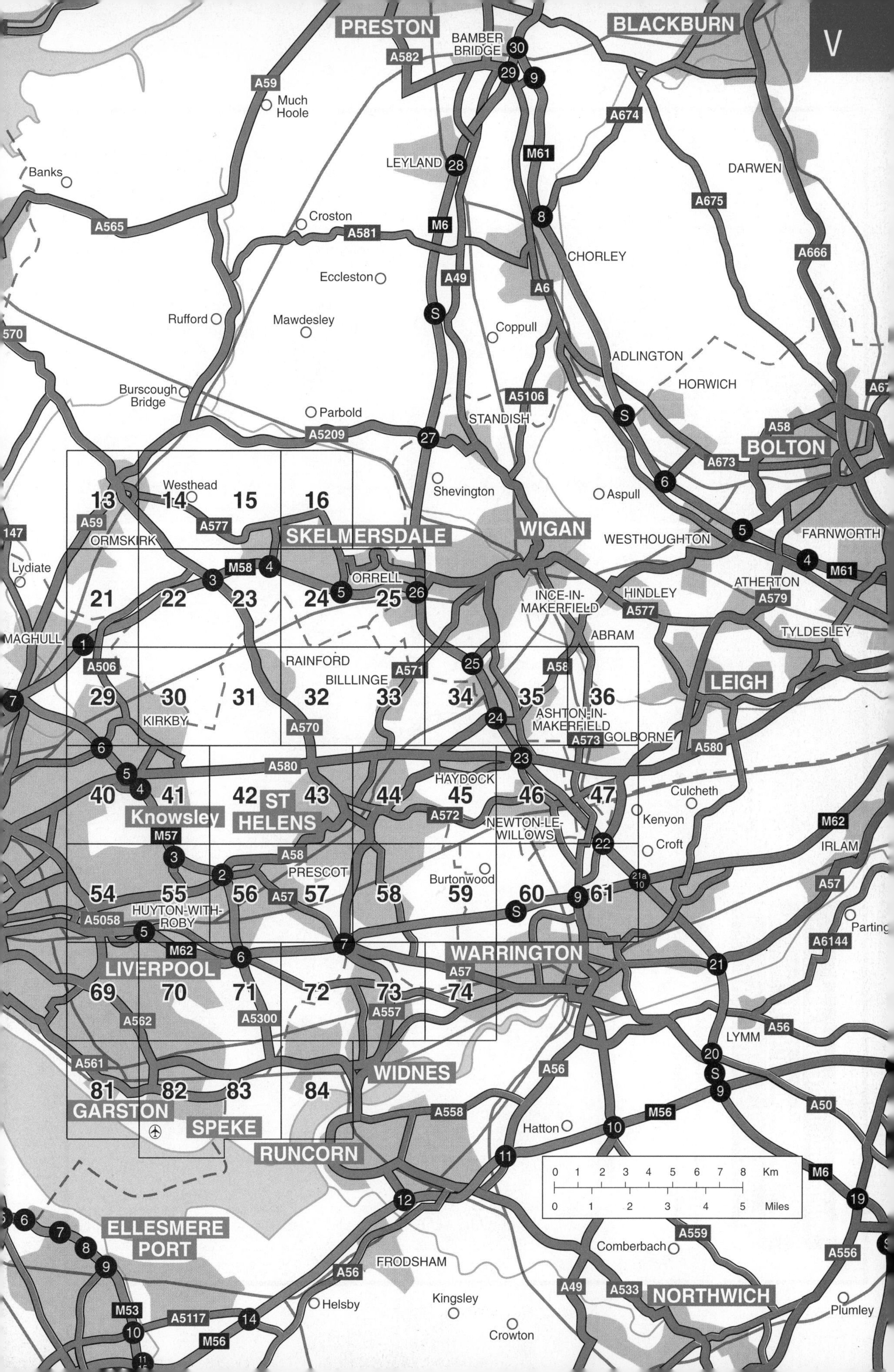
PRESTON
BAMBER BRIDGE
BLACKBURN
A582
A59
Much Hoole
A674
M61
LEYLAND
DARWEN
Banks
A675
A565
Croston
A581
M6
A666
CHORLEY
Eccleston
A49
A6
Rufford
Mawdesley
Coppull
570
ADLINGTON
HORWICH
Burscough Bridge
A5106
Parbold
STANDISH
A58
BOLTON
A5209
A673
Westhead
Shevington
Aspull
A59
A577
SKELMERSDALE
WIGAN
WESTHOUGHTON
FARNWORTH
ORMSKIRK
147
M58
Lydiate
ORRELL
M61
INCE-IN-MAKERFIELD
HINDLEY
ATHERTON
A577
A579
MAGHULL
ABRAM
TYLDESLEY
A506
RAINFORD
BILLLINGE
A571
LEIGH
KIRKBY
ASHTON-IN-MAKERFIELD
A570
A573
GOLBORNE
A580
A580
HAYDOCK
Culcheth
Kenyon
Knowsley
ST HELENS
A572
NEWTON-LE-WILLOWS
M57
M62
Croft
IRLAM
A58
PRESCOT
Burtonwood
A57
A57
HUYTON-WITH-ROBY
A5058
Partington
A6144
M62
WARRINGTON
LIVERPOOL
A57
A557
A5300
A562
A56
LYMM
A561
WIDNES
A56
GARSTON
SPEKE
A558
M56
A50
Hatton
RUNCORN
0 1 2 3 4 5 6 7 8 Km
0 1 2 3 4 5 Miles
M6
ELLESMERE PORT
A559
Comberbach
FRODSHAM
A556
A56
A49
A533
NORTHWICH
Helsby
Kingsley
Plumley
M53
A5117
M56
Crowton
13
14
15
16
21
22
23
24
25
29
30
31
32
33
34
35
36
40
41
42
43
44
45
46
47
54
55
56
57
58
59
60
61
69
70
71
72
73
74
81
82
83
84

Major administrative and post code boundaries of Merseyside

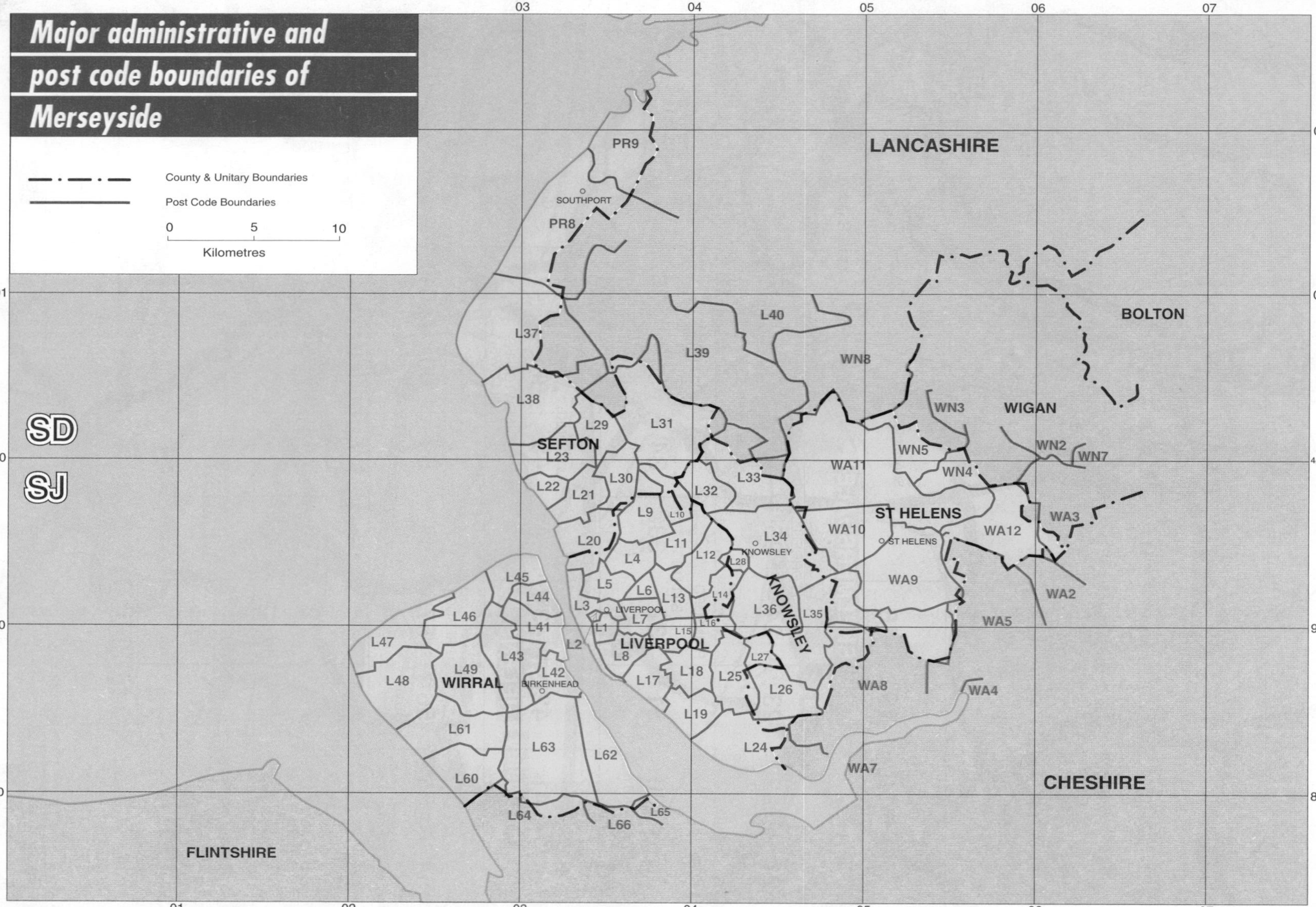

2

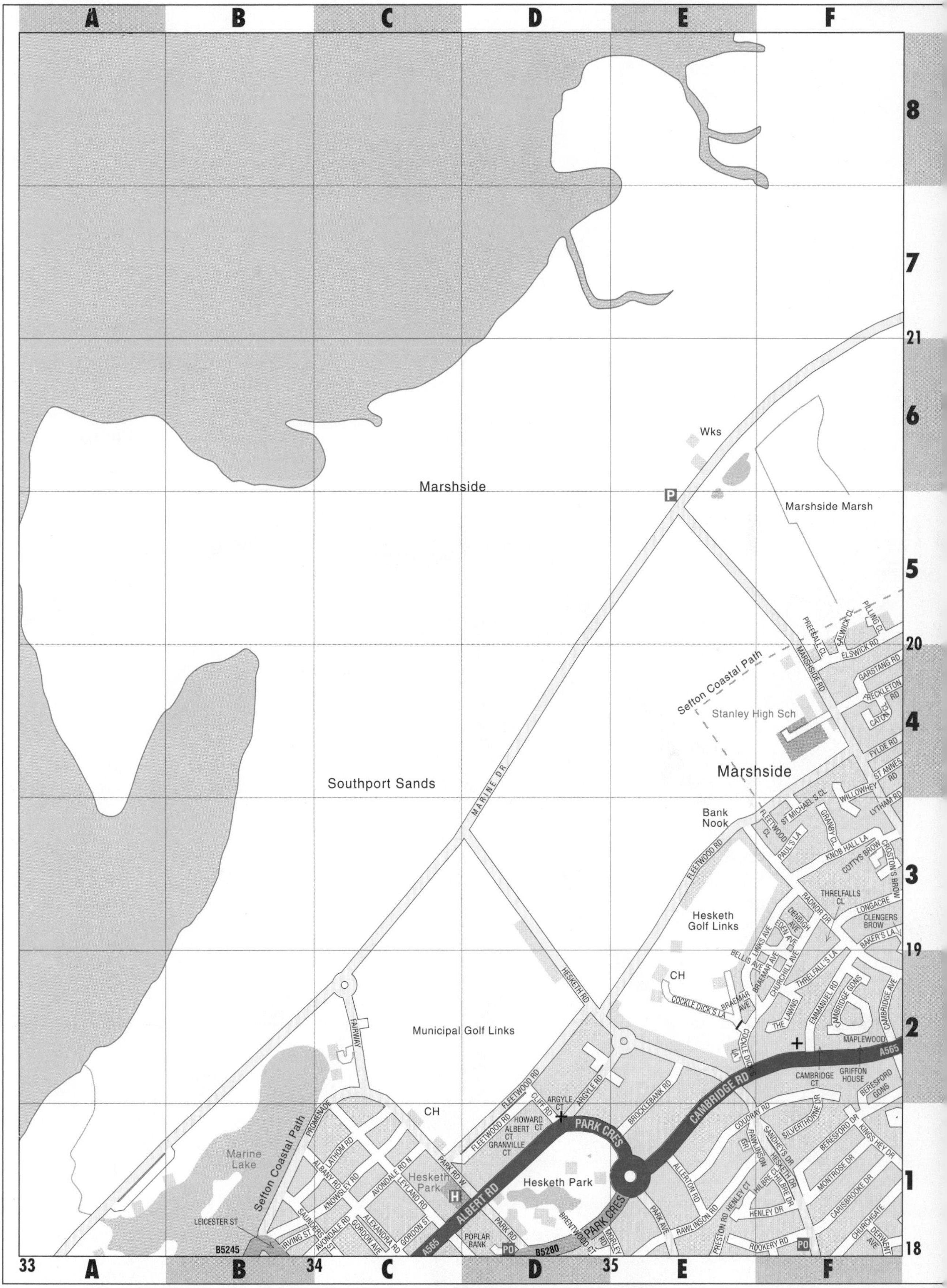
A
B
C
D
E
F
8
7
21
6
5
20
4
3
19
2
1
18
33
34
35
Marshside
Southport Sands
Marshside Marsh
Wks
MARINE DR
Sefton Coastal Path
Stanley High Sch
Marshside
Bank Nook
Hesketh Golf Links
CH
Municipal Golf Links
Hesketh Park
Marine Lake
MARSHSIDE RD
PREESALL CL
SALWICK CL
PILLING CL
ELSWICK RD
GARSTANG RD
RECKLETON RD
CATON CL
FYLDE RD
ST ANNES RD
LYTHAM RD
WILLOWHEY
FLEETWOOD CL
ST MICHAEL'S CL
GRANBY CL
PAUL'S LA
KNOB HALL LA
COTTYS BROW
CROSTON'S BROW
THRELFALLS CL
LONGACRE
CLENGERS BROW
BAKER'S LA
RADNOR DR
DENBIGH AVE
EDEN AVE
LINKS AVE
BELLIS AVE
BRAEMAR AVE
CHURCHILL AVE
THRELFALL'S LA
EMMANUEL RD
CAMBRIDGE GDNS
CAMBRIDGE AVE
MAPLEWOOD
THE LAWNS
COCKLE DICK'S LA
FLEETWOOD RD
HESKETH RD
FAIRWAY
CAMBRIDGE RD
A565
CAMBRIDGE CT
GRIFFON HOUSE
BERESFORD GDNS
SILVERTHORNE DR
COUDRAY RD
RAWLINSON GR
SANDHEYS DR
HESKETH DR
HILBRE DR
BERESFORD DR
KINGS HEY DR
MONTROSE DR
CARISBROOKE DR
CHURCHGATE
DERWENT AVE
HENLEY CT
HENLEY DR
ROOKERY RD
PO
PRESTON RD
RAWLINSON RD
ALLERTON RD
PARK AVE
BROCKLEBANK RD
ARGYLE RD
ARGYLE CT
CLIFF RD
HOWARD CT
ALBERT CT
GRANVILLE CT
PARK CRES
ALBERT RD
PARK RD W
PARK RD
POPLAR BANK
B5280
BRENTWOOD CT
MORLEY RD
PROMENADE
LATHOM RD
ALBANY RD
KNOWSLEY RD
AVONDALE RD N
LEYLAND RD
SAUNDERS ST
AVONDALE RD
GORDON AVE
ALEXANDRA RD
GORDON ST
IRVING ST
LEICESTER ST
B5245
H
P

4

2

1

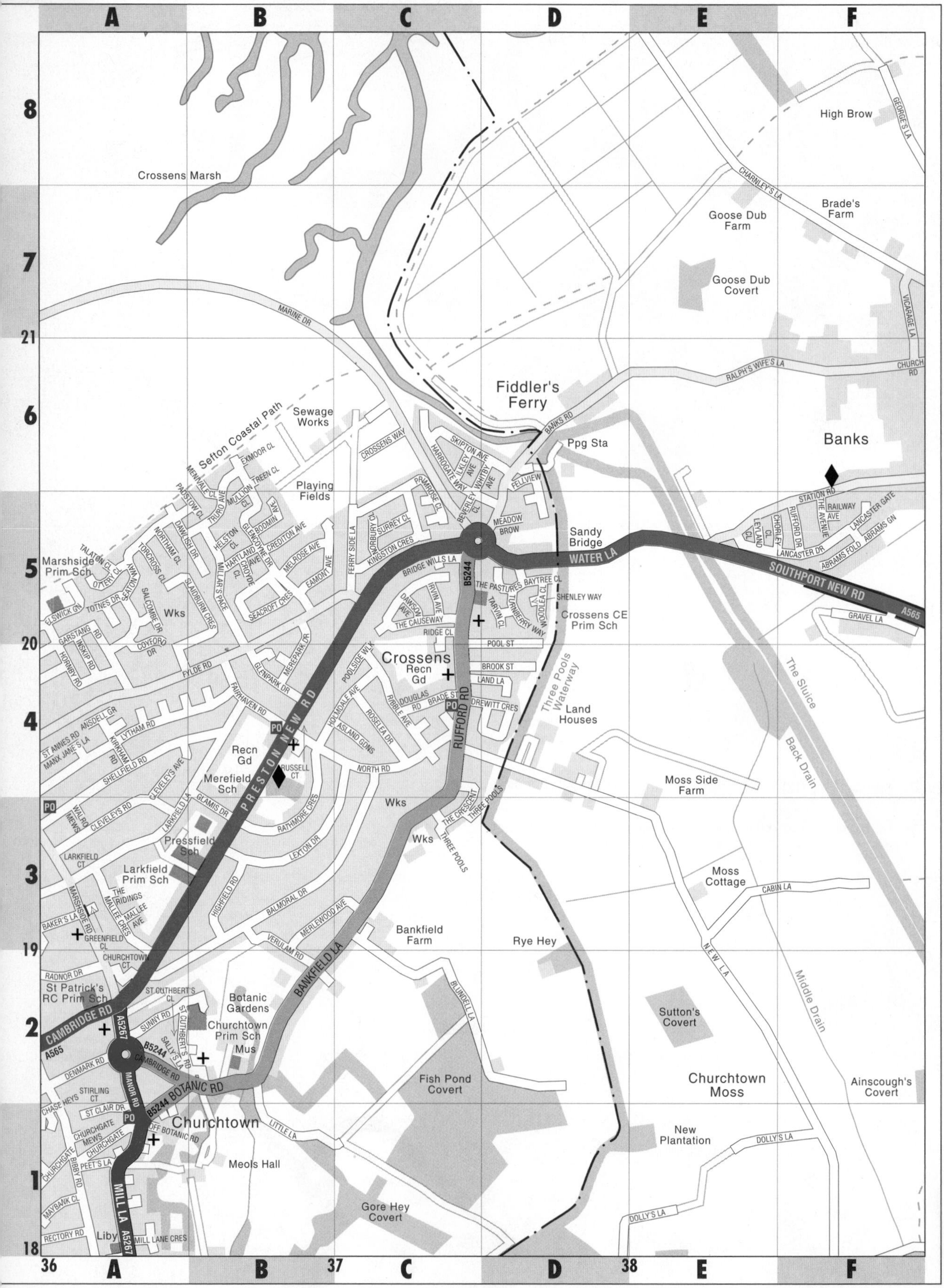

A
B
C
D
E
F
8
7
21
6
5
20
4
3
19
2
1
18
36
37
38
Crossens Marsh
High Brow
GEORGE'S LA
CHARNLEY'S LA
Goose Dub Farm
Brade's Farm
Goose Dub Covert
VICARAGE LA
MARINE DR
RALPH'S WIFE'S LA
CHURCH RD
Fiddler's Ferry
Banks
BANKS RD
Ppg Sta
Sefton Coastal Path
Sewage Works
CROSSENS WAY
SKIPTON AVE
HARROGATE WAY
ILKLEY AVE
WHITBY AVE
FELLVIEW
EXMOOR CL
TREEN CL
MENIVALE CL
PADSTOW CL
MULLION CL
TRURO AVE
BODMIN AVE
Playing Fields
PRIMROSE CL
BEVERLEY CL
STATION RD
THE AVENUE
RAILWAY AVE
LANCASTER GATE
ABRAMS GN
ABRAMS FOLD
LANCASTER DR
RUFFORD DR
CHORLEY CL
LEYLAND CL
MEADOW BROW
Sandy Bridge
WATER LA
SOUTHPORT NEW RD
A565
GRAVEL LA
FERRY SIDE LA
NORBURY CL
SURREY CL
KINGSTON CRES
NORTHAM CL
DAWLISH DR
HELSTON CL
GLENCOYNE DR
CREDITON AVE
HARTLAND CL
CROYDE CL
MELROSE AVE
EAMONT AVE
TALATON CL
Marshside Prim Sch
OTTERY CL
SEATON WAY
TORCROSS CL
SLAIDBURN CRES
MILLAR'S PACE
SEACROFT CRES
BRIDGE WILLS LA
B5244
THE PASTURES
BAYTREE CL
WOODLEA CL
SHENLEY WAY
TARVIN CL
TURNBERRY WAY
DAWSON AVE
IRVIN AVE
THE CAUSEWAY
Crossens CE Prim Sch
ELSWICK GN
TOTNES DR
SALCOMBE DR
Wks
GARSTANG RD
INSKIP RD
COYFORD DR
HORNBY RD
RIDGE CL
POOL ST
BROOK ST
LAND LA
DREWITT CRES
Crossens
Recn Gd
POOLSIDE WLK
FYLDE RD
GLENPARK DR
MEREPARK DR
FAIRHAVEN RD
HOLMDALE AVE
ROSELEA DR
RIBBLE AVE
DOUGLAS RD
BRADE ST
PO
RUFFORD RD
Three Pools Waterway
Land Houses
The Sluice
Back Drain
ST ANNES RD
ANSDELL GR
LYTHAM RD
MANX JANE'S LA
KIRKHAM RD
SHELLFIELD RD
ASLAND GDNS
NORTH RD
PRESTON NEW RD
Recn Gd
RUSSELL CT
Merefield Sch
CLEVELEYS AVE
Moss Side Farm
WALRO MEWS
CLEVELEYS RD
LARKFIELD LA
GLAMIS DR
RATHMORE CRES
THE CRESCENT
THREE POOLS
LARKFIELD CT
Pressfield Sch
LEXTON DR
Larkfield Prim Sch
MARSHSIDE RD
THE RIDINGS
MALLEE CRES
MALLEE AVE
HIGHFIELD RD
BALMORAL DR
MERLEWOOD AVE
Moss Cottage
CABIN LA
BAKER'S LA
GREENFIELD CL
Bankfield Farm
Rye Hey
VERULAM RD
CHURCHTOWN CT
NEW LA
RADNOR DR
BANKFIELD LA
Middle Drain
St Patrick's RC Prim Sch
ST CUTHBERT'S CL
Botanic Gardens
BLUNDELL LA
Sutton's Covert
CAMBRIDGE RD
A5267
SUNNY RD
ST CUTHBERT'S RD
Churchtown Prim Sch
SALLY'S LA
Mus
DENMARK RD
CAMBRIDGE RD
Fish Pond Covert
Churchtown Moss
Ainscough's Covert
MANOR RD
BOTANIC RD
CHASE HEYS
STIRLING CT
ST CLAIR DR
Churchtown
OFF BOTANIC RD
LITTLE LA
New Plantation
DOLLY'S LA
CHURCHGATE MEWS
CHURCHGATE
PEET'S LA
BIBBY RD
Meols Hall
MAYBANK CL
MILL LA
Gore Hey Covert
RECTORY RD
Liby
MILL LANE CRES

1

5

4

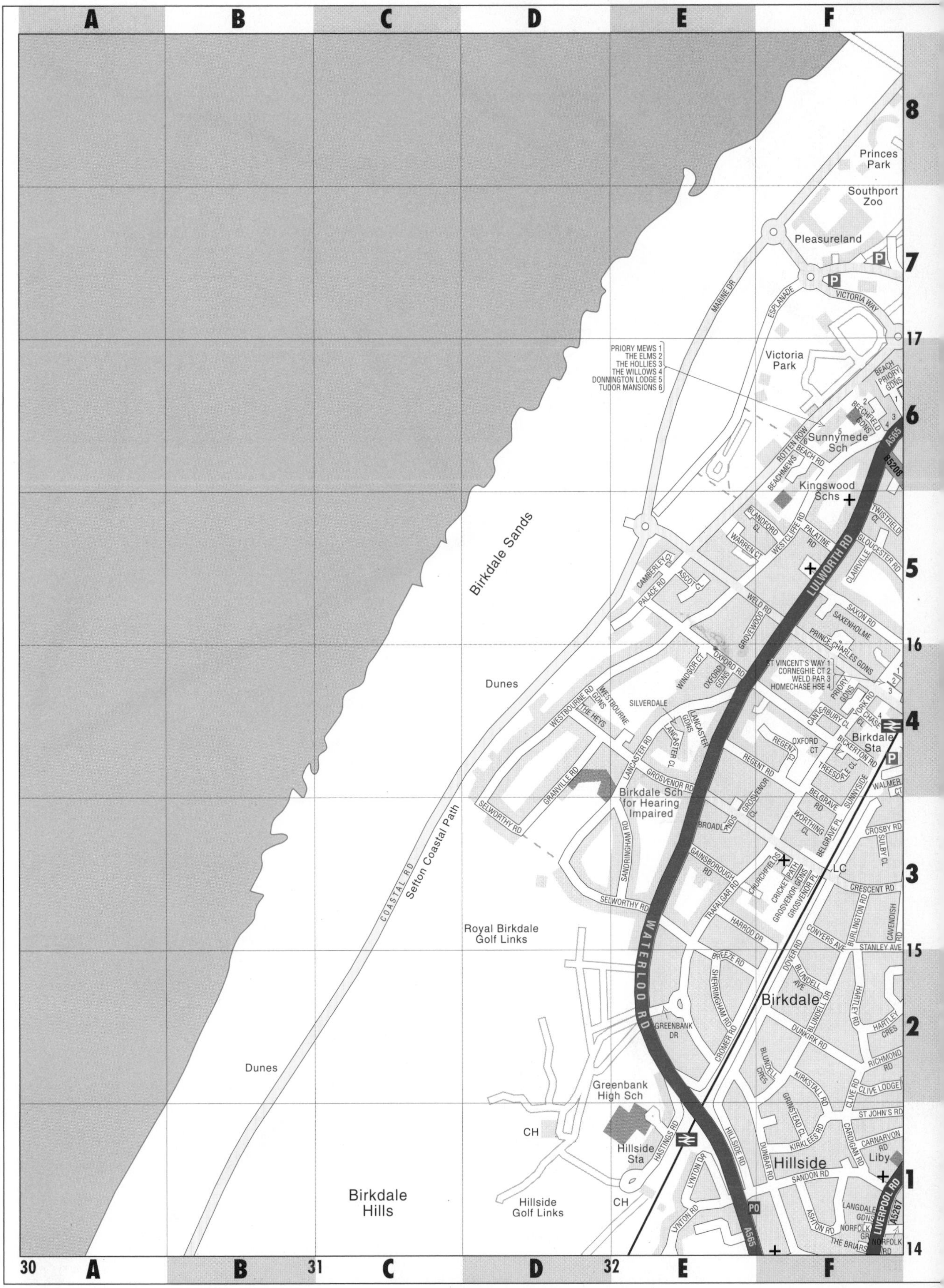
A
B
C
D
E
F
8
7
17
6
5
16
4
3
15
2
1
14
30
31
32
Princes Park
Southport Zoo
Pleasureland
P
VICTORIA WAY
ESPLANADE
MARINE DR
Victoria Park
PRIORY MEWS 1
THE ELMS 2
THE HOLLIES 3
THE WILLOWS 4
DONNINGTON LODGE 5
TUDOR MANSIONS 6
BEACH PRIORY GDNS
BEECHFIELD GDNS
Sunnymede Sch
ROTTEN ROW
BEACHMEWS
BEACH RD
A565
B5208
Kingswood Schs
BLANDFORD CL
WARREN CT
WESTCLIFFE RD
PALATINE RD
LULWORTH RD
TWISTFIELD CL
GLOUCESTER RD
CLAIRVILLE
CAMBERLEY CL
PALACE RD
ASCOT CL
WELD RD
GROVEWOOD
SAXON RD
SAXENHOLME
PRINCE CHARLES GDNS
Birkdale Sands
ST VINCENT'S WAY 1
CORNEGHIE CT 2
WELD PAR 3
HOMECHASE HSE 4
WINDSOR CT
OXFORD RD
OXFORD GDNS
PRIORY GDNS
YORK RD
CHASE
CANTERBURY CL
Birkdale Sta
SILVERDALE
WESTBOURNE RD
WESTBOURNE GDNS
THE HEYS
LANCASTER GDNS
LANCASTER CL
LANCASTER RD
REGENT CL
OXFORD CT
BICKERTON RD
REGENT RD
TREESDALE CL
SUNNYSIDE
WALMER CT
Dunes
GRANVILLE RD
GROSVENOR RD
Birkdale Sch for Hearing Impaired
SELWORTHY RD
SANDRINGHAM RD
BROADLANDS
GROSVENOR CL
BELGRAVE RD
WORTHING CL
BELGRAVE PL
CROSBY RD
SULBY CL
GAINSBOROUGH RD
CHURCHFIELDS
CRICKET PATH
GROSVENOR GDNS
GROSVENOR PL
LC
CRESCENT RD
COASTAL RD
Sefton Coastal Path
TRAFALGAR RD
HARROD DR
BURLINGTON RD
CAVENDISH
Royal Birkdale Golf Links
WATERLOO RD
CONYERS AVE
STANLEY AVE
BREEZE RD
DOVER RD
BLUNDELL AVE
SHERRINGHAM RD
Birkdale
BLUNDELL DR
HARTLEY RD
HARTLEY CRES
GREENBANK DR
CROMER RD
DUNKIRK RD
BLUNDELL CRES
RICHMOND RD
KIRKSTALL RD
CLIVE RD
CLIVE LODGE
Dunes
Greenbank High Sch
GRIMSTEAD CL
ST JOHN'S RD
KIRKLEES RD
CARDIGAN RD
CARNARVON RD
CH
HASTINGS RD
HILLSIDE RD
Hillside Sta
DUNBAR RD
Hillside
Liby
LYNTON DR
SANDON RD
LIVERPOOL RD
A5267
Birkdale Hills
Hillside Golf Links
CH
LYNTON RD
PO
ASHTON RD
LANGDALE GDNS
NORFOLK
THE BRIARS
NORFOLK RD

7
4

3
1

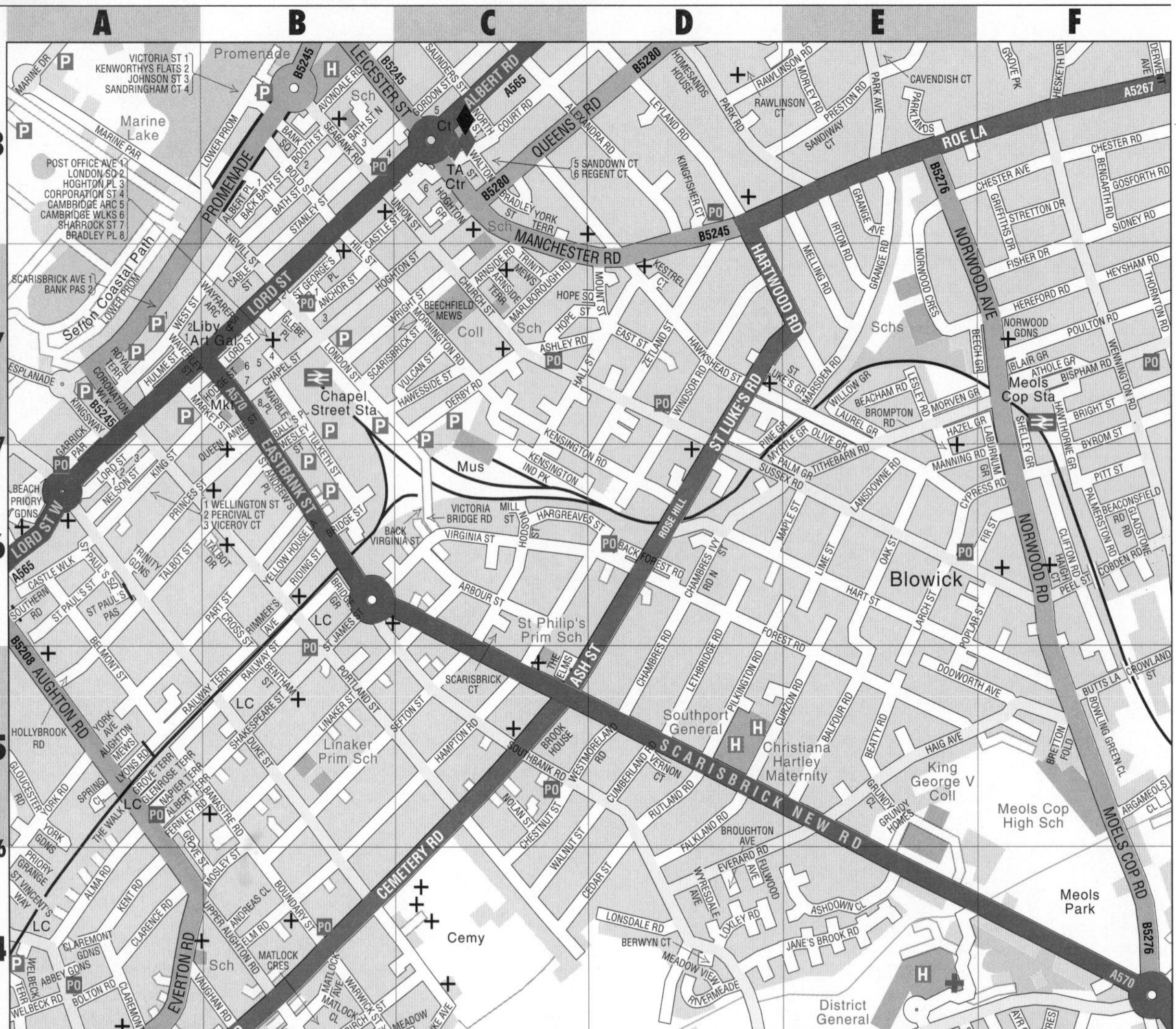
A
B
C
D
E
F
SOUTHPORT
Promenade
Marine Lake
Sefton Coastal Path
VICTORIA ST 1
KENWORTHYS FLATS 2
JOHNSON ST 3
SANDRINGHAM CT 4
POST OFFICE AVE 1
LONDON SQ 2
HOGHTON PL 3
CORPORATION ST 4
CAMBRIDGE ARC 5
CAMBRIDGE WLKS 6
SHARROCK ST 7
BRADLEY PL 8
SCARISBRICK AVE 1
BANK PAS 2
1 WELLINGTON ST
2 PERCIVAL CT
3 VICEROY CT
5 SANDOWN CT
6 REGENT CT
MARINE DR
MARINE PAR
LOWER PROM
PROMENADE
LORD ST
LORD ST W
EASTBANK ST
LEICESTER ST
ALBERT RD
QUEENS RD
MANCHESTER RD
ROE LA
HARTWOOD RD
ST LUKE'S RD
ROSE HILL
ASH ST
NORWOOD AVE
NORWOOD RD
SCARISBRICK NEW RD
MOELS COP RD
CEMETERY RD
EASTBOURNE RD
AUGHTON RD
LIVERPOOL RD
EVERTON RD
KEW RD
MOSS RD
BIRKDALE COP
A565
A570
A5267
B5245
B5280
B5276
B5208
B5243
Chapel Street Sta
Meols Cop Sta
Liby & Art Gal
Mkt
Mus
Coll
Schs
Blowick
St Philip's Prim Sch
Linaker Prim Sch
Southport General
Christiana Hartley Maternity
King George V Coll
Meols Cop High Sch
Meols Park
District General
Cemy
Birkdale Prim Sch
Christ The King Sch
Allot Gdns
Hollybrook Farm
Fine Jane's Farm
Fine Jane's Brook
Blowick Moss
Boundary Brook
Sandy Brook
Bedford Park
Moss Farm
Sch
Liby
33
34
35
14
15
16
17
1
2
3
4
5
6
7
8

3
8

2

A
B
C
D
E
F
ROE LA A5267
BAMBER GDNS
HIGH PARK PL
CHURCH CL
CHESTER RD
VERNON RD
SIDNEY RD
HEYSHAM RD
OLD PARK LA
High Park
HIGH PARK RD
WARREN RD
FARM CL
TARLETON RD
DEVONSHIRE RD
POULTON RD
Bishops David Sheppard CE Sch
LAWSON ST
BISPHAM RD
SCOTT ST
NEWTON ST
MILTON ST
TEDDER AVE
VICTORY AVE
WAVELL AVE
RUSSELL AVE
RUSSELL RD
MONTGOMERY AVE
WAVELL CL
SALISBURY ST
CANNING RD
ROSEBERY ST
COBDEN RD
ENTERPRISE WORKSHOPS
A.K.BSN PK
CROWLAND CL
CROWLAND ST
Wks
WENNINGTON RD
CH
OLD LINKS CL
FINE JANE'S WAY
FOSTERS CL
MOSS LA
PITTS HOUSE LA
Southport Old Links (Golf Course)
Recn Gd
Three Pools Waterway
Pool House Farm
Pitts House Covert
Brook Farm Bridge
DOLLY'S LA
STRAIGHT UP LA
Peet's Farm
Wyke Hey Farm
LONG MEANYGATE
Hooton's Cottages
Middle Drain
WYKE WOOD LA
Wyke House Farm
The Old Pool
WYKE LA
Big Wood
THE AVENUE
Twist's Covert
Hodge's Farm
FOUL LA
Wyke Thorn Farm
Heath Covert
PERCH POOL LA
THE MEOLS COP CTR
NEW FOUL LA
Sheepfold Farm
Sandy Brook
New House Farm
Pool Hey Crossing
Shaw's Farm
Scarisbrick Moss
SCARISBRICK NEW RD
POOL HEY LA
Pool Hey
Wyke Cop Crossing
Perch Pool Covert
Nursery
Drummersdale Drain
WOODMOSS LA
High Brows Covert
WYKE COP RD
Wyke Road Farm
Crem
Brown Edge
BROWN EDGE CL
SOUTHPORT RD
Black Brook
Sandy Brook
Sandy Brook Farm
HARES LA
TURNING LA
Boundary Farm
TINSLEY'S LA
Carr Cross
RIMMER GN
SNAPE GN
CAT TAIL LA
Snape Green
A570
8
7
17
6
5
16
4
3
15
2
1
14
36
37
38

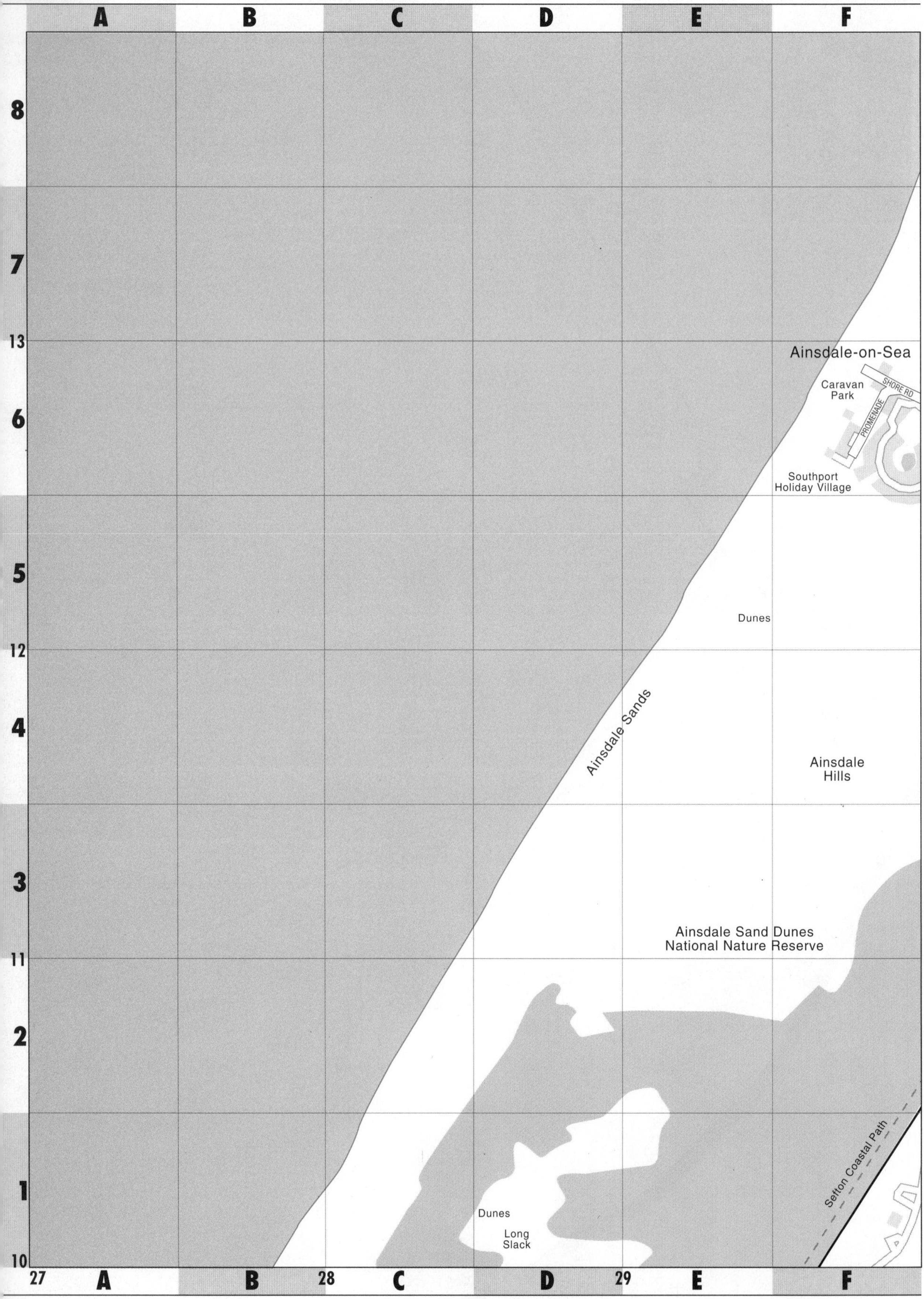
Ainsdale-on-Sea
Caravan Park
SHORE RD
PROMENADE
Southport Holiday Village
Dunes
Ainsdale Sands
Ainsdale Hills
Ainsdale Sand Dunes National Nature Reserve
Sefton Coastal Path
Dunes
Long Slack

9

3
8

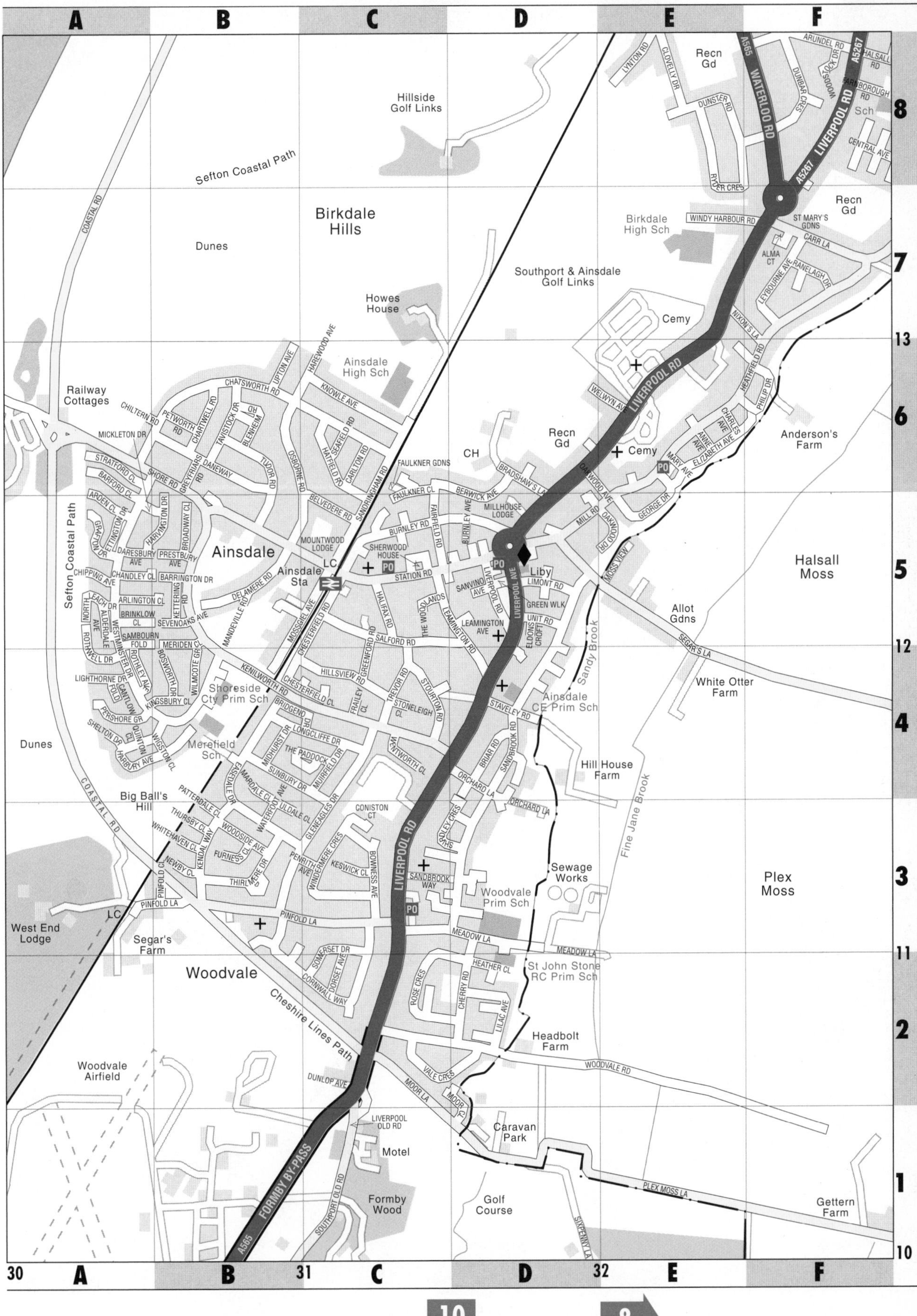
A
B
C
D
E
F
8
7
13
6
5
12
4
3
11
2
1
10
30
31
32
Recn Gd
Hillside Golf Links
Sefton Coastal Path
Birkdale Hills
Dunes
COASTAL RD
Birkdale High Sch
Southport & Ainsdale Golf Links
Howes House
Cemy
Ainsdale High Sch
Railway Cottages
CH
Recn Gd
Anderson's Farm
Ainsdale
Ainsdale Sta
LC
Liby
Halsall Moss
Allot Gdns
Sandy Brook
White Otter Farm
Shoreside Cty Prim Sch
Ainsdale CE Prim Sch
Merefield Sch
Hill House Farm
Big Ball's Hill
Fine Jane Brook
Sewage Works
Plex Moss
Woodvale Prim Sch
West End Lodge
Segar's Farm
Woodvale
St John Stone RC Prim Sch
Cheshire Lines Path
Headbolt Farm
Woodvale Airfield
Caravan Park
Motel
Formby Wood
Golf Course
Gettern Farm
A565
WATERLOO RD
A5267
LIVERPOOL RD
LIVERPOOL AVE
FORMBY BY-PASS
WINDY HARBOUR RD
CARR LA
SEGAR'S LA
WOODVALE RD
PLEX MOSS LA
MEADOW LA
PINFOLD LA
MOOR LA
STATION RD
KENILWORTH RD
SOUTHPORT OLD RD
LIVERPOOL OLD RD
DUNLOP AVE
SIXPENNY LA
PO

10
8

7
4

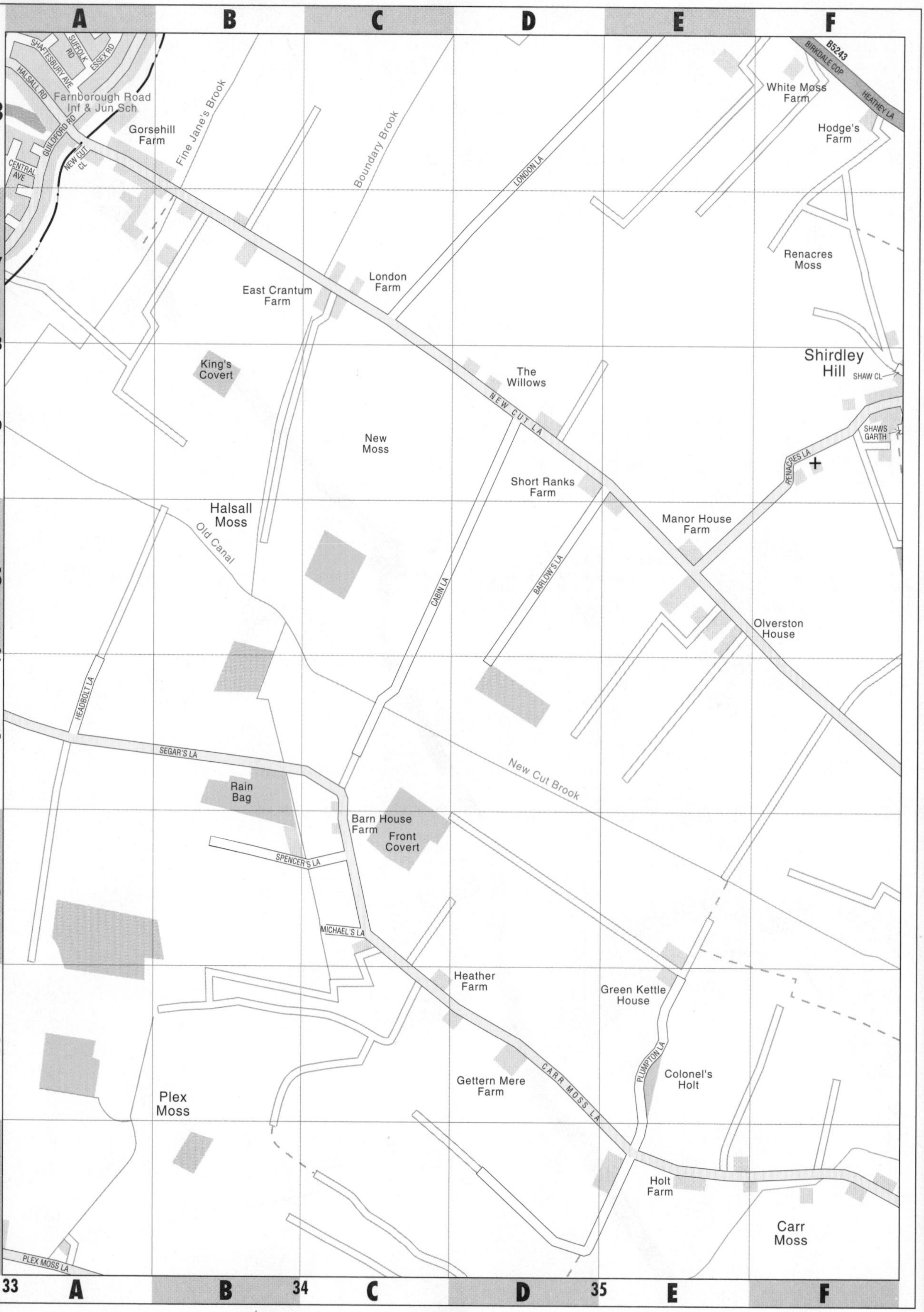
A
B
C
D
E
F
8
7
13
6
5
12
4
3
11
2
1
10
33
34
35
SHAFTESBURY AVE
SUFFOLK RD
ESSEX RD
HALSALL RD
Farnborough Road Inf & Jun Sch
GUILDFORD RD
NEW CUT CL
CENTRAL AVE
Gorsehill Farm
Fine Jane's Brook
Boundary Brook
LONDON LA
B5243
BIRKDALE COP
HEATHEY LA
White Moss Farm
Hodge's Farm
Renacres Moss
East Crantum Farm
London Farm
Shirdley Hill
SHAW CL
King's Covert
The Willows
NEW CUT LA
SHAWS GARTH
RENACRES LA
New Moss
Short Ranks Farm
Halsall Moss
Old Canal
Manor House Farm
BARLOW'S LA
CABIN LA
Olverston House
HEADBOLT LA
SEGAR'S LA
New Cut Brook
Rain Bag
Barn House Farm
Front Covert
SPENCER'S LA
MICHAEL'S LA
Heather Farm
Green Kettle House
PLUMPTON LA
CARR MOSS LA
Colonel's Holt
Gettern Mere Farm
Plex Moss
Holt Farm
Carr Moss
PLEX MOSS LA

7
11

6
10

A
B
C
D
E
F
8
7
09
6
5
08
4
3
07
2
1
06
27
28
29
Cloven-le-Dale
LC
Woodvale Airfield
Fisherman's Path
Formby Hills
Golf Links
Freshfield Caravan Pk
Picnic Area
CH
Clarence House Sch
LITTLE BREWERY LA
BREWERY LA
OLD LA
PARADISE LA
KENTON CL
ST ANNE'S CL
ST ANNE'S RD
ST ANNE'S PATH
YORK CL
WEST LA
STANLEY RD
FISHERMANS CL
ARGARMEOLS RD
RIMMER'S AVE
MASSAM'S LA
CANTERBURY CL
WRIGLEYS CL
WRIGLEYS LA
STANLAWE RD
MERSEY AVE
GREGSON'S AVE
CUMMINS AVE
QUEENS AVE
RED BARNES
MAYFIELD CT
ARGARMEOLS GR
THE BIRCHES
MONTAGU RD
GOLF RD
VICTORIA WAY
SHIREBURN RD
FAIRWAYS CT
BADGERS RAKE
TOWER END
VICTORIA RD
Freshfield Sta
LOWSWOOD
TIMMS LA
TIMMS CL
CRICKET PATH
GREEN LA
GRANGE LA
Freshfield
GORES LA
DEANS CT
BORROWDALE
COLLEGE PATH
HAZELBANK GDNS
DERBY RD
PIERCEFIELD RD
FIRS CRES
FIRS CL
SQUIRREL GN
BIRCH GN
LENTON AVE
VICARAGE CL
FRESHFIELD CT
OLD TOWN LA
BRECON CT
RYMERS GN
MANOR LODGE
BYRON CL
GRABURN RD
WILLOW GR
Sefton Coastal Path
GORSE WAY
PROCTOR RD
ST PETER'S AVE
FIRS LINK
LARCH WAY
OAKFIELD DR
COLLEGE CL
HOLMWOOD DR
VICARAGE RD
VAUGHAN CL
ST GEORGE'S RD
OLD MILL LA
FORMBY GDNS
Sandfield Farm
DUNES DR
HARINGTON RD
ST PETER'S CL
Formby High Sch
COLLEGE AVE
BARKFIELD LA
ALDERSON CRES
BLUNDELL AVE
LARKHILL LA
WICKS CRES
WICKS GREEN CL
WELD DR
BEECH DR
HOLWOOD DR
HOLWOOD GDNS
BARKFIELD AVE
FRESHFIELD RD
LONG LA
DAVENHAM RD
WICKS GN
WARREN GN
INCE CRES
LONSDALE RD
HALSALL LA
CLIFDEN CT
COPPICE LEYS
FORMBY
HOLMWOOD CL
Holy Trinity CE Prim Sch
THE PAGE CT
THE GALLERY
FURNESS AVE
SCHOOL AVE
SCHOOL LA
HARINGTON GN
HARINGTON CL
WICKS LA
ROSEMARY LA
THE CLOISTERS
WICKS GDNS
BUTTERMERE CL
ENNERDALE CL
GRISEDALE CL
LENTON CL
HEYWOOD CL
ORMS WAY
MICHAELS CL
CHAPEL LA
SUMNER RD
THREE TUNS LA
St Jerome's RC Prim Sch
DELPH LA
GREENLOON'S DR
Woodlands Prim Sch
WOODLANDS RD
TARN RD
ENNERDALE RD
GRANTON CL
BROWS LA
ELBOW LA
CROPTON RD
SPRUCE WAY
FOXHILL CL
GRASMERE RD
RYDAL AVE
GREENLOON'S WALK
DENHURST DR
HAZLEHURST CL
EDENHURST CL
KIRKLAKE BANK
ASHDALE
SPRINGFIELD CL
DERWENT AVE
WOODLANDS CL
ESKDALE CL
ESKDALE DR
LANGDALE AVE
MARSH BROWS
BROWS CL
DUKES WAY
ASHURST CT
DUKE ST
PHILLIPS CL
MEADOW CROFT
ELMDALE CL
CONISTON RD
MERE RD
LANGDALE CL
KIRKLAKE RD
FORMBY BRIDGE
Formby Sta
Liby
CHURCH GN
CHURCH WAY
ST LUKE'S DR
BUSHBY'S PK
BROOKS WAY
BROOKS RD
WARD AVE
CHINDIT CL
QUEENS CROFT
SEFTON RD
FORMBY ST
KINGS CL
KINGS RD
MEOLS CL
RAVENSCROFT
WALKER CL
GLENDALE WAY
PHILLIP'S LA
TYRERS CL
DICKINSON RD
DICKINSON CL
NORBURN CRES
BIRKEY LA
BUSHBY'S LA
QUEEN'S RD
TRAP HILL
Eccles Crossing
RAVEN MEOLS LA
NURSERY DR
HAREBELL CL
LIFEBOAT RD
Shorrocks Hill
LIME TREE WAY
PINEWOOD CL
SEALAND CL
SEALAND AVE
FOSTER RD
ANDREWS YORT
ANDREWS CL
BUCKINGHAM GR
KENSINGTON RD
SANDRINGHAM RD
WINDSOR RD
PARK AVE
PARK WAY
CASTLE DR
Bill's La
ASHCROFT RD
KENT RD
ST LUKE'S CHURCH RD
MAPLE CL
ELM DR
PINEWOOD AVE
St Luke's Sch
JUBILEE RD
ELSON RD
GEORGIAN PL
ROSTRON CRES
HAMPTON RD
BALMORAL DR
EDINBURGH RD
LANCASTER RD
MARINA RD
Formby Point Caravan Pk
BEECHWOOD DR
ASH GR
CEDAR DR
SYCAMORE GR
CHESTNUT WAY
ASPEN GR
MILFORD CL
CAMBRIDGE RD
FUNCHAL AVE
CARR'S CRES W
CARR'S CRES
CRESCENT AVE
ECCLES RD
OSBORNE RD
HOGGS HILL LA
ALTCAR LA
MAYFIELD AVE
HEYDON CL
HADSTOCK AVE
STAPLETON RD
BURWELL AVE
BARTON HEYS RD
SUTTON RD
KEW RD
PARK RD
BELVEDERE DR
Sewage Works
ALEXANDRA RD
ELSWORTH CL
SANDHURST CL
TADLOW CL
MELDRETH CL
ORWELL CL
STAPLETON CL

17
10

9
7

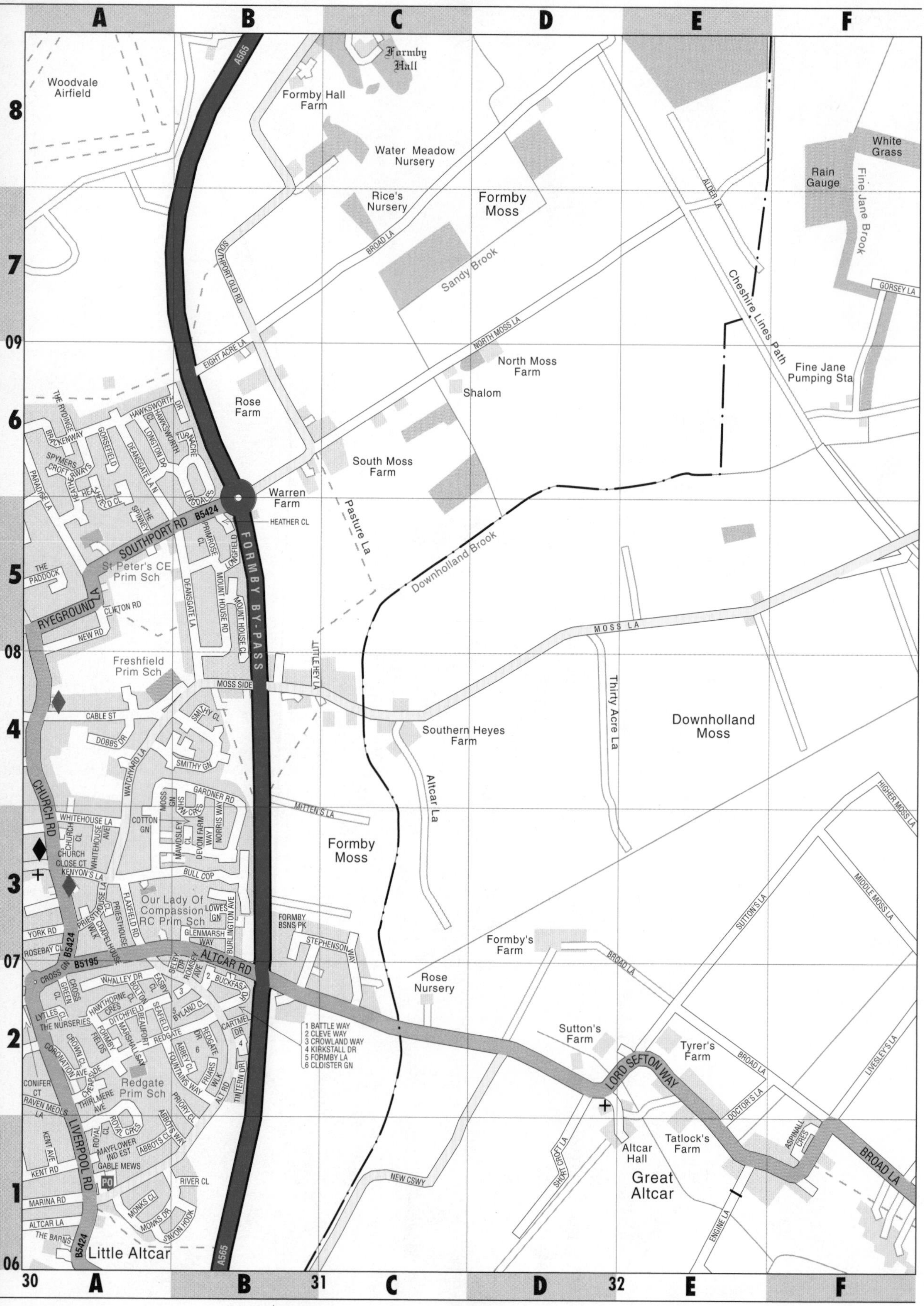
A
B
C
D
E
F
8
7
09
6
5
08
4
3
07
2
1
06
30
31
32
Woodvale Airfield
Formby Hall
Formby Hall Farm
Water Meadow Nursery
Rice's Nursery
Formby Moss
BROAD LA
Sandy Brook
SOUTHPORT OLD RD
White Grass
Rain Gauge
Fine Jane Brook
ALDER LA
Cheshire Lines Path
GORSEY LA
NORTH MOSS LA
EIGHT ACRE LA
North Moss Farm
Shalom
Fine Jane Pumping Sta
Rose Farm
South Moss Farm
Warren Farm
HEATHER CL
Pasture La
Downholland Brook
FORMBY BY-PASS
A565
B5424
SOUTHPORT RD
St Peter's CE Prim Sch
RYEGROUND LA
CLIFTON RD
NEW RD
THE PADDOCK
PARADISE LA
THE RYDINGS
BRACKENWAY
SPYMERS CROFT
HEATHERWAYS
GORSEFIELD
DEANSGATE LA N
HAWKSWORTH DR
LONGTON DR
TURNACRE
LINGDALES
THE SPINNEY
PRIMROSE CL
LONGFIELD
MOUNT HOUSE RD
MOUNT HOUSE CL
DEANSGATE LA
Freshfield Prim Sch
MOSS SIDE
LITTLE HEY LA
MOSS LA
Thirty Acre La
Downholland Moss
CABLE ST
DOBBS DR
SMITHY CL
SMITHY GN
WATCHYARD LA
Southern Heyes Farm
Altcar La
MITTEN'S LA
GARDNER RD
NORRIS WAY
DEVON FARM WAY
MAWDSLEY CL
COTTON GN
CHURCH RD
WHITEHOUSE LA
WHITEHOUSE AVE
CHURCH CL
CHURCH CLOSE CT
KENYON'S LA
BULL COP
Formby Moss
HIGHER MOSS LA
MIDDLE MOSS LA
SUTTON'S LA
Our Lady Of Compassion RC Prim Sch
LOWES GN
GLENMARSH WAY
BURLINGTON AVE
FORMBY BSNS PK
STEPHENSON WAY
PRIESTHOUSE LA
PRIESTHOUSE CL
FLAXFIELD RD
CHAPELHOUSE WALK
YORK RD
ROSEBAY CL
CROSS GN
B5195
ALTCAR RD
Formby's Farm
BROAD LA
Rose Nursery
WHALLEY DR
BOLTON RD
EASBY CL
SELBY DR
ROMSEY AVE
BUCKFAST DR
CARTMEL DR
HAWTHORNE CRES
DITCHFIELD
BEAUFORT
SEAFIELD
BYLAND CL
REDGATE
ABBEY CL
LYTLES CL
THE NURSERIES
CROSS GREEN CL
CROWN CL
FORMBY FIELDS
MARSHALLS CL
1 BATTLE WAY
2 CLEVE WAY
3 CROWLAND WAY
4 KIRKSTALL DR
5 FORMBY LA
6 CLOISTER GN
Sutton's Farm
Tyrer's Farm
LORD SEFTON WAY
BROAD LA
LIVESLEY'S LA
DOCTOR'S LA
CORONATION AVE
FOUNTAINS WAY
FRIARS WLK
ALT RD
TINTERN DR
PRIORY CL
Redgate Prim Sch
THIRLMERE AVE
CONIFER CT
RAVEN MEOLS LA
KENT AVE
LIVERPOOL RD
ROYAL CL
ROYAL CRES
MAYFLOWER IND EST
ABBOTS CL
ABBOTS WAY
GABLE MEWS
KENT RD
PO
RIVER CL
MARINA RD
MONKS CL
MONKS DR
SAXON HOOK
ALTCAR LA
THE BARNS
Little Altcar
NEW CSWY
SHORT CROFT LA
Altcar Hall
Great Altcar
Tatlock's Farm
ASPINALL CRES
ENGINE LA

9
18

8
12

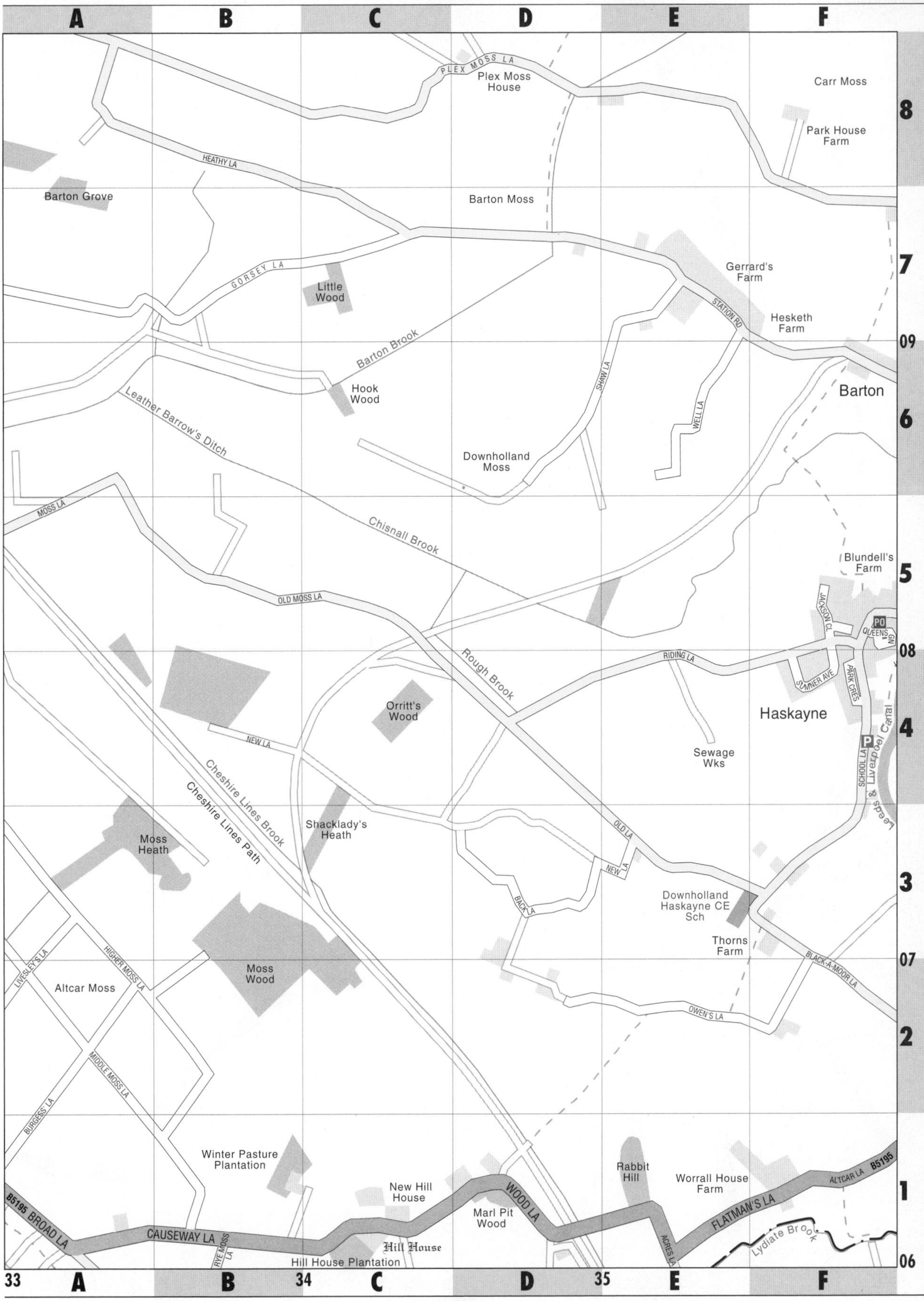
A
B
C
D
E
F
8
7
09
6
5
08
4
3
07
2
1
06
33
34
35
PLEX MOSS LA
Plex Moss House
Carr Moss
Park House Farm
HEATHY LA
Barton Grove
Barton Moss
GORSEY LA
Little Wood
Gerrard's Farm
STATION RD
Hesketh Farm
Barton Brook
Hook Wood
SHAW LA
WELL LA
Barton
Leather Barrow's Ditch
Downholland Moss
MOSS LA
Chisnall Brook
Blundell's Farm
OLD MOSS LA
JACKSON CL
PO
QUEENS
GN
RIDING LA
SUMNER AVE
PARK CRES
Rough Brook
Orritt's Wood
Haskayne
Leeds & Liverpool Canal
P
NEW LA
SCHOOL LA
Sewage Wks
Cheshire Lines Brook
Cheshire Lines Path
Shacklady's Heath
Moss Heath
OLD LA
NEW LA
BACK LA
Downholland Haskayne CE Sch
Thorns Farm
BLACK-A-MOOR LA
LIVESLEY'S LA
HIGHER MOSS LA
Altcar Moss
Moss Wood
OWEN'S LA
MIDDLE MOSS LA
BURGESS' LA
Winter Pasture Plantation
Rabbit Hill
Worrall House Farm
B5195
ALTCAR LA
New Hill House
WOOD LA
FLATMAN'S LA
B5195 BROAD LA
CAUSEWAY LA
RYE MOSS LA
Marl Pit Wood
ACRES LA
Lydiate Brook
Hill House
Hill House Plantation

19
12

11

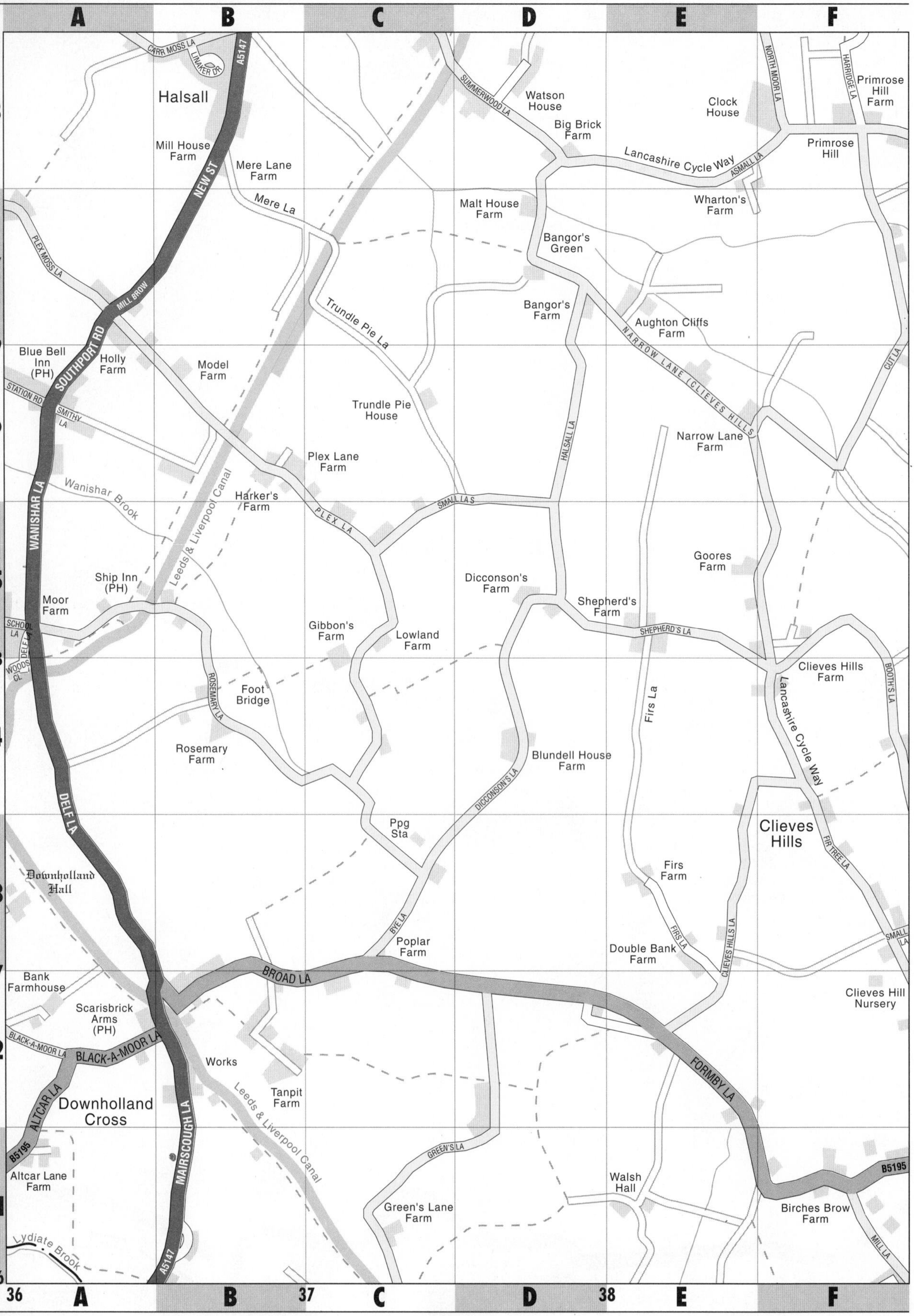
A
B
C
D
E
F
8
7
09
6
5
08
4
3
07
2
1
06
36
37
38
Halsall
CARR MOSS LA
LINAKER DR
A5147
NEW ST
Mill House Farm
Mere Lane Farm
Mere La
SUMMERWOOD LA
Watson House
Big Brick Farm
Lancashire Cycle Way
ASMALL LA
NORTH MOOR LA
Clock House
HARRIDGE LA
Primrose Hill Farm
Primrose Hill
Wharton's Farm
Malt House Farm
Bangor's Green
PLEX MOSS LA
MILL BROW
SOUTHPORT RD
Trundle Pie La
Bangor's Farm
Aughton Cliffs Farm
NARROW LANE (CLIEVES HILLS)
CUT LA
Blue Bell Inn (PH)
Holly Farm
Model Farm
STATION RD
SMITHY LA
Trundle Pie House
HALSALL LA
Narrow Lane Farm
Plex Lane Farm
Wanishar Brook
WANISHAR LA
Harker's Farm
PLEX LA
SMALL LA S
Leeds & Liverpool Canal
Goores Farm
Dicconson's Farm
Ship Inn (PH)
Moor Farm
Shepherd's Farm
SCHOOL LA
DELF LA
WOODS CL
Gibbon's Farm
Lowland Farm
SHEPHERD'S LA
Clieves Hills Farm
BOOTH'S LA
Foot Bridge
ROSEMARY LA
Firs La
Lancashire Cycle Way
Rosemary Farm
Blundell House Farm
DELF LA
DICCONSON'S LA
Ppg Sta
Clieves Hills
FIR TREE LA
Downholland Hall
Firs Farm
BYE LA
Poplar Farm
Double Bank Farm
FIRS LA
CLIEVES HILLS LA
SMALL LA
Bank Farmhouse
BROAD LA
Clieves Hill Nursery
Scarisbrick Arms (PH)
BLACK-A-MOOR LA
BLACK-A-MOOR LA
Works
FORMBY LA
ALTCAR LA
Downholland Cross
Tanpit Farm
Leeds & Liverpool Canal
MAIRSCOUGH LA
B5195
GREEN'S LA
Altcar Lane Farm
Walsh Hall
B5195
Birches Brow Farm
Green's Lane Farm
MILL LA
Lydiate Brook
A5147

11

20

14

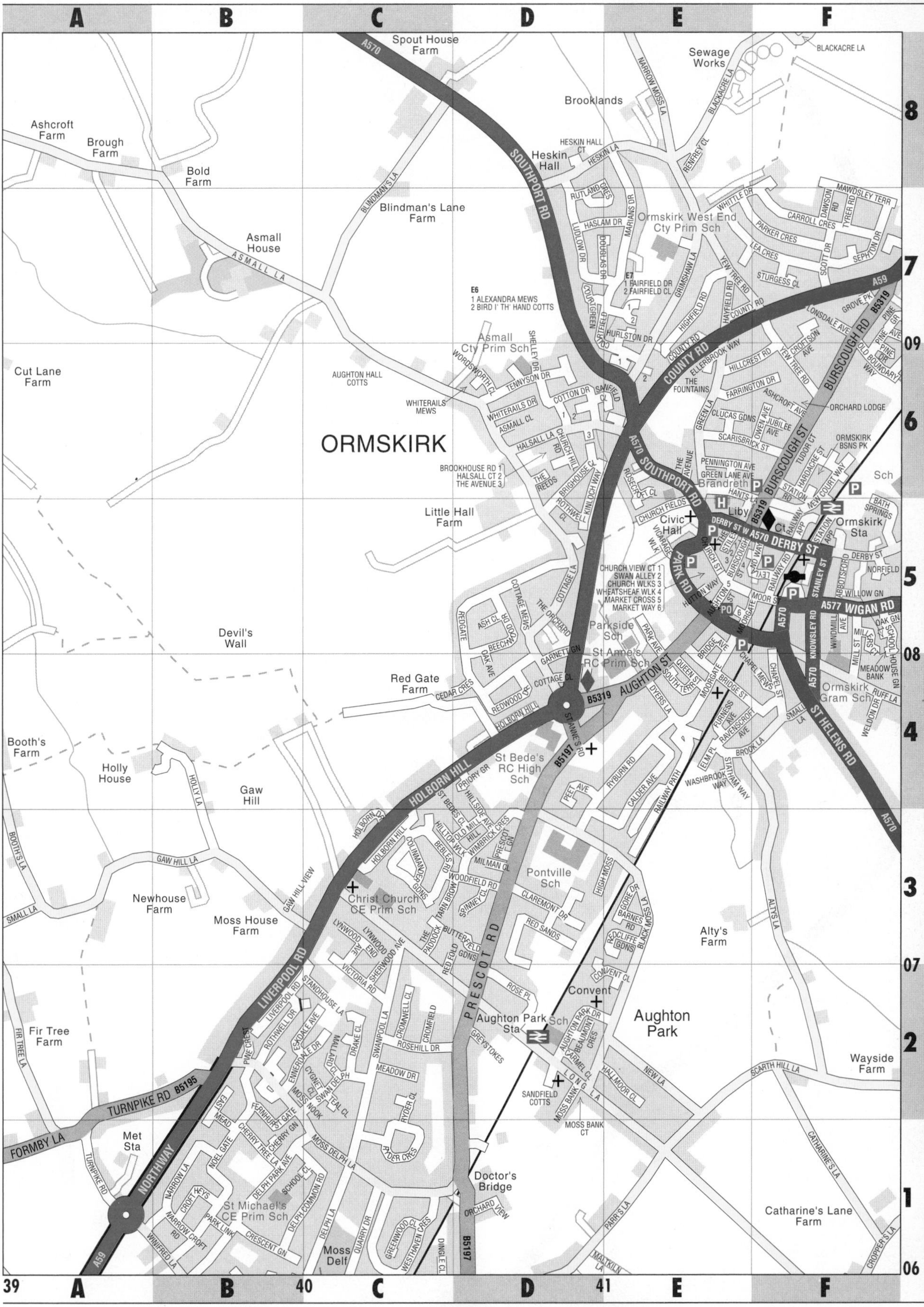
A
B
C
D
E
F
8
7
09
6
5
08
4
3
07
2
1
06
39
40
41
Spout House Farm
A570
Sewage Works
BLACKACRE LA
Brooklands
NARROW MOSS LA
BLACKACRE LA
Ashcroft Farm
Brough Farm
Bold Farm
Heskin Hall
HESKIN HALL CT
HESKIN LA
RENFREY CL
SOUTHPORT RD
BLINDMAN'S LA
Blindman's Lane Farm
RUTLAND CRES
HASLAM DR
MARIANS DR
Ormskirk West End Cty Prim Sch
WHITTLE DR
MAWDSLEY TERR
CARROLL CRES
DAWSON RD
TYRER RD
PARKER CRES
LEA CRES
SEPHTON DR
STURGESS CL
SCOTT DR
Asmall House
ASMALL LA
LUDLOW DR
DOUGLAS DR
COURTGREEN
GRIMSHAW LA
YEW TREE RD
HAYFIELD RD
COUNTY RD
HIGHFIELD RD
E7
1 FAIRFIELD DR
2 FAIRFIELD CL
E6
1 ALEXANDRA MEWS
2 BIRD I' TH' HAND COTTS
A59
GROVE PK
LONSDALE AVE
B5319
PINE AVE
PINE DR
OLD BOUNDARY WAY
BURSCOUGH RD
Asmall Cty Prim Sch
SHELLEY DR
HURLSTON DR
COUNTY RD
ELLERBROOK WAY
HILLCREST RD
CROFTSON AVE
Cut Lane Farm
AUGHTON HALL COTTS
WORDSWORTH CL
TENNYSON DR
COTTON DR
SANFIELD CL
THE FOUNTAINS
FARRINGTON DR
ASHCROFT AVE
WHITERAILS MEWS
WHITERAILS DR
ASMALL CL
CLUCAS GDNS
OWEN AVE
JUBILEE AVE
ORCHARD LODGE
ORMSKIRK
HALSALL LA
CHURCH HILL RD
SCARISBRICK ST
BURSCOUGH ST
TUDOR CT
ORMSKIRK BSNS PK
A570
THE AVENUE
PENNINGTON AVE
GREEN LANE AVE
HARDACRE ST
NEW COURT WAY
BROOKHOUSE RD 1
HALSALL CT 2
THE AVENUE 3
THE REEDS
BRIGHOUSE CL
KINLOCH WAY
ROSECROFT CL
SOUTHPORT RD
Brandreth
HANTS LA
STATION RD
Sch
ROTHWELL CL
CHURCH FIELDS
Civic Hall
Liby
B5319
Ct
RAILWAY APP
BATH SPRINGS
Little Hall Farm
VICARAGE WLK
DERBY ST W
A570 DERBY ST
STATION APP
Ormskirk Sta
PARK RD
CHURCH ST
DERBY ST
NORFIELD
CHURCH VIEW CT 1
SWAN ALLEY 2
CHURCH WLKS 3
WHEATSHEAF WLK 4
MARKET CROSS 5
MARKET WAY 6
COTTAGE LA
HUTTON WAY
AUGHTON ST
MOOR ST
PO
MOORGATE
STANLEY ST
WILLOW GN
A577 WIGAN RD
ABBOTSFORD
COTTAGE MEWS
THE ORCHARD
ASH CL
BEECH
OAK AVE
REDGATE
Devil's Wall
Parkside Sch
PARK AVE
St Anne's RC Prim Sch
GARNETT GN
KNOWSLEY RD
WINDMILL AVE
MILL ST
SCHOOL HOUSE GN
OAK GN
08
Red Gate Farm
CEDAR CRES
REDWOOD DR
COTTAGE CL
HOLBORN HILL
B5319
AUGHTON ST
DYERS LA
QUEEN ST
SOUTH TERR
BRIDGE AVE
BRIDGE ST
CHAPEL MEWS
CHAPEL ST
MEADOW BANK
Ormskirk Gram Sch
RUFF LA
WELDON DR
ST HELENS RD
ST ANNE'S RD
FURNESS AVE
RAVENSCROFT AVE
SMALL LA
Booth's Farm
Holly House
HOLLY LA
St Bede's RC High Sch
B5197
RYBURN RD
ELM PL
BROOK LA
WASHBROOK WAY
STATHAM WAY
Gaw Hill
HOLBORN HILL
PRIORY GR
HILLSIDE AVE
ST BEDE'S CL
PEET AVE
CALDER AVE
RAILWAY PATH
A570
BOOTH'S LA
GAW HILL LA
HOLBORN HILL
HILLTOP WLK
OLD MILL HILL
WIMBRICK CRES
PRESCOT GN
MILMAN CL
COLUMBA GDNS
BEBLES RD
WOODFIELD RD
Pontville Sch
HIGH MOSS
SMALL LA
Newhouse Farm
GAW HILL VIEW
Christ Church CE Prim Sch
TARN BROW
SPINNEY CL
CLAREMONT DR
GORE DR
BARNES RD
RED SANDS
REDCLIFFE GDNS
BLACK MOSS LA
Moss House Farm
LYNWOOD AVE
LYNWOOD END
SHERWOOD AVE
THE PADDOCK
BUTTERFIELD GDNS
RED FOLD
PRESCOT RD
Alty's Farm
VICTORIA RD
LIVERPOOL RD
STANDHOUSE LA
ROSE PL
CONVENT CL
Convent
Aughton Park
Fir Tree Farm
FIR TREE LA
LIVERPOOL RD
ROTHWELL DR
ESKDALE AVE
PINE CREST
SWANPOOL LA
CROMWELL CL
CROMFIELD
ROSEHILL DR
Aughton Park Sta
Sch
GREYSTOKES
AUGHTON PARK DR
BEAUMONT CRES
CARMEL CL
ALTYS LA
Wayside Farm
ENNERDALE DR
MALLARD CL
DRAKE CL
CYGNET CL
SWAN DELPH
TEAL CL
MEADOW DR
LONG LA
HALLMOOR CL
NEW LA
SCARTH HILL LA
TURNPIKE RD
B5195
EAST MEAD
FERNHURST GATE
MOSS NOOK
SANDFIELD COTTS
MOSS BANK
MOSS BANK CT
FORMBY LA
Met Sta
NOEL GATE
CHERRY TREE LA
CHERRY GN
MOSS DELPH LA
RYDER CL
RYDER CRES
CATHARINE'S LA
TURNPIKE RD
NORTHWAY
NARROW LA
DELPH PARK AVE
SCHOOL CL
DELPH COMMON RD
Doctor's Bridge
ORCHARD VIEW
CROFT HEYS
NARROW CROFT RD
PARK LINK
St Michael's CE Prim Sch
CRESCENT GN
DELPH LA
QUARRY DR
GREENWOOD CL
WESTHAVEN CRES
DINGLE CL
B5197
PARR'S LA
Catharine's Lane Farm
A59
WINIFRED LA
Moss Delf
MALKIN LA
CROPPER'S LA

21

14

13

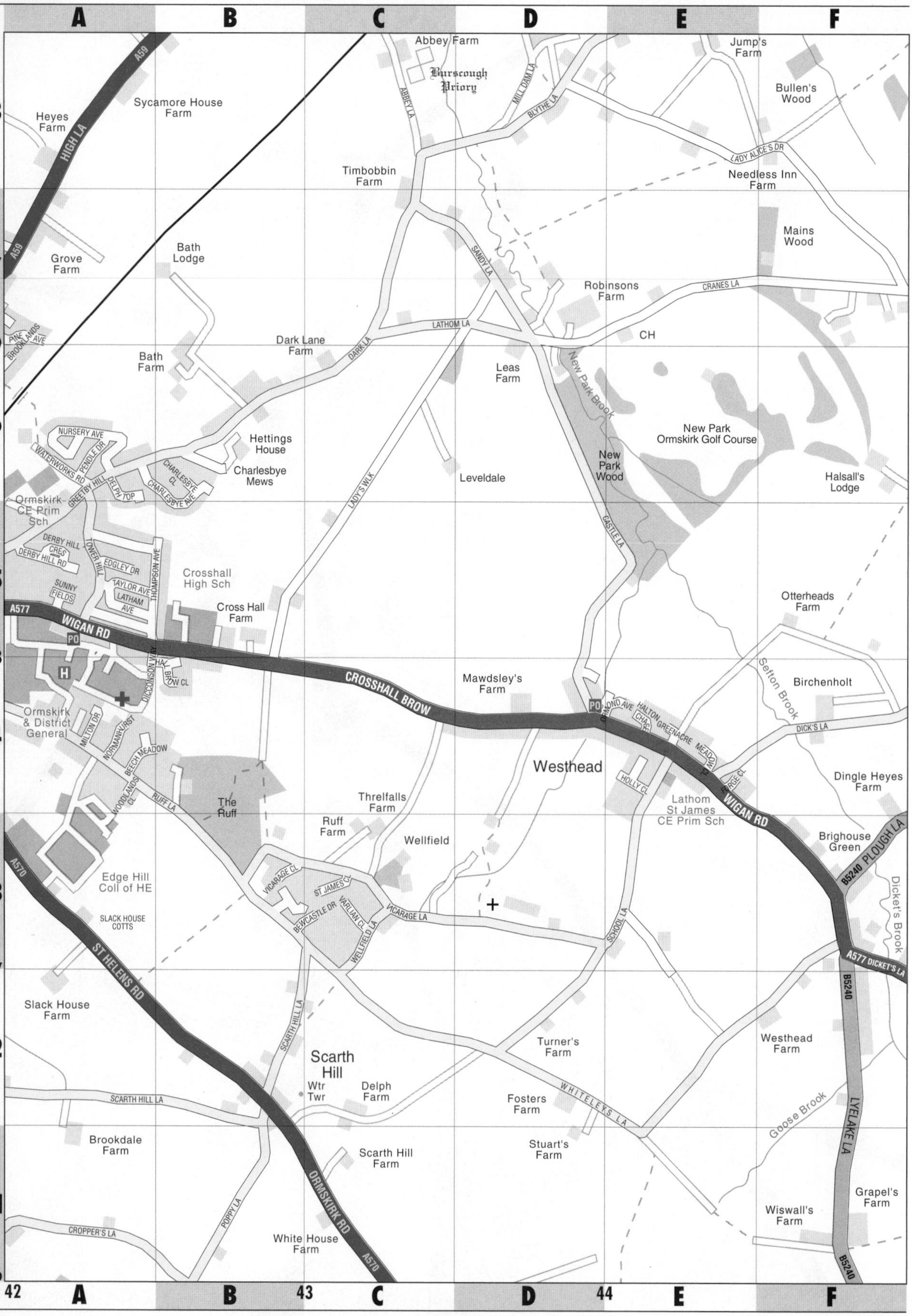
A
B
C
D
E
F
8
7
09
6
5
08
4
3
07
2
1
06
42
43
44
Heyes Farm
Sycamore House Farm
Abbey Farm
Burscough Priory
Jump's Farm
Bullen's Wood
Timbobbin Farm
Needless Inn Farm
Mains Wood
Grove Farm
Bath Lodge
Robinsons Farm
Dark Lane Farm
Bath Farm
CH
Leas Farm
New Park Brook
New Park Ormskirk Golf Course
Hettings House
Charlesbye Mews
New Park Wood
Leveldale
Halsall's Lodge
Ormskirk CE Prim Sch
Crosshall High Sch
Cross Hall Farm
Otterheads Farm
Mawdsley's Farm
Birchenholt
Sefton Brook
Ormskirk & District General
Westhead
Dingle Heyes Farm
The Ruff
Threlfalls Farm
Ruff Farm
Lathom St James CE Prim Sch
Wellfield
Brighouse Green
Edge Hill Coll of HE
Dicket's Brook
SLACK HOUSE COTTS
Slack House Farm
Turner's Farm
Westhead Farm
Scarth Hill
Wtr Twr
Delph Farm
Fosters Farm
Goose Brook
Brookdale Farm
Scarth Hill Farm
Stuart's Farm
Grapel's Farm
Wiswall's Farm
White House Farm
A59
HIGH LA
ABBEY LA
MILL DAM LA
BLYTHE LA
LADY ALICE'S DR
SANDY LA
CRANES LA
LATHOM LA
DARK LA
PINE
BROOKLANDS AVE
NURSERY AVE
PENDLE DR
WATERWORKS RD
GREETBY HILL
DELPH TOP
CHARLESBYE CL
CHARLESBYE AVE
LADY'S WLK
CASTLE LA
DERBY HILL CRES
DERBY HILL RD
TOWER HILL
EDGLEY DR
THOMPSON AVE
TAYLOR AVE
LATHAM AVE
SUNNY FIELDS
A577
WIGAN RD
PO
H
DICCONSON WAY
HAL BROW CL
CROSSHALL BROW
DIAMOND AVE
HALTON CHAS
GREENACRE
MEAD
DICK'S LA
FORGE CL
HOLLY CL
MILTON DR
NORMAN WAY
BEECH MEADOW
WOODLANDS CL
RUFF LA
A570
VICARAGE CL
ST JAMES CL
BEWCASTLE DR
VARLIAN CL
WELLFIELD LA
VICARAGE LA
SCHOOL LA
B5240
PLOUGH LA
A577 DICKET'S LA
ST HELENS RD
SCARTH HILL LA
WHITELEYS LA
LYELAKE LA
POPPY LA
CROPPER'S LA
ORMSKIRK RD

13

22

16

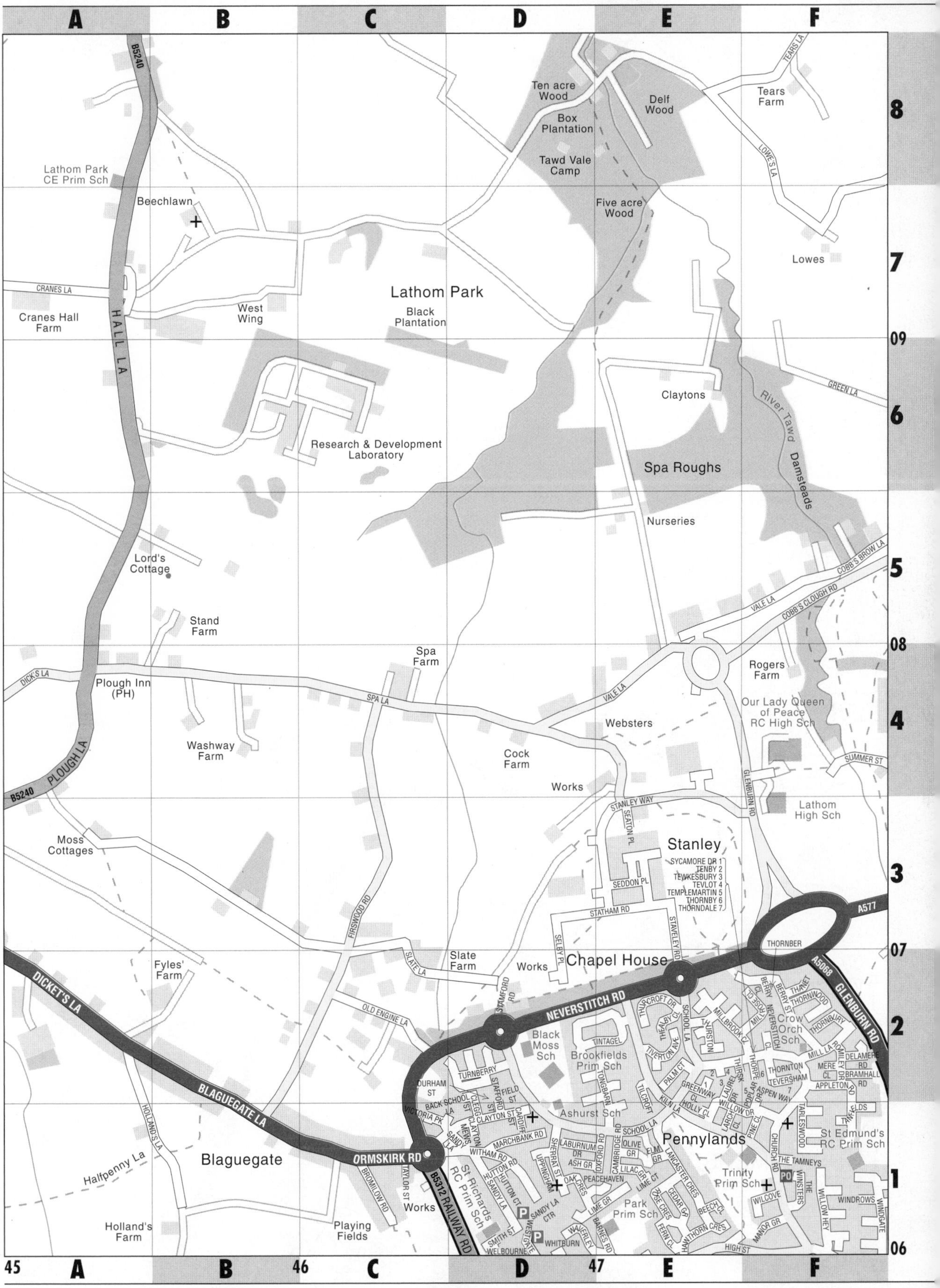

A
B
C
D
E
F
8
7
09
6
5
08
4
3
07
2
1
06
45
46
47
B5240
Ten acre Wood
Box Plantation
Delf Wood
Tawd Vale Camp
Tears Farm
TEARS LA
LOWE'S LA
Lathom Park CE Prim Sch
Beechlawn
Five acre Wood
Lowes
CRANES LA
Lathom Park
Cranes Hall Farm
HALL LA
West Wing
Black Plantation
Claytons
GREEN LA
River Tawd
Research & Development Laboratory
Spa Roughs
Damsteads
Nurseries
Lord's Cottage
COBB'S BROW LA
VALE LA
COBB'S CLOUGH RD
Stand Farm
Spa Farm
Rogers Farm
DICK'S LA
Plough Inn (PH)
SPA LA
VALE LA
Our Lady Queen of Peace RC High Sch
Websters
Washway Farm
Cock Farm
SUMMER ST
PLOUGH LA
B5240
Works
GLENBURN RD
STANLEY WAY
Lathom High Sch
Moss Cottages
SEATON PL
Stanley
SYCAMORE DR 1
TENBY 2
TEWKESBURY 3
TEVLOT 4
TEMPLEMARTIN 5
THORNBY 6
THORNDALE 7
SEDDON PL
STATHAM RD
A577
FIRSWOOD RD
SELBY PL
STAVELEY RD
THORNBER
Fyles' Farm
SLATE LA
Slate Farm
Works
Chapel House
A5068
GLENBURN RD
DICKET'S LA
STAMFORD RD
NEVERSTITCH RD
OLD ENGINE LA
Black Moss Sch
Brookfields Prim Sch
Crow Orch Sch
BLAGUEGATE LA
TURNBERRY
DURHAM ST
BACK SCHOOL LA
VICTORIA PK
CLAYTON ST
FIELD ST
Ashurst Sch
SCHOOL LA
KILN LA
HOLLAND'S LA
MARCHBANK RD
WITHAM RD
Pennylands
St Edmund's RC Prim Sch
Halfpenny La
Blaguegate
ORMSKIRK RD
BROMILOW RD
TAYLOR ST
B5312 RAILWAY RD
St Richards RC Prim Sch
THE TAMNEYS
Trinity Prim Sch
PEACEHAVEN
Park Prim Sch
WINDROWS
Works
Holland's Farm
Playing Fields
SMITH ST
WELBOURNE
WHITBURN
HIGH ST
MANOR GR
WILCOVE

23

16

15

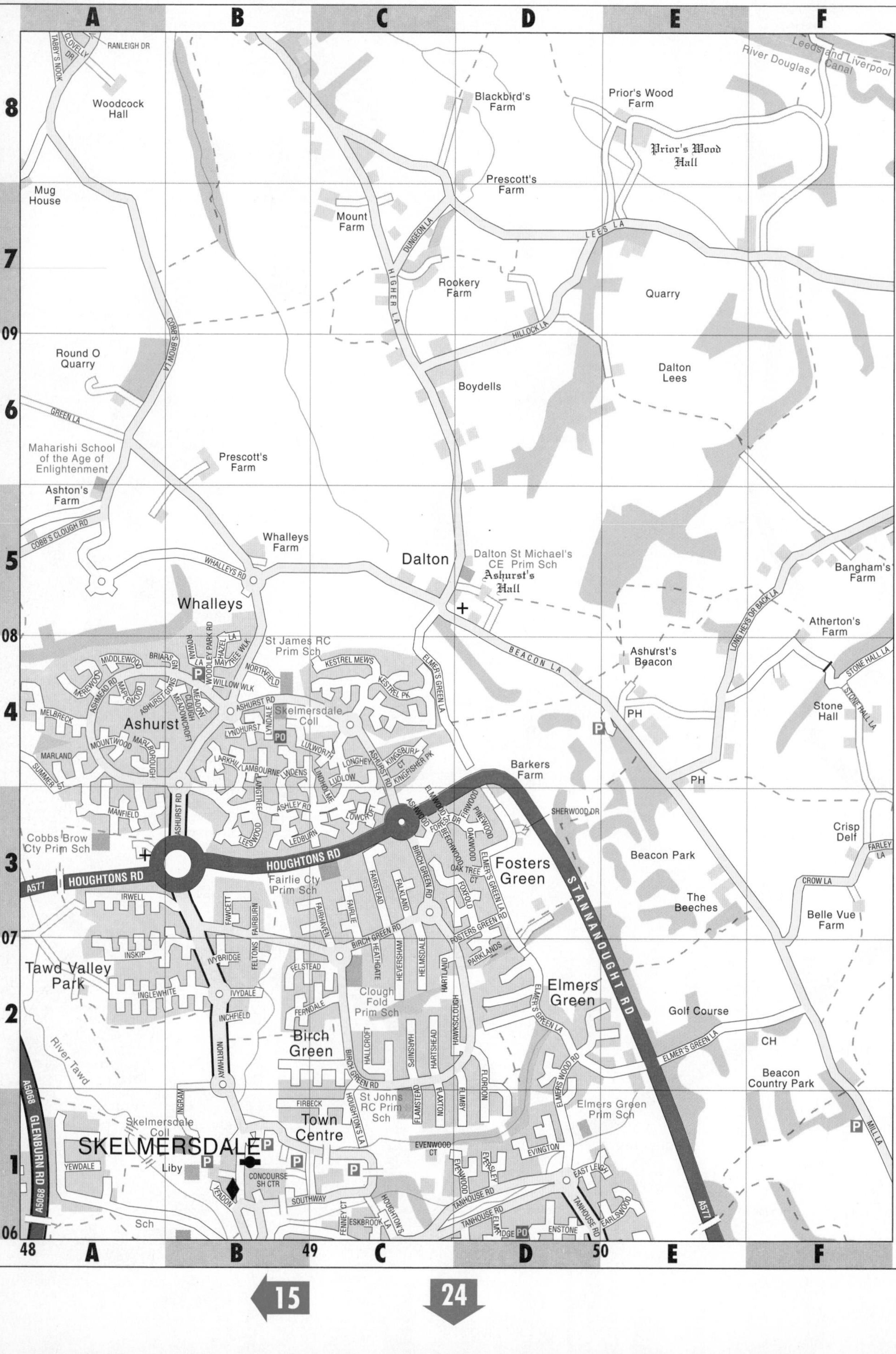
A
B
C
D
E
F
8
7
09
6
5
08
4
3
07
2
1
06
48
49
50
Tabby's Nook
Clovelly Dr
Ranleigh Dr
Woodcock Hall
River Douglas
Leeds and Liverpool Canal
Blackbird's Farm
Prior's Wood Farm
Prior's Wood Hall
Mug House
Prescott's Farm
Mount Farm
Dungeon La
Lees La
Higher La
Rookery Farm
Quarry
Hillock La
Cobb's Brow La
Round O Quarry
Boydells
Dalton Lees
Green La
Maharishi School of the Age of Enlightenment
Prescott's Farm
Ashton's Farm
Cobb's Clough Rd
Whalleys Farm
Dalton
Dalton St Michael's CE Prim Sch
Ashurst's Hall
Bangham's Farm
Whalleys Rd
Whalleys
Long Heys or Back La
Atherton's Farm
St James RC Prim Sch
Beacon La
Ashurst's Beacon
Stone Hall La
Kestrel Mews
Kestrel Pk
Stone Hall
Elmer's Green La
Middlewood
Briars Gn
Rowan La
Hazel La
Woodley Park Rd
Maytree Wlk
Northfield
Willow Wlk
Merewood
Ashmead Rd
Maplewood
Ashurst Gdns
Meadowcroft
Clough
Meadow
Ashurst Rd
Lyndale
Skelmersdale Coll
Melbreck
Ashurst
PH
PO
Lyndhurst
Lulworth
Mountwood
Marlborough
Marland
Kingsbury Ct
Kingfisher Pk
Larkhill
Lambourne
Lindens
Longhey
Summer St
Langtree
Lindholme
Ludlow
Barkers Farm
PH
Manfield
Ashley Rd
Ashwood
Elmwood
Forest Dr
Firwood
Pinewood
Sherwood Dr
Cobbs Brow Cty Prim Sch
Leeswood
Ledburn
Lowcroft
Beechwood
Oakwood
Crisp Delf
Beacon Park
Houghtons Rd
Oak Tree Ct
Fosters Green
Farley La
A577
Houghtons Rd
Fairlie Cty Prim Sch
Fairstead
Falkland
Birch Green Rd
Foxfold
Elmer's Green La
Crow La
Irwell
Fawcett
Fairburn
Fairhaven
Fairlie
Stannanought Rd
The Beeches
Belle Vue Farm
Fosters Green Rd
Birch Green Rd
Inskip
Ivybridge
Feltons
Heathgate
Heversham
Helmsdale
Hartland
Parklands
Tawd Valley Park
Felstead
Elmers Green
Inglewhite
Ivydale
Clough Fold Prim Sch
Hawksclough
Elmer's Green La
Golf Course
Inchfield
Ferndale
Birch Green
River Tawd
Northway
Hallcroft
Harsnips
Hartshead
CH
Birch Green Rd
Elmer's Green La
Elmers Wood Rd
Beacon Country Park
A5068
Glenburn Rd
Ingram
Firbeck
Houghton's La
St Johns RC Prim Sch
Flamstead
Plaxton
Flimby
Flordon
Elmers Green Prim Sch
Skelmersdale Coll
Town Centre
Evington
Mill La
SKELMERSDALE
Evenwood Ct
Yewdale
Liby
Concourse Sh Ctr
Evenwood
Eversley
East Leigh
Yeadon
Southway
Fenney Ct
Houghton's
Tanhouse Rd
Sch
Eskbrook La
Tanhouse Rd
Elmridge
Enstone
Tanhouse Rd
Earlswood
A577

15
24

9
18

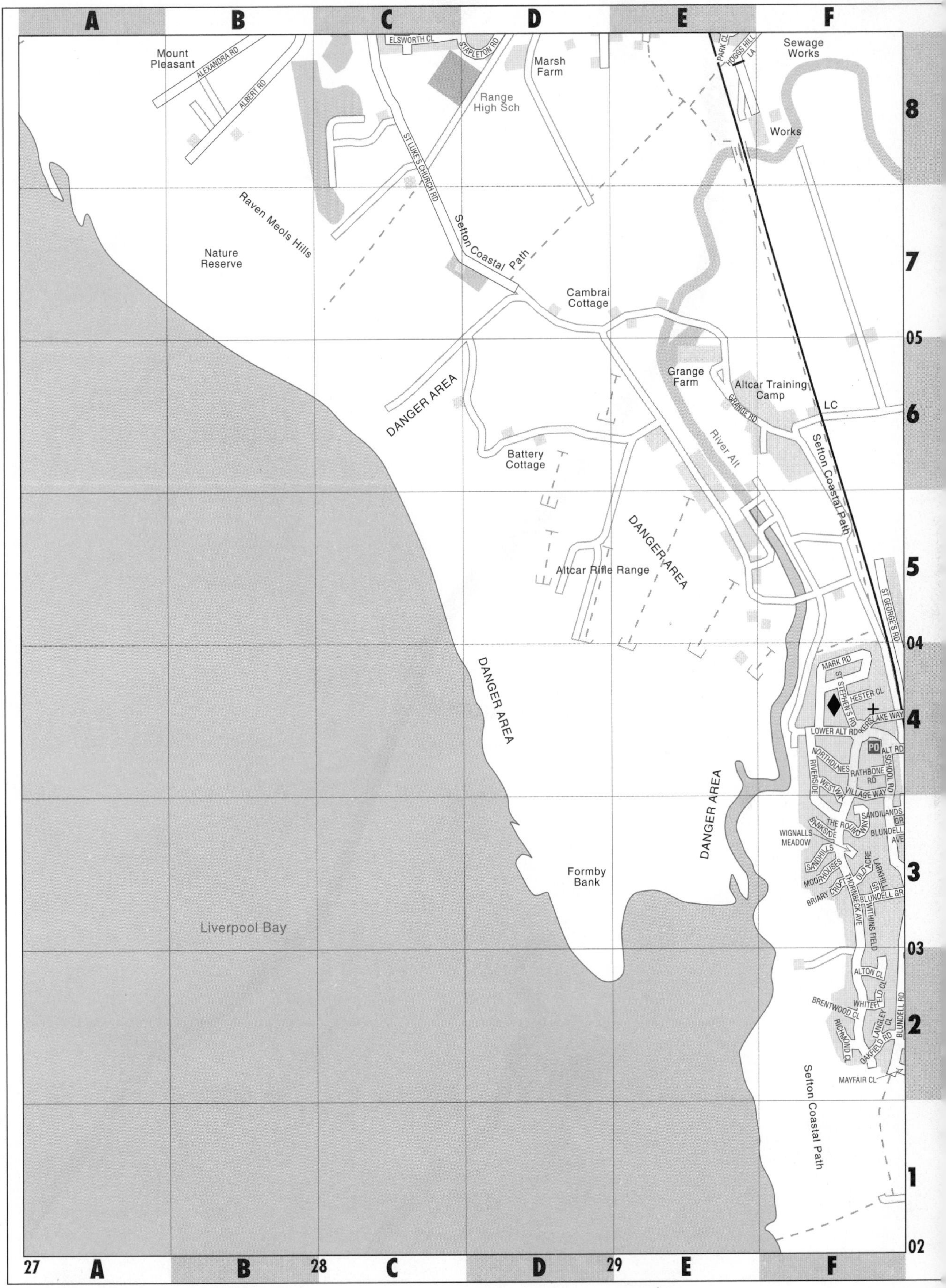
A
B
C
D
E
F
Mount Pleasant
ALEXANDRA RD
ALBERT RD
ELSWORTH CL
STAPLETON RD
Marsh Farm
Range High Sch
PARK CL
HOGGS HILL LA
Sewage Works
Works
ST LUKE'S CHURCH RD
Raven Meols Hills
Nature Reserve
Sefton Coastal Path
Cambrai Cottage
DANGER AREA
Grange Farm
Altcar Training Camp
GRANGE RD
LC
River Alt
Battery Cottage
Sefton Coastal Path
DANGER AREA
Altcar Rifle Range
ST GEORGE'S RD
DANGER AREA
MARK RD
ST STEPHEN'S RD
HESTER CL
LAKE WAY
LOWER ALT RD
PO
ALT RD
NORTHDUNES
RATHBONE RD
SCHOOL RD
RIVERSIDE
WEST WAY
VILLAGE WAY
DANGER AREA
SANDILANDS GR
THE ROUNDWAY
BANKSIDE
BLUNDELL AVE
WIGNALLS MEADOW
SANDHILLS
MOORHOUSES
OLD ACRE
LARKHILL GR
BRIARY CROFT
THORNBECK AVE
BLUNDELL GR
WITHINS FIELD
Formby Bank
Liverpool Bay
ALTON CL
BRENTWOOD CL
WHITEFIELD CL
LANGLEY CL
BLUNDELL RD
RICHMOND CL
OAKFIELD RD
MAYFAIR CL
Sefton Coastal Path
8
7
05
6
5
04
4
3
03
2
1
02
27
28
29

18

17
10

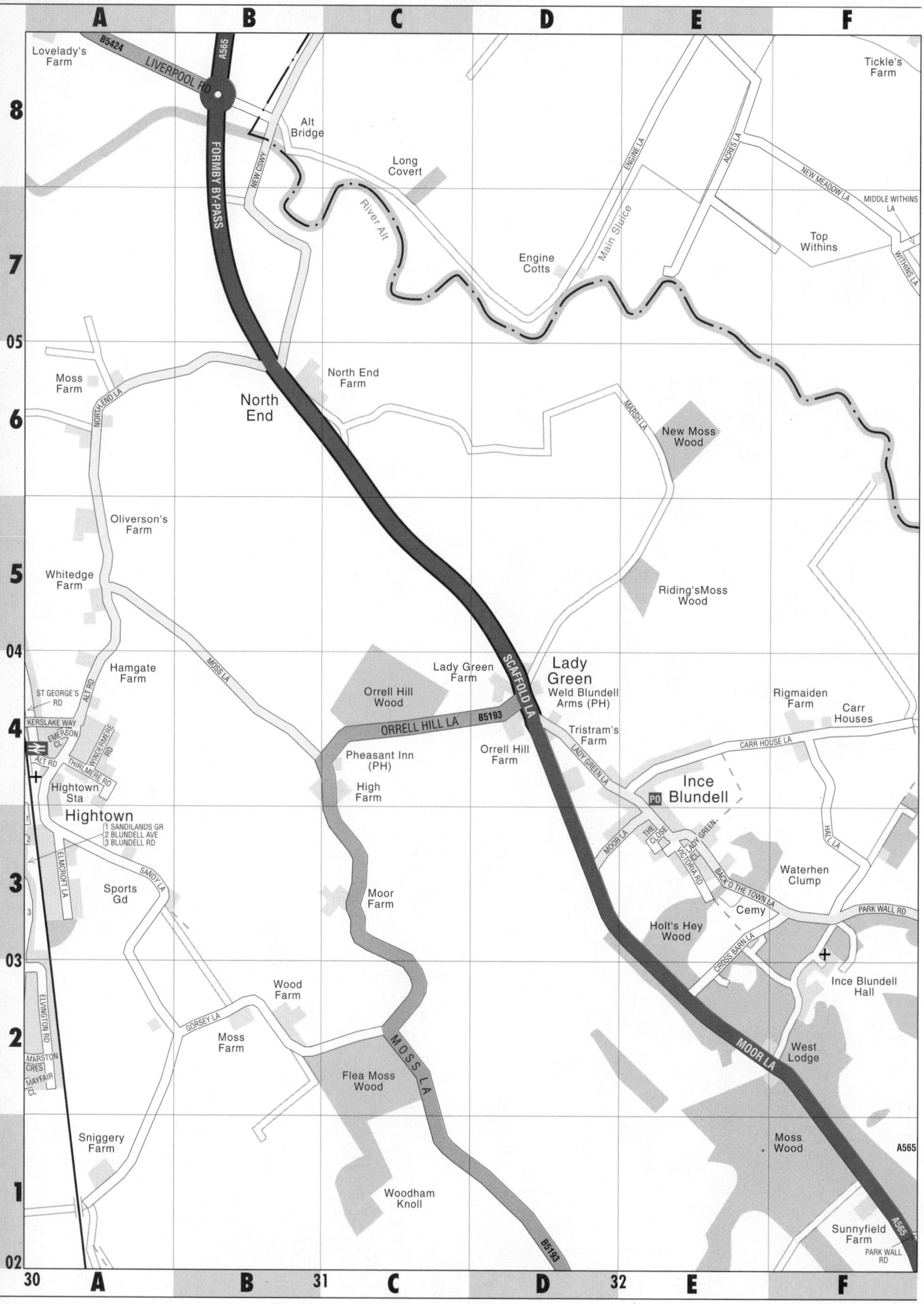
A
B
C
D
E
F
8
7
05
6
5
04
4
3
03
2
1
02
30
31
32
Lovelady's Farm
B5424
LIVERPOOL RD
A565
FORMBY BY-PASS
NEW CSWY
Alt Bridge
Long Covert
River Alt
ENGINE LA
Main Sluice
Engine Cotts
ACRES LA
NEW MEADOW LA
MIDDLE WITHINS LA
Top Withins
WITHINS LA
Tickle's Farm
Moss Farm
NORTH END LA
North End Farm
North End
MARSH LA
New Moss Wood
Oliverson's Farm
Whitedge Farm
Riding'sMoss Wood
Hamgate Farm
MOSS LA
ALT RD
ST GEORGE'S RD
KERSLAKE WAY
EMERSON CL
WINDERMERE RD
THIRLMERE RD
Hightown Sta
Hightown
1 SANDILANDS GR
2 BLUNDELL AVE
3 BLUNDELL RD
ELMCROFT LA
Sports Gd
SANDY LA
Orrell Hill Wood
ORRELL HILL LA
B5193
Lady Green Farm
SCAFFOLD LA
Lady Green
Weld Blundell Arms (PH)
Tristram's Farm
Orrell Hill Farm
Pheasant Inn (PH)
High Farm
LADY GREEN LA
Rigmaiden Farm
Carr Houses
CARR HOUSE LA
PO
Ince Blundell
HALL LA
MOOR LA
THE CLOSE
LADY GREEN CL
VICTORIA RD
BACK O' THE TOWN LA
Waterhen Clump
Cemy
PARK WALL RD
Moor Farm
Holt's Hey Wood
CROSS BARN LA
Ince Blundell Hall
ELVINGTON RD
MARSTON CRES
MAYFAIR CL
Wood Farm
GORSEY LA
Moss Farm
MOSS LA
Flea Moss Wood
MOOR LA
West Lodge
Sniggery Farm
Moss Wood
A565
Woodham Knoll
B5193
Sunnyfield Farm
A565
PARK WALL RD

17
26

11
20

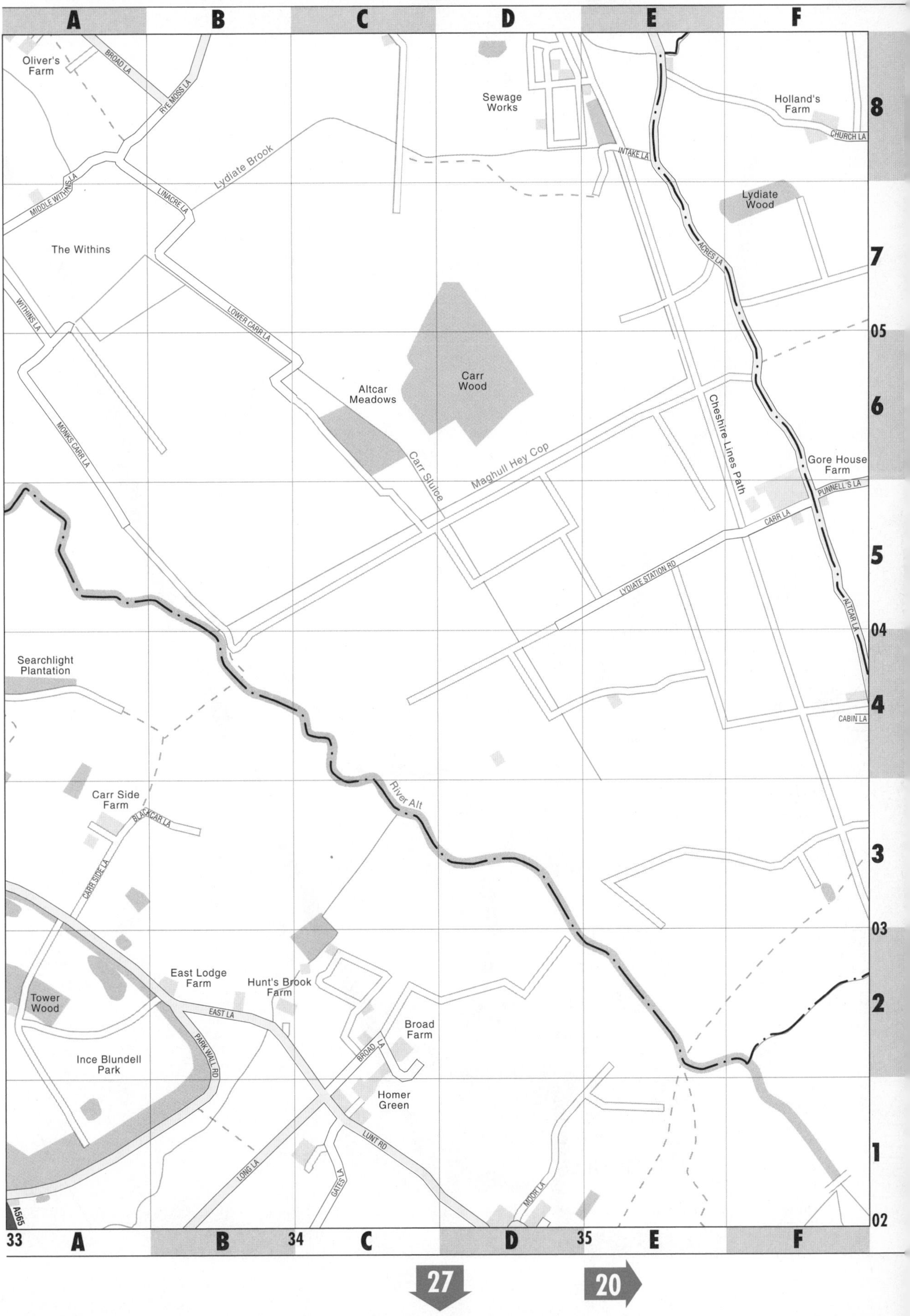
A
B
C
D
E
F
Oliver's Farm
BROAD LA
RYE MOSS LA
Sewage Works
Holland's Farm
CHURCH LA
8
INTAKE LA
Lydiate Brook
MIDDLE WITHINS LA
LINACRE LA
Lydiate Wood
The Withins
ACRES LA
7
WITHINS LA
LOWER CARR LA
05
Carr Wood
Altcar Meadows
6
MONKS CARR LA
Cheshire Lines Path
Gore House Farm
Carr Sluice
Maghull Hey Cop
PUNNELL'S LA
CARR LA
5
LYDIATE STATION RD
ALTCAR LA
04
Searchlight Plantation
4
CABIN LA
River Alt
Carr Side Farm
BLACKCAR LA
3
CARR SIDE LA
03
East Lodge Farm
Hunt's Brook Farm
Tower Wood
2
EAST LA
Broad Farm
PARK WALL RD
Ince Blundell Park
BROAD LA
Homer Green
LUNT RD
1
LONG LA
GATES LA
MOOR LA
A565
02
33
A
B
34
C
D
35
E
F

27
20

19
12

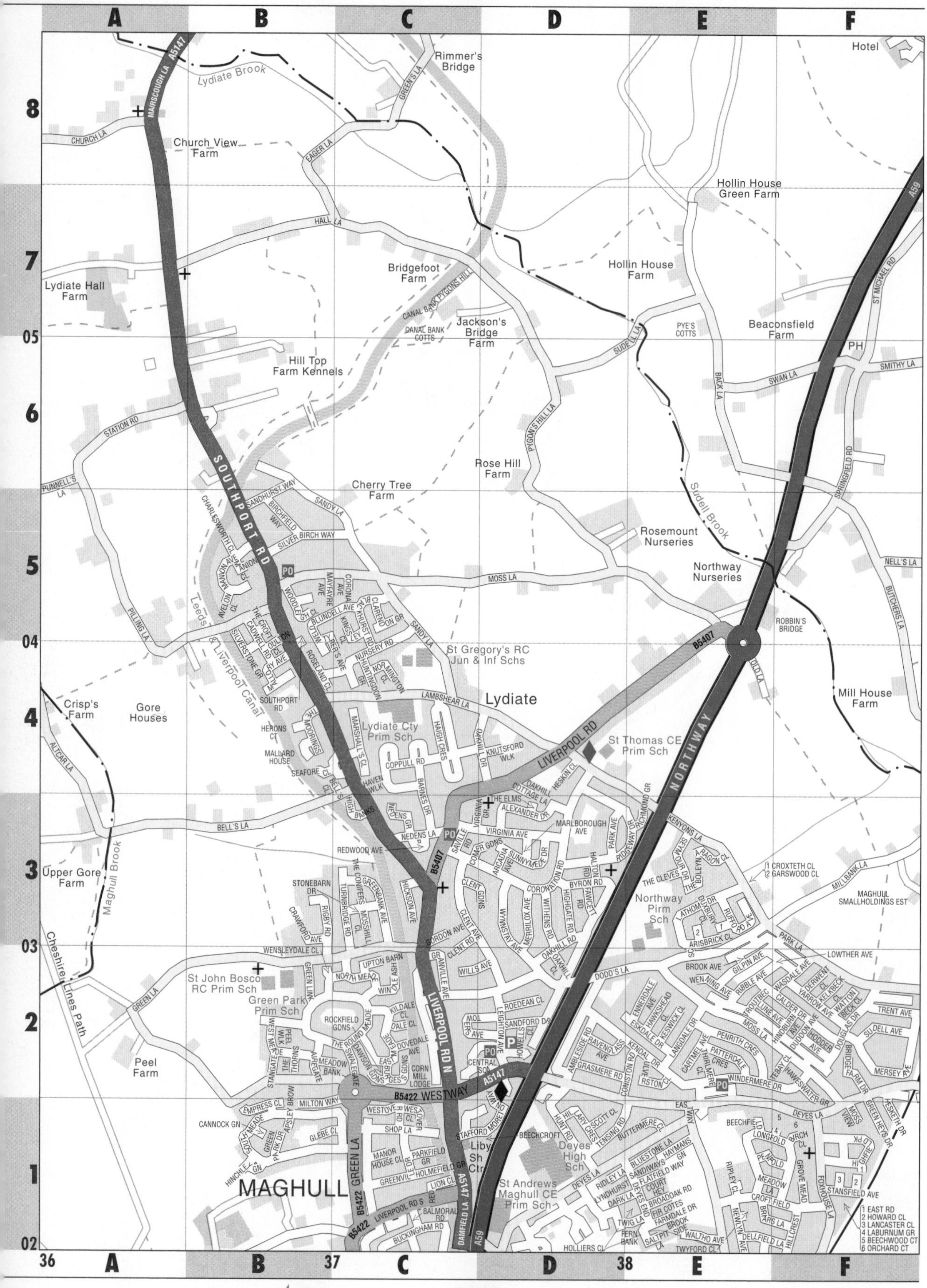
A
B
C
D
E
F
8
7
05
6
5
04
4
3
03
2
1
02
36
37
38
Hotel
Rimmer's Bridge
Lydiate Brook
MAIRSCOUGH LA
A5147
GREEN'S LA
CHURCH LA
Church View Farm
EAGER LA
Hollin House Green Farm
A59
HALL LA
Bridgefoot Farm
Hollin House Farm
Lydiate Hall Farm
CANAL BANK PYGONS HILL
CANAL BANK COTTS
Jackson's Bridge Farm
PYE'S COTTS
Beaconsfield Farm
ST MICHAEL RD
SUDELL LA
PH
SMITHY LA
Hill Top Farm Kennels
SWAN LA
BACK LA
STATION RD
PYGON'S HILL LA
SOUTHPORT RD
Rose Hill Farm
SPRINGFIELD RD
PUNNELL'S LA
Cherry Tree Farm
SANDHURST WAY
SANDY LA
BIRCHFIELD WAY
Sudell Brook
SILVER BIRCH WAY
Rosemount Nurseries
Northway Nurseries
NELL'S LA
MOSS LA
PO
Leeds & Liverpool Canal
PILLING LA
BUTCHERS LA
ROBBIN'S BRIDGE
B5407
SANDY LA
NURSERY RD
St Gregory's RC Jun & Inf Schs
OLD LA
LAMBSHEAR LA
Lydiate
Mill House Farm
Crisp's Farm
Gore Houses
SOUTHPORT RD
HERONS CT
MALLARD HOUSE
Lydiate Cty Prim Sch
HAIGH CRES
KNUTSFORD WLK
LIVERPOOL RD
St Thomas CE Prim Sch
NORTHWAY
ALTCAR LA
COPPULL RD
SEAFORE CL
HAVEN WLK
BARNES DR
OAKHILL COTTAGE LA
HESKIN CL
THE ELMS
ALEXANDER DR
MARLBOROUGH AVE
RICHMOND GR
KENYONS LA
BELL'S LA
NEDENS LA
VIRGINIA AVE
PARK AVE
REDWOOD AVE
SAVILLE RD
COMER GDNS
SUNNYMEDE DR
1 CROXTETH CL
2 GARSWOOD CL
MILLBANK LA
Upper Gore Farm
Maghull Brook
STONEBARN DR
THE CONIFERS
HICKSON AVE
CLENT GDNS
CORONATION RD
BYRON RD
THE CLEVES
THE BOLEYN
MAGHULL SMALLHOLDINGS EST
RIGBY RD
TURNBRIDGE RD
MOSSHILL CL
WYNSTAY AVE
MERRILOX AVE
WITHENS RD
HIGHGATE RD
FAWCETT RD
Northway Prim Sch
LATHOM DR
DUXBURY CL
CRAWFORD AVE
GORDON AVE
CLENT RD
CLENT AVE
ARISBRICK CL
PARK LA
Cheshire Lines Path
WENSLEYDALE CL
UPTON BARN
WILLS AVE
OAKHILL CL
DODD'S LA
BROOK AVE
GILPIN AVE
LOWTHER AVE
St John Bosco RC Prim Sch
GREEN LINK
NORTH MEADE
WINDLE ASH
GRANVILLE AVE
ENNERDALE AVE
HAWKSHEAD CL
WENNING AVE
RIBBLE AVE
WASDALE AVE
DERWENT CL
KELBECK CL
YARROW AVE
WATTON BECK CL
TRENT AVE
GREEN LA
Green Park Prim Sch
KILDALE CL
DALE CL
ROEDEAN CL
ESKDALE DR
KESWICK CL
LANGDALE DR
TROUTBECK
LUNE AVE
CALDER DR
HINDBURN AVE
DUDDON AVE
HODDER AVE
DOUGLAS DR
ROCKFIELD GDNS
DOVEDALE AVE
LIVERPOOL RD N
SANDFORD DR
LEIGHTON AVE
HOWELLS CL
AMBLESIDE RD
RAVENGLASS AVE
KENDAL DR
MOSS LA
PENRITH CRES
CARTMEL AVE
PATTERDALE CRES
TEBAY CL
SUDELL AVE
BRIDGE FARM DR
MERSEY AVE
Peel Farm
STANGATE
WEST MEADE
PEEL WLK
THE THORNS
AIRESGATE
MEADOW BANK
SWALEGATE
DAWSON GDNS
CORN MILL LODGE
CENTRAL SQ
GRASMERE RD
CONISTON RD
ULVERSTON
THIRLMERE CL
WINDERMERE DR
HAWESWATER GR
B5422 WESTWAY
MILTON WAY
EMPRESS CL
WESTOVER RD
WESTOVER CL
DEYES LA
CANNOCK GN
SOUTHMEADE
APSLEY BROW
GREEN PARK DR
GLEBE CL
SHOP LA
STAFFORD MORETON
BEECHCROFT
HILLARY CRES
SCOTT CL
TENSING RD
BUTTERMERE CL
BEECHFIELD
LONGFOLD
BIRCH CL
MOSS VIEW
GREEN HEYS DR
HESKETH DR
Liby
Sh Ctr
Deyes High Sch
BLUESTONE LA
HAYMANS GN
RIPLEY CL
GROVE MEAD
FOXHOUSE LA
MANOR HOUSE CL
PARKFIELD GR
HOLMEFIELD GR
GREENVILLE DR
HINCHLEY GN
St Andrews Maghull CE Prim Sch
DEYES LA
RIDLEY LA
SANDIWAYS
FLATFIELD WAY
MEADOW LA
STANSFIELD AVE
MAGHULL
B5422 GREEN LA
LION CL
LYNDHURST
DARK LA
COURT HEY
BROADOAK RD
CROFT FIELD
BRIARS LA
HILLCREST
1 EAST RD
2 HOWARD CL
3 LANCASTER CL
4 LABURNUM GR
5 BEECHWOOD CT
6 ORCHARD CT
LIVERPOOL RD S
BALMORAL RD
FIR COTES
FARMDALE DR
BROOK SIDE
TWIG LA
FERN BANK
SALTPIT LA
WALTHO AVE
NEWLYN AVE
DELLFIELD LA
BUCKINGHAM RD
DAMFIELD LA
HOLLIERS CL
TWYFORD CL

19
28

13
22

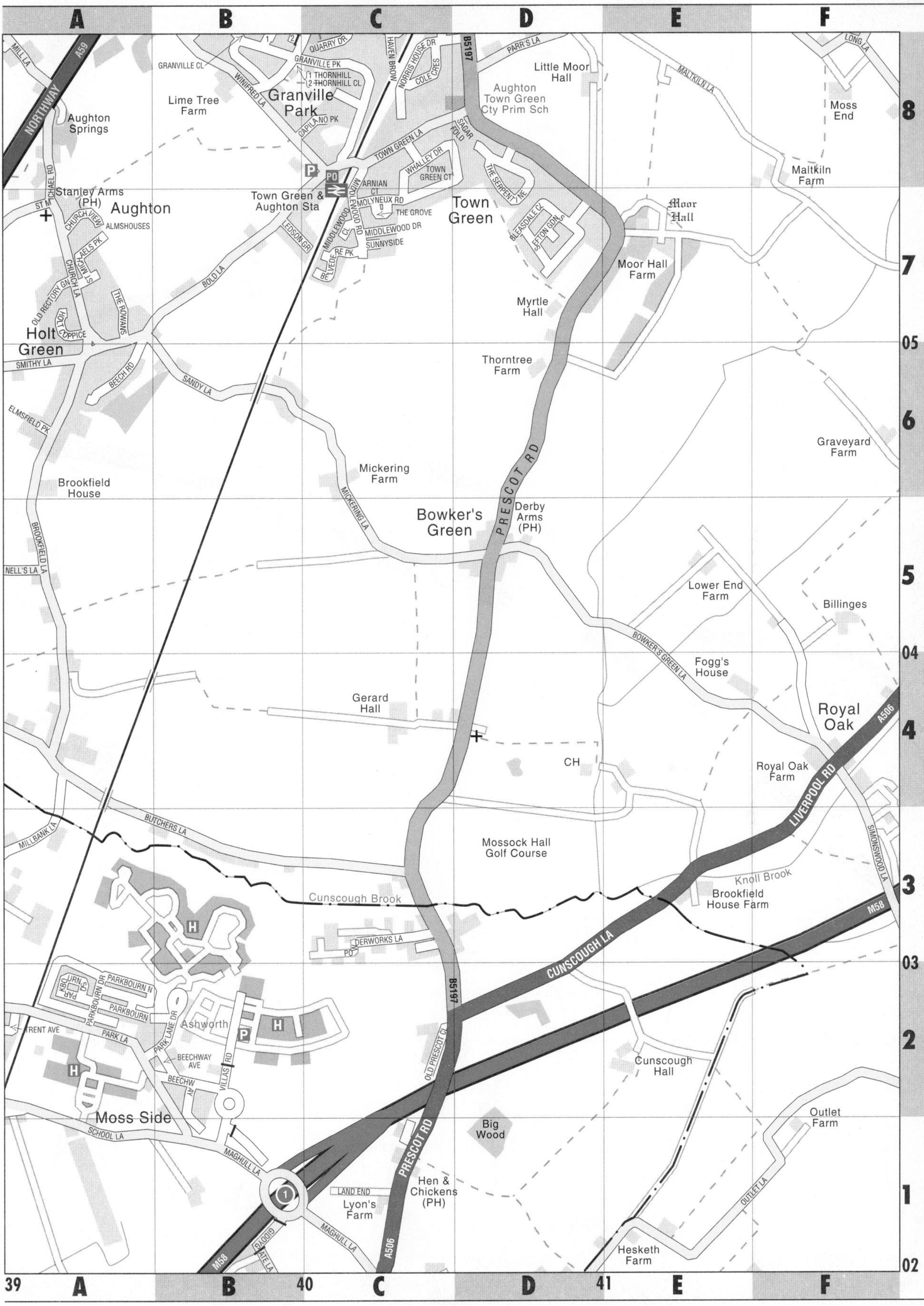
A
B
C
D
E
F
8
7
05
6
5
04
4
3
03
2
1
02
39
40
41
NORTHWAY
A59
MILL LA
Aughton Springs
GRANVILLE CL
WINIFRED LA
Lime Tree Farm
QUARRY DR
GRANVILLE PK
1 THORNHILL
2 THORNHILL CL
Granville Park
CAPILANO PK
HAVEN BROW
NORRIS HOUSE DR
COLE CRES
B5197
PARR'S LA
Little Moor Hall
Aughton Town Green Cty Prim Sch
MALTKILN LA
LONG LA
Moss End
Maltkiln Farm
SAGAR FOLD
TOWN GREEN LA
WHALLEY DR
TOWN GREEN CT
THE SERPENTINE
Stanley Arms (PH)
Aughton
Town Green & Aughton Sta
ARNIAN CT
MOLYNEUX RD
THE GROVE
Town Green
BLEASDALE CL
SEFTON GDNS
Moor Hall
ST M
MICHAEL RD
CHURCH VIEW
ALMSHOUSES
MIDDLEWOOD DR
MIDDLEWOOD CL
SUNNYSIDE
LEDSON GR
BELVEDERE PK
Moor Hall Farm
CHURCH LA
OLD RECTORY GN
HOLT COPPICE
THE ROWANS
BOLD LA
Myrtle Hall
Holt Green
SMITHY LA
BEECH RD
SANDY LA
Thorntree Farm
ELMSFIELD PK
Graveyard Farm
Brookfield House
Mickering Farm
MICKERING LA
Bowker's Green
PRESCOT RD
Derby Arms (PH)
BROOKFIELD LA
NELL'S LA
Lower End Farm
Billinges
BOWKER'S GREEN LA
Fogg's House
Gerard Hall
Royal Oak
A506
CH
Royal Oak Farm
LIVERPOOL RD
MILLBANK LA
BUTCHERS LA
Mossock Hall Golf Course
SIMONSWOOD LA
Knoll Brook
Cunscough Brook
Brookfield House Farm
M58
H
DERWORKS LA
PO
CUNSCOUGH LA
PARKBOURN DR
PARKBOURN N
PARKBOURN
PARK LANE DR
Ashworth
P
TRENT AVE
PARK LA
BEECHWAY AVE
VILLAS RD
BEECHW AY
OLD PRESCOT CL
Cunscough Hall
Moss Side
SCHOOL LA
Big Wood
Outlet Farm
MAGHULL LA
1
LAND END
Lyon's Farm
Hen & Chickens (PH)
OUTLET LA
GIDDYGATE LA
Hesketh Farm

29
22

21
14

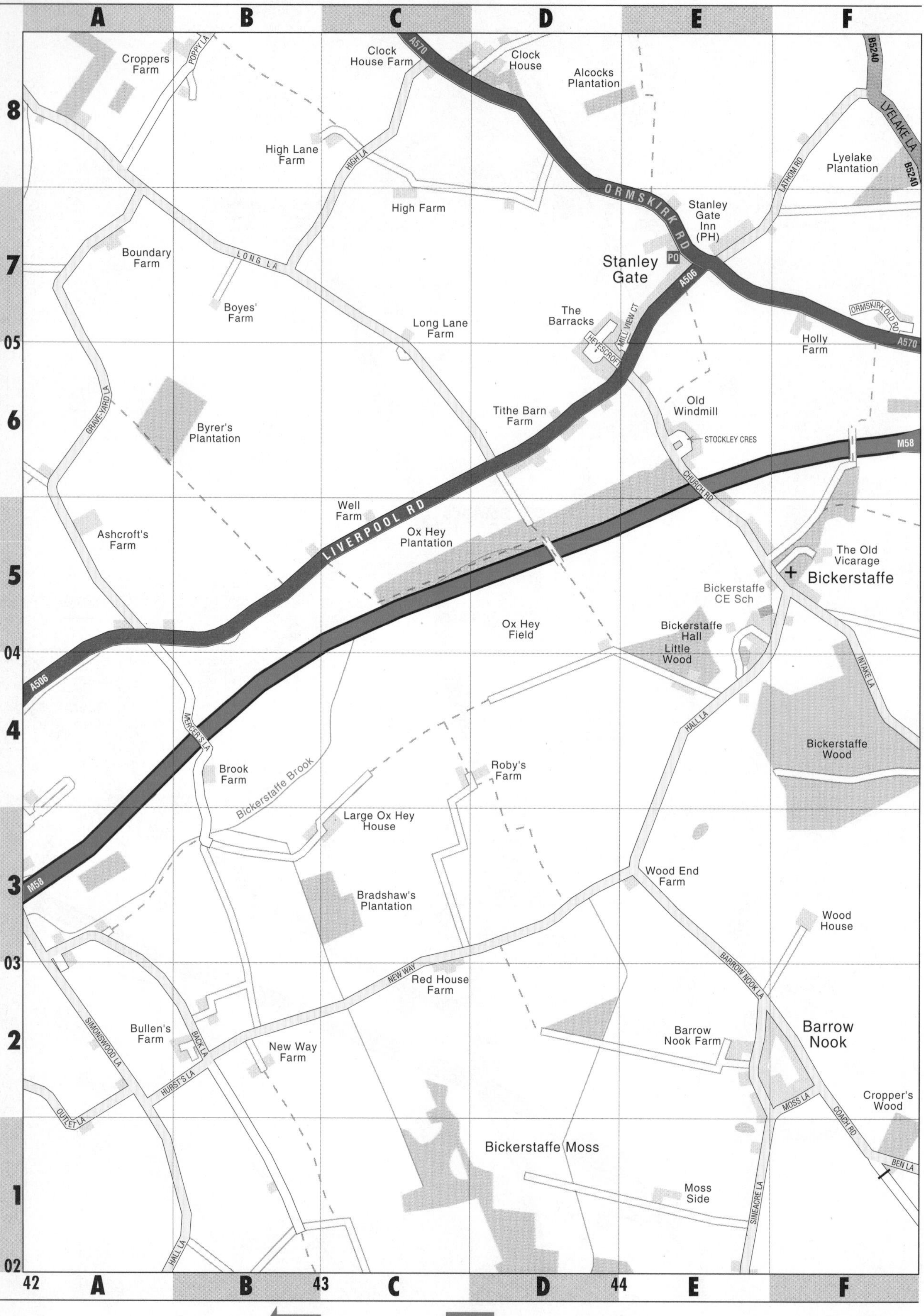
A
B
C
D
E
F
Croppers Farm
POPPY LA
Clock House Farm
A570
Clock House
Alcocks Plantation
B5240
LYELAKE LA
8
High Lane Farm
HIGH LA
Lyelake Plantation
LATHOM RD
High Farm
ORMSKIRK RD
Stanley Gate Inn (PH)
Boundary Farm
LONG LA
PO
7
Stanley Gate
A506
Boyes' Farm
Long Lane Farm
The Barracks
MILL VIEW CT
HEYESCROFT
ORMSKIRK OLD RD
Holly Farm
05
Old Windmill
GRAVE-YARD LA
Tithe Barn Farm
6
Byrer's Plantation
STOCKLEY CRES
M58
CHURCH RD
Well Farm
LIVERPOOL RD
Ox Hey Plantation
Ashcroft's Farm
The Old Vicarage
5
Bickerstaffe
Bickerstaffe CE Sch
Ox Hey Field
Bickerstaffe Hall
04
Little Wood
INTAKE LA
A506
HALL LA
MERCER'S LA
4
Bickerstaffe Wood
Roby's Farm
Brook Farm
Bickerstaffe Brook
Large Ox Hey House
3
M58
Wood End Farm
Bradshaw's Plantation
Wood House
03
NEW WAY
Red House Farm
BARROW NOOK LA
Barrow Nook
2
Bullen's Farm
SIMONSWOOD LA
BACK LA
New Way Farm
Barrow Nook Farm
HURST'S LA
MOSS LA
COACH RD
Cropper's Wood
OUTLET LA
Bickerstaffe Moss
BEN LA
1
Moss Side
SINEACRE LA
HALL LA
02
42
43
44

15
24

A B C D E F

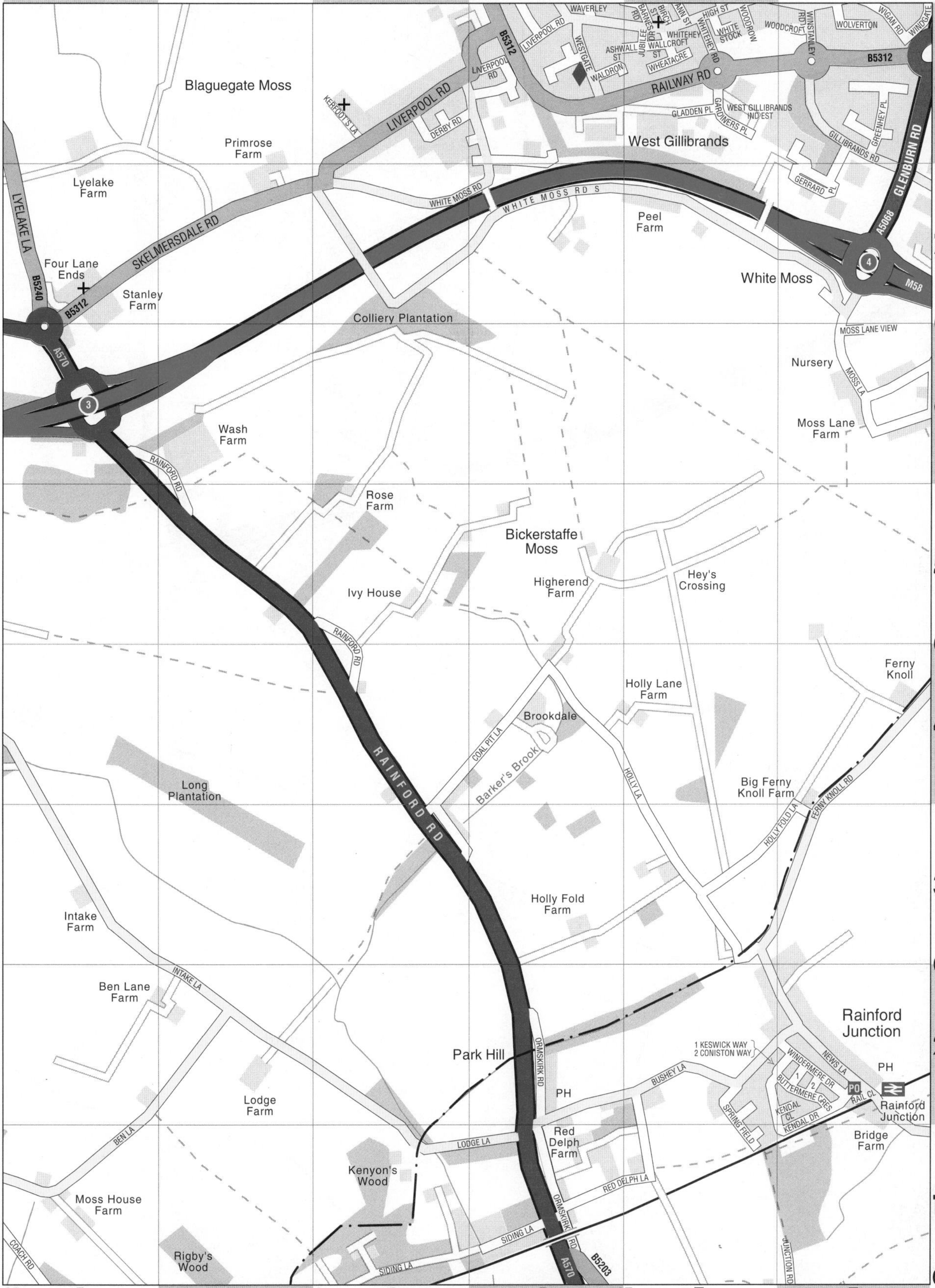

A B C D E F

31
24

23
16

A
B
C
D
E
F
8
7
05
6
5
04
4
3
03
2
1
02
48
49
50
A5068
B5312
GRIMSHAW RD
SOUTHWAY
Glenburn High Sch
Skelmersdale Coll (Westbrook Ctr)
ESKDALE
ESKBANK
Delphside Prim Sch
TANHOUSE RD
ELSWICK
ELMSTEAD
ELMRIDGE
TAWD RD
Hillside Cty Prim Sch
ENNERDA
EGERTON
CASTER CL
EAVESDALE
St Marks RC Prim Sch
A577
HART'S LA
GLEBE RD
GRATTON PL
East Gillibrands
THE MOUNT
GREENWAY AVE
HILLCREST
ORMSKIRK RD
Tawd Bridge
Tanhouse
GRIMSHAW RD
FIR TREE CL
LYNWOOD CL
TANHOUSE RD
B5312
A577 WINDMILL
PARSONAGE BROW
DENSHAW
NEWGATE RD
DENHOLME
Holland Moor
GARNETT PL
GRIMROD PL
WHITELEDGE RD
SPENCERS LA
AMBERGATE
GORSEY
AMERSHAM
DANIELS LA
DIGMOOR DR
Skelmersdale Sports Ctr
DIGMOOR RD
BANKFIELD
BLYTHEWOOD
St Mathew's RC Prim Sch
BLAYDON PK
Holland Moor Prim Sch
GILLIBRANDS RD
BANKSBARN
BLAKEHALL
WHITSTONE DR
COLINTON
CORNBROOK
STANNANOUGHT RD
MARTINS LA
ORMSKIRK RD
BACK LA
BARNFIELD DR
LIMEFIELD DR
A577
M58
ABBEYSTEAD
ACREGATE
BEECHTREES
NEWLYN DR
NIXONS LA
MEADOW CL
MOOR DR
Moorside Prim Sch
ORMSKIRK RD
DARFIELD
DAYBROOK
MOSS LA
WHITELEDGE RD
ABBEYWOOD
BIRLEYWOOD
BEAVERS LA
Bishop Martin CE Prim Sch
CHERRYCROFT
CHARNOCK
DANBERS
RAVENHEAD WAY
Little Digmoor Cty Sch
BEARNCROFT
BACK LA
CLAY BROW RD
BEECHWOOD CT
Digmoor
ALDERLEY
BIRKRIG
CASTLEHEY
Playing Fields
BELFIELD
DIGMOOR RD
St Luke's RC Prim Sch
CARFIELD
BRIERFIELD
CHEQUER LA
PENNINE PL
HOLLAND MOSS
Moss Farm
NIPE LA
PIKELAW PL
PILLING PL
POTTER PL
PENKETH PL
Moss Side Farm
River Tawd
PEEL RD
5
CHEQUER LA
TOWER HILL RD
M58
PRESCOTT RD
PIMBO RD
PIT HEY PL
POTTER PL
PEEL RD
East Pimbo
CHEQUER CL
Hotel
PADDOCK RD
PROSPECT PL
A577
FERNY KNOLL RD
West Pimbo
Ind Est
PAXTON PL
Ind Est
PRIORSWOOD PL
Holland Moss
PRESTWOOD PL
PINFOLD PL
PRESCOTT RD
Upholland Sta
Moor Side Farm
DUKE'S WOOD LA
PENROSE PL
Barton House
PENDLE PL
Lower Balcony Farm
Nursery
LC
Balcarres Farm
Crawford Village Prim Sch
LONG LA
PIMBO LA
DUKE'S WOOD LA
MANOR HOUSE DR
Millets
Maggots Nook
Red House Farm
Crawford
PO
CRAWFORD RD
OAKLEIGH
The Crawford (PH)
Billinge Bounty Farm
Strawberry Cottage
Black Brook
Scythe Stone Delph Farm
NEWS LA
MAGGOTS NOOK RD
Maddocks
REEDS BROW
LANGWOOD LA
Hay's House
48
A
B
49
C
D
50
E
F

A
B
C
D
E
F
8
7
6
5
4
3
2
1
05
04
03
02
51
52
53
Windmill (dis)
Hall Green
Newgate
Works
ORMSKIRK RD
MILL LA
DINGLE RD
GROVE RD
PARLIAMENT ST
SCHOOL LA
ORRELL RD
St Thomas Sch
Up Holland
Dean Wood Golf Course
Hotel
CH
ORRELL
Orrell Post
St Peter's RC High Sch
GATHURST RD
B5206
M6
A577
M58
Liby
Higher Tower Hill Farm
Mast
Well Cross Farm
TOWER HILL RD
Tontine
MOOR RD
Orrell Holgate Prim Sch
Orrell Sta
St James' RC Prim Sch
Far Moor
The Lawns Farm
Upholland Tunnel
Orrell St James' Rd Cty Jun & Inf Sch
Up Holland High Sch
Lower Pimbo
PIMBO LA
ST JAMES' RD
GANTLEY RD
UPHOLLAND RD
Orrell Water Park
Farrar's Farm
Higher Pimbo Farm
Pimbo Bushes
Higher End
Winstanley Coll
WINSTANLEY RD
Greenslate Farm
Billings
Works
BISPHAM HALL BSNS PK
SMETHURST RD
Moss Wood
Mountains Farm
Bispham Hall
Heaton House
Longshaw
New House Farm
Longshaw Bottom
PARK RD
Brownlow Farm
Promised Land Farm
Brownlow
HALL LA
EDGE HALL RD
26

18

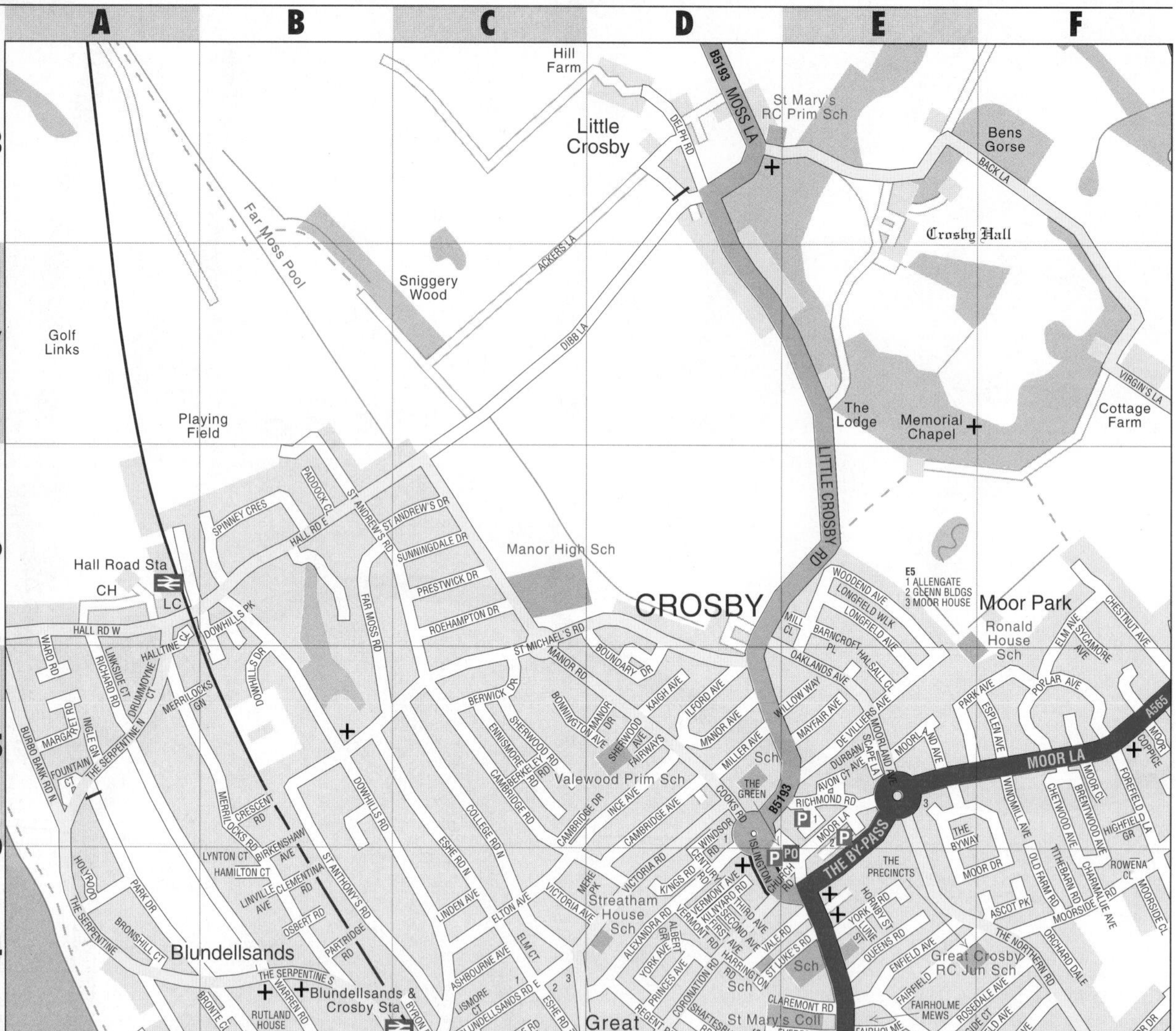
A
B
C
D
E
F
8
7
01
6
5
00
4
3
99
2
1
98
30
31
32
Hill Farm
Little Crosby
B5193 MOSS LA
St Mary's RC Prim Sch
Bens Gorse
BACK LA
Crosby Hall
DELPH RD
Far Moss Pool
ACKERS LA
Sniggery Wood
Golf Links
DIBB LA
The Lodge
Memorial Chapel
Cottage Farm
VIRGIN'S LA
Playing Field
LITTLE CROSBY RD
Manor High Sch
Hall Road Sta
CH
LC
CROSBY
E5
1 ALLENGATE
2 GLENN BLDGS
3 MOOR HOUSE
Moor Park
Ronald House Sch
HALL RD W
HALL RD E
SPINNEY CRES
PADDOCK CL
ST ANDREW'S RD
ST ANDREW'S DR
SUNNINGDALE DR
PRESTWICK DR
ROEHAMPTON DR
ST MICHAEL'S RD
MANOR RD
BOUNDARY DR
FAR MOSS RD
DOWHILLS PK
DOWHILLS DR
MERRILOCKS GN
HALLTINE CL
WARD RD
RICHARD RD
LINKSIDE CT
DRUMMOYNE CT
THE SERPENTINE N
FOUNTAIN CT
INGLE GN
MARGARET RD
BURBO BANK RD N
BERWICK DR
ENNISMORE RD
SHERWOOD RD
BONNINGTON AVE
MANOR DR
SHERWOOD AVE
KAIGH AVE
ILFORD AVE
FAIRWAYS
Valewood Prim Sch
CAMBRIDGE RD
CAMBRIDGE DR
CAMBRIDGE AVE
INCE AVE
MILLER AVE
MANOR AVE
WILLOW WAY
MAYFAIR AVE
DE VILLIERS AVE
OAKLANDS AVE
WOODEND AVE
LONGFIELD WLK
LONGFIELD AVE
BARNCROFT PL
HALSALL CL
MILL CL
DURBAN AVE
SCAPE LA
MOORLAND AVE
MOOR LA
A565
MOOR COPPICE
PARK AVE
ESPLEN AVE
POPLAR AVE
ELM AVE
SYCAMORE AVE
CHESTNUT AVE
WINDMILL AVE
CHETWOOD AVE
BRENTWOOD AVE
MOOR CL
FOREFIELD LA
HIGHFIELD RD
HIGHFIELD GR
THE BYWAY
MOOR DR
OLD FARM RD
TITHEBARN RD
CHARMALUE AVE
ROWENA CL
MOORSIDE AVE
MOORSIDE CL
ASCOT PK
THE GREEN
B5193
RICHMOND RD
AVON CT
THE BY-PASS
THE PRECINCTS
ISLINGTON
CHURCH RD
COOKS RD
WINDSOR RD
CRESCENT RD
MERRILOCKS RD
BIRKENSHAW AVE
LYNTON CT
HAMILTON CT
LINVILLE AVE
CLEMENTINA RD
ST ANTHONY'S RD
DOWHILLS RD
COLLEGE RD N
ESHE RD N
LINDEN AVE
ELTON AVE
VICTORIA AVE
VICTORIA RD
MERE PK
Streatham House Sch
KINGS RD
VERMONT AVE
THIRD AVE
SECOND AVE
FIRST AVE
KILNYARD RD
VALE RD
ST LUKE'S RD
YORK ST
HORNBY ST
QUEENS RD
ENFIELD AVE
Great Crosby RC Jun Sch
THE NORTHERN RD
ORCHARD DALE
HOLYROOD
THE SERPENTINE
PARK DR
BRONSHILL CT
Blundellsands
OSBERT RD
PARTRIDGE RD
THE SERPENTINE S
WARREN RD
Blundellsands & Crosby Sta
BYRON RD
RUTLAND HOUSE
BRONTE CL
ASHBOURNE AVE
LISMORE CT
BLUNDELLSANDS RD E
ESHE RD
ELM CT
ALEXANDRA RD
ALBERT GR
YORK AVE
PRINCES AVE
CORONATION RD
HARRINGTON RD
Sch
CLAREMONT RD
EVEREST RD
St Mary's Coll
FAIRHOLME MEWS
FAIRHOLME RD
ROSEDALE AVE
SEAFIELD AVE
MOORGATE AVE
HILL ST
BLAIR IND EST
TREVOR DR
Great Crosby
Liby
SHAFTESBURY AVE
KIMBERLEY DR
MARYFIELD
PRESELAND RD
DEVON CL
CHANNEL RD
CHANNEL REACH
ALMACS CL
GAYWOOD CL
NICHOLAS RD
NEWSTEAD AVE
SEATHWAITE CL
St Mary's Coll Prep Sch
BLUNDELLSANDS RD W
AGNES RD
ELSINORE CT
ABBOTSFORD RD
KENILWORTH RD
NANHOE RD
WAVERLEY RD
MIDLOTHIAN DR
CARNEGIE AVE
BROMPTON AVE
WARWICK AVE
CARL'S CL
THE SPUR
WOODVILLE AVE
THE CLOISTERS
THE CLOSE
CORONATION DR
LIVERPOOL RD
Sacred Heart RC High Sch
STIRLING AVE
WILLEDSTAN AVE
BALMORAL AVE
MELROSE AVE
STRATHMORE DR
MUSKER ST
MUSKER GDNS
STALEY AVE
KERSHAW AVE
MORNINGSIDE
DESMOND GR
BROWNMOOR LA
HAZEL GR
WINEVA GDNS
Sefton Coastal Path
RAMLEH CL
CHEYNE CL
THE DOWNS
Sch
Brighton le Sands
St Nicholas CE Prim Sch
BURBO CRES
BURBO BANK RD S
WESTON CT
BURBO MANSIONS
MERSEY RD
MERSEY CT
ABBOTSFORD
ROSSETT RD
CROSENDER RD
JUBILEE RD
SUNNYSIDE RD
COLLEGE RD
BROOKFIELD AVE
LANCASTER AVE
TUDOR RD
KINGSWOOD DR
MARLBOROUGH RD
SAXON RD
NORMAN RD
MYERS RD W
BELVIDERE RD
BELVIDERE PK
COLLEGE AVE
ROTHESAY DR
CAITHNESS DR
WHITHAM AVE
KELVINSIDE
MYERS CT
MYERS RD E
BROWNMOOR PK
GRASMERE GDNS
RYDAL AVE
DERWENT RD
BUTTERMERE GDNS
Sacred Heart RC High Sch
Merchant Taylors' Sch
MARINERS RD
HARLECH RD
BRIDGE RD
MERTON GR
CAVENDISH RD
DEVONSHIRE RD
SOMERSET RD
PINEHURST AVE
ROSEBERY AVE
WORCESTER AVE
SHREWSBURY AVE
LICHFIELD AVE
CANTERBURY AVE
BROOKE RD E
CEDAR GR
LAUREL GR
ALDER GR
MYRTLE GR
PINE GR
REGINA AVE
PARK VIEW
RIVERSLEA RD
BALLIOL RD
TRINITY GR
BRIGHTON VALE
WARREN HOUSE RD
GREEN LA
HASTINGS RD
SUDBURY RD
ENDSLEIGH RD
HOLDEN RD
BACK MERSEY VIEW
MERSEY VIEW
SELSDON RD
LEOPOLD RD
HEATHFIELD RD
BROOKE RD W
COURTENAY AVE
COURTENAY RD
SOMERVILLE RD
SOMERVILLE GR
LC
D3
1 WINCHESTER AVE
2 COLLEGE GN
Waterloo
MARLDON AVE
GROSVENOR AVE
MORNINGTON AVE
HATHERLEY AVE
DUDLEY AVE
DUDDINGSTON AVE
CRANMORE AVE
STUART RD
RUTHERGLEN AVE
GLENBY AVE
PARKWAY
ALLENBY AVE
DORBETT DR
KINGSWAY
MILTON RD
MOLYNEUX RD
GALLOWAY RD
WINSTANLEY RD
BACK WINSTANLEY RD
GLENWYLLIN RD
ROYTON RD
MIDDLETON RD
PARKFIELD
KINGSWOOD AVE
QUEENSWAY
HIGHWAY
LAWTON RD
FERNDALE RD
ROCKLAND RD
ASHLAR RD
FIR RD
SYCAMORE RD
THORNDALE RD
OAKDALE RD
ASHDALE RD
BIRCHDALE RD
EASTBOURNE RD 1
WORTHING ST 2
SUSSEX ST 3
WESTWARD VIEW 4
HOLDEN TERR 5
HOLDEN GR 6
HOLDEN RD E 7
PURLEY RD 8
RIVER BANK 9
GLENBANK
BEACH BANK
OXFORD DR
SANDHEYS GR
SANDHEYS AVE
PORTLAND AVE
LULWORTH AVE
SANDHEYS TERR
SEAVIEW TERR
GORDON AVE
HARBORD RD
OXFORD RD
MANLEY RD
BURDETT RD
SERVITE CL
BROWNING AVE
SWEDEN GR
DENMARK ST
Sch
ST JOHN'S CL
JOHN'S RD
CORONA RD
ARGO RD
LYRA RD
NORMA RD
FAIRBAIRN RD
HICKS RD
THE CRESCENT
GARTH CT
HAIGH RD
Chesterfield High Sch Annexe
Waterloo EMI Day
Liby
Civic Hall
CROSBY RD N
BEACH LAWN
BLUCHER ST
MURAT GR
MURAT ST
PICTON RD
ADELAIDE TERR
WELLINGTON ST
MIDLAND ST
EAST ST
MASON ST
MOUNT PLEASANT
ST JOHN'S PL
MOUNT RD
SANDON ST
KING ST
HYDE RD
CROSS ST
BRIGHTON RD
ELM HOUSE
LORNE ST
SOUTH RD
HAMERFIELD RD
CURZON RD
WILLOUGHBY RD
GLENDOWER RD
NEVILLE RD
BACK SOUTH RD
HOUGHTON RD
HOUGHMONT
HOUGHMONT AVE
PARK RD
PARK CT
ESHELBY CL
RONALD CL
RONALD RD
GEVES GDNS
ST MARY'S RD
1 PARKHOLME
2 PARK CT
3 LEESWOOD
BACK MOUNT ST 1
CANNING ST 2
WELBECK CT 3
Boating Lake
MARINE CRES
SANDHEYS AVE
LC
P
PO
H
30
00

37

19
28
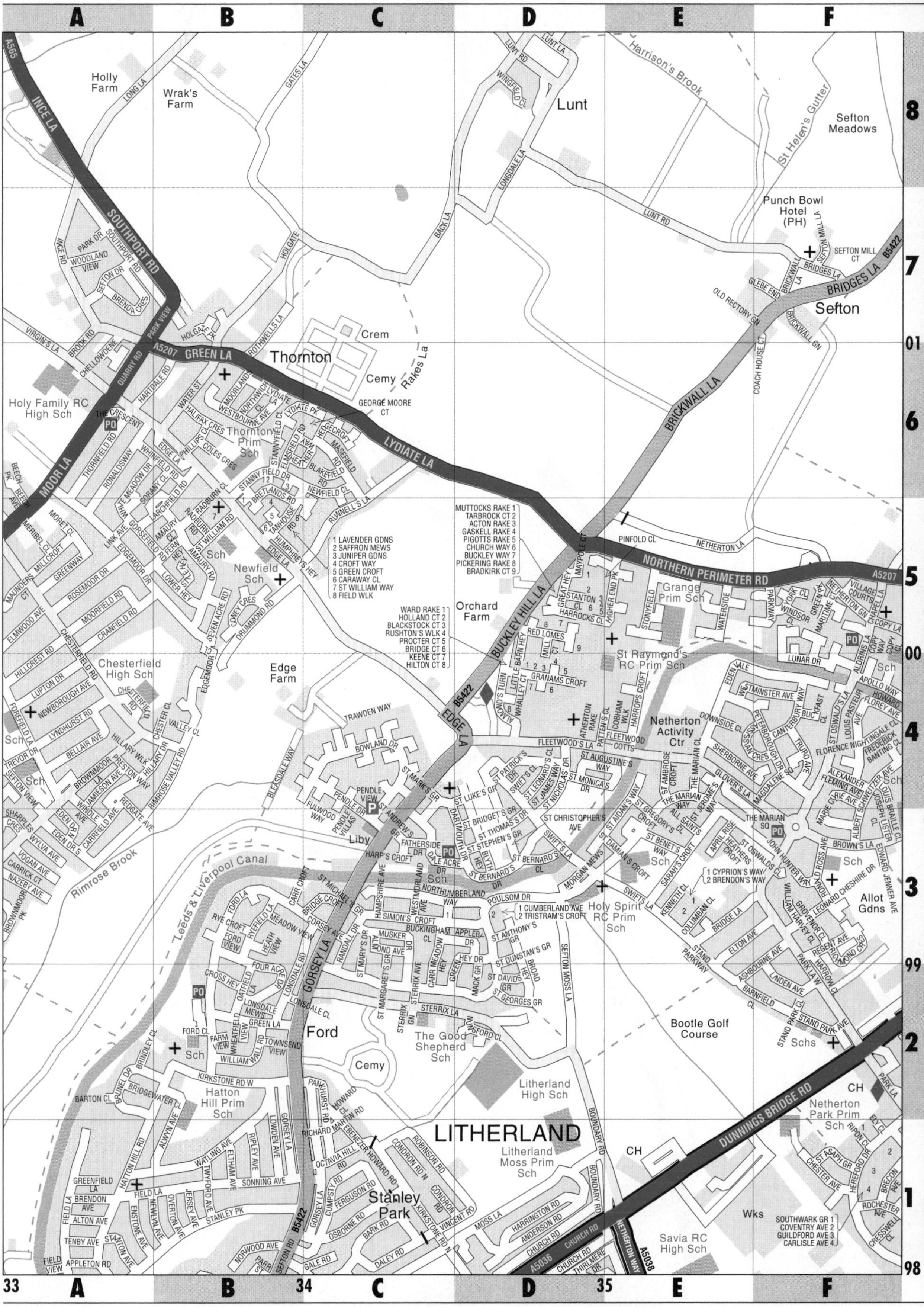
A
B
C
D
E
F
8
7
01
6
5
00
4
3
99
2
1
98
33
34
35
Holly Farm
Wrak's Farm
Lunt
Harrison's Brook
St Helen's Gutter
Sefton Meadows
Punch Bowl Hotel (PH)
Sefton
INCE LA
SOUTHPORT RD
A565
LONG LA
GATES LA
LUNT RD
LUNT LA
WINGFIELD CL
LONGDALE LA
BACK LA
HOLGATE
SEFTON MILL LA
SEFTON MILL CT
BRIDGES LA
B5422
OLD RECTORY GN
GLEBE END
BRICKWALL LA
BRICKWALL GN
COACH HOUSE CT
Crem
Cemy
Rakes La
Thornton
A5207 GREEN LA
LYDIATE LA
GEORGE MOORE CT
VIRGIN'S LA
BROOK RD
CHELLOWDENE
QUARRY RD
PARK VIEW
HOLGATE PK
ROTHWELLS LA
HARTDALE RD
WATER ST
MOORLANDS
NORTHWICK
WESTBOURNE AVE
LYDIATE PK
HALIFAX CRES
PHILLIPS CL
COLES CRES
Thornton Prim Sch
Holy Family RC High Sch
THE CRESCENT
PO
MOOR LA
THORNFIELD RD
RONALDSWAY
WHINFIELD RD
EDGE LA
MEADOW DR
SORANY CL
LARCHFIELD RD
RADBURN CL
BECH PK
MORET CL
MERIBEL CL
MILLCROFT
GREENWAY
LINK AVE
GORSEFIELD RD
EDGEMOOR DR
AMAURY RD
ST WILLIAM RD
Sch
Newfield Sch
BRETLANDS RD
TANHOUSE
STANNY FIELD DR
HUMPHREYS HEY
RUNNELL'S LA
NEWFIELD CL
BLAKEFIELD RD
MASEFIELD
1 LAVENDER GDNS
2 SAFFRON MEWS
3 JUNIPER GDNS
4 CROFT WAY
5 GREEN CROFT
6 CARAWAY CL
7 ST WILLIAM WAY
8 FIELD WLK
MAUNDERS CT
ELMWOOD AVE
ROSEMOOR DR
MOORFIELD RD
CRANFIELD RD
LOWER HEY
SEVEN ACRE RD
DRUMMOND RD
COWEY CRES
HILLCREST RD
CHESTERFIELD RD
LUPTON DR
NEWBOROUGH AVE
LYNDHURST RD
Chesterfield High Sch
CHESTERFIELD RD
EDGEMOOR CL
CHESTER CL
VALLEY CL
FOREFIELD LA
TREVOR DR
SEFTON VIEW
BELLAIR AVE
BROWNMOOR LA
HILLARY WLK
HILLARY DR
RIMROSE VALLEY RD
PRESTON WAY
JAMIESON AVE
WINDLE AVE
CARRFIELD AVE
REDGATE AVE
EDEN DR N
EDEN DR S
SHARPLES CRES
WYLVA AVE
VOGAN AVE
CARRICK CT
NAZEBY AVE
BROWNMOOR PK
Rimrose Brook
Leeds & Liverpool Canal
Edge Farm
Orchard Farm
MUTTOCKS RAKE 1
TARBROCK CT 2
ACTON RAKE 3
GASKELL RAKE 4
PIGOTTS RAKE 5
CHURCH WAY 6
BUCKLEY WAY 7
PICKERING RAKE 8
BRADKIRK CT 9
WARD RAKE 1
HOLLAND CT 2
BLACKSTOCK CT 3
RUSHTON'S WLK 4
PROCTER CT 5
BRIDGE CT 6
KEENE CT 7
HILTON CT 8
BUCKLEY HILL LA
EDGE LA
MAYPOLE CT
PINFOLD CL
NETHERTON LA
NORTHERN PERIMETER RD
A5207
GREAT HEY
STANTON CL
HIGHER END PK
HARROCKS CL
RED LOMES
MILL CT
LITTLE BARN HEY
WHALLEY CT
GRANAMS CROFT
ALMOND'S TURN
ATHERTON RAKE
PATTEN'S CL
COBHAM WLK
HARROPS CROFT
STONYFIELD
Grange Prim Sch
St Raymond's RC Prim Sch
WATERSIDE
PARKWAY
YORK CL
WINDSOR CL
GREEN PK
MARITIME CT
NETHERTON GN
VILLAGE COURTS
CHAPEL LA
COPY LA
LUNAR DR
ALDRINS LA
COPY WAY
APOLLO WAY
HOWARD FLOREY AVE
EDEN VALE
WESTMINSTER AVE
Netherton Activity Ctr
DOWNSIDE CL
PETERBOROUGH DR
CANTERBURY WAY
BUCKFAST CL
TRURO AVE
ST OSWALD'S LA
LOUIS PASTEUR AVE
FREDERICK BANTING CL
FLORENCE NIGHTINGALE CL
SHERBORNE AVE
GLOVER'S LA
MAGDALENE SQ
ALEXANDER FLEMING AVE
MARIE CURIE AVE
ALBERT SCHWEITZER AVE
LOUIS BRAILLE CL
JOSEPH LISTER CL
EDWARD JENNER AVE
BROWN'S LA
TRAWDEN WAY
BOWLAND DR
BLEASDALE WAY
PENDLE VIEW
PENDLE DR
FULWOOD WAY
PENDLE VILLAS
ST MARK'S GR
ST ANDREW'S GR
Liby
FLEETWOOD'S LA
FLEETWOOD COTTS
ST AUGUSTINE'S WAY
ST MONICA'S DR
ST NICHOLAS' DR
ST LEONARD'S CL
ST JAMES WAY
SWIFT'S CL
ST PATRICK'S DR
ST LUKE'S GR
DARTMOUTH DR
ST BRIDGET'S GR
ST THOMAS'S DR
ST STEPHEN'S GR
ST CHRISTOPHER'S AVE
ST BERNARD'S CL
SWIFT'S LA
ST AIDAN'S WAY
ST AMBROSE CROFT
THE MARIAN CL
THE MARIAN WAY
ALL SAINTS CL
ST JEROME'S WAY
ST GREGORY'S CROFT
ST BENET'S WAY
ST DAMIAN'S CROFT
MORGAN MEWS
SARAH'S CROFT
APRIL RISE
HEATHERS CROFT
ST OSWALDS CL
THE MARIAN SQ
JOHN HUNTER WAY
RONALD ROSS AVE
LEONARD CHESHIRE DR
1 CYPRION'S WAY
2 BRENDON'S WAY
Allot Gdns
HARP'S CROFT
FATHERSIDE DR
DALE ACRE DR
BLYTH HEY
NORTHUMBERLAND WAY
POULSOM DR
1 CUMBERLAND AVE
2 TRISTRAM'S CROFT
Holy Spirit RC Prim Sch
KENNETH CL
COLUMBAN CL
BRIDGE LA
ELTON AVE
STAND PARKWAY
ASHBOURNE AVE
WILLIAM HARVEY CL
GROSVENOR CL
REGENT AVE
HAROLD CL
LINDEN AVE
PARK LA W
BARNFIELD CL
STAND PARK CL
STAND PARK AVE
Schs
FORD LA
RYE CROFT
FORD VIEW
RIEFIELD
MEADOW VIEW
HEATH VIEW
CARR CROFT
BRIDGE CROFT
ST MICHAEL'S GR
CORSEY AVE
HAMPSHIRE AVE
WESTMORLAND AVE
SIMON'S CROFT
BUCKINGHAM CL
APPLEBY CL
MUSKER DR
ST MARY'S DR
RANDALL DR
ST MARGARET'S GR
STERRIX AVE
CARR MEADOW HEY
GREEN HEY DR
MACK GR
ST ANTHONY'S
ST DUNSTAN'S GR
BROAD HEY
ST DAVID'S GR
ST GEORGES GR
SEFTON MOSS LA
CROSS HEY
FOUR ACRE DR
OATFIELD LA
LONSDALE MEWS
LONSDALE RD
GORSEY LA
LONSDALE CL
STERRIX LA
STERRIX GN
MUNSFORD CL
Ford
The Good Shepherd Sch
Cemy
FORD CL
FARM VIEW
WHEATFIELD VIEW
GREEN LA
TOWNSEND VIEW
WILLIAM WALL RD
KIRKSTONE RD W
Hatton Hill Prim Sch
BARTON CL
BRUNEL DR
BRINDLEY CL
BRIDGEWATER CL
ALWYN AVE
WATLING AVE
ELTHAM AVE
RIPLEY AVE
LOWDEN AVE
GORSEY LA
SONNING AVE
HATTON HILL RD
GREENFIELD LA
BRENDON AVE
ALTON AVE
TENBY AVE
FIELD VIEW
APPLETON RD
FIELD LA
ENSTONE AVE
NEWLYN AVE
OVERTON AVE
TWYFORD AVE
JERSEY AVE
STANLEY PK
STANTON AVE
NORWOOD AVE
PARR ST
SEFTON RD
B5422
GALE RD
PANKHURST RD
HOWARD CL
MARTIN RD
RICHARD RD
EBENEZER HOWARD RD
OCTAVIA HILL RD
CUMPSTY RD
GORSEY LA
FERGUSON RD
OSBORNE RD
Stanley Park
BARK RD
DALEY RD
KIRKSTONE RD N
CONDRON RD N
ROBINSON RD
CONDRON RD S
VINCENT RD
LITHERLAND
Litherland High Sch
Litherland Moss Prim Sch
MOSS LA
HARRINGTON RD
ANDERSON RD
CHURCH RD
A5036
THIRLMERE DR
BOUNDARY RD
NETHERTON WAY
A5038
CH
Bootle Golf Course
Savia RC High Sch
DUNNINGS BRIDGE RD
Wks
Netherton Park Prim Sch
PARK LA
ELY CL
RIPON CL
ST ASAPH GR
CHESTER AVE
HEREFORD DR
BRECON AVE
ROCHESTER AVE
CRESSWELL CL
SOUTHWARK GR 1
COVENTRY AVE 2
GUILDFORD AVE 3
CARLISLE AVE 4
38
28

27
20

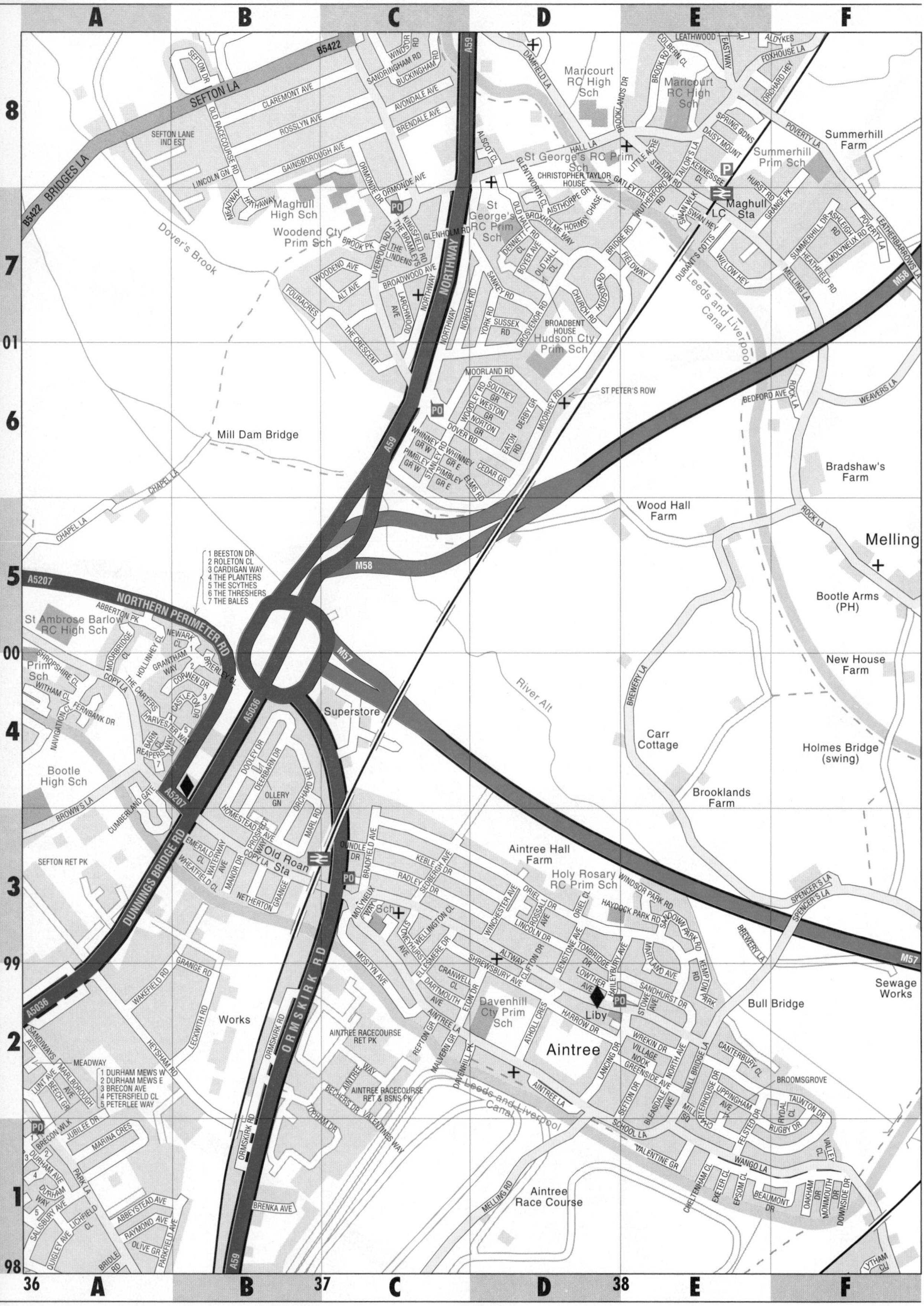
A
B
C
D
E
F
8
7
01
6
5
00
4
3
99
2
1
98
36
37
38
SEFTON LA
B5422
BRIDGES LA
SEFTON DR
CLAREMONT AVE
ROSSLYN AVE
GAINSBOROUGH AVE
OLD RACECOURSE RD
SEFTON LANE IND EST
LINCOLN GN
WINDSOR RD
SANDRINGHAM RD
BUCKINGHAM RD
AVONDALE AVE
BRENDALE AVE
ORMONDE DR
ORMONDE AVE
A59
NORTHWAY
Maghull High Sch
Woodend Cty Prim Sch
MEADWAY
HATHAWAY
Dover's Brook
BROOK PK
WOODEND AVE
ALT AVE
FOURACRES
THE CRESCENT
LIVERPOOL RD S
THE LINDENS
THE BRAMBLES
KINGSFIELD RD
GLENHOLM RD
BROADWOOD AVE
LARCHWOOD AVE
Maricourt RC High Sch
DAMFIELD LA
BROOKLANDS DR
ALSCOT CL
HALL LA
St George's RC Prim Sch
CHRISTOPHER TAYLOR HOUSE
St George's RC Prim Sch
GLENTWORTH CL
OLD HALL RD
BROXHOLME WAY
AISTHORPE GR
HORNBY CHASE
GATLEY DR
LITTLE ACRE
STATION RD
RUTHERFORD RD
BRIDGE RD
FIELDWAY
CHURCH RD
HUDSON RD
DENNETT CL
BOYER AVE
OLD HALL CL
SANKEY RD
NORFOLK RD
YORK RD
SUSSEX RD
GROSVENOR RD
BROADBENT HOUSE
Hudson Cty Prim Sch
MOORLAND RD
SOUTHEY GR
WESTON GR
NORTON GR
WOODLEY RD
DERBY GR
EATON RD
MOORHEY RD
ST PETER'S ROW
DOVER RD
WHINNEY GR W
WHINNEY GR E
PIMBLEY GR W
PIMBLEY GR E
STANLEY RD
CEDAR GR
ELMS RD
LEATHWOOD
ALDYKES
FOXHOUSE LA
ORCHARD HEY
COLBERN CL
BROOK RD
EASTWAY
SPRING GDNS
DAISY MOUNT
TAILOR'S LA
KENNESSEE CL
POVERTY LA
Summerhill Farm
Summerhill Prim Sch
HURST RD
GRANGE PK
Maghull Sta
LC
SWAN WLK
SWAN HEY
DURANT'S COTTS
WILLOW HEY
MELLING LA
SUMMERHILL DR
ASHLEIGH RD
HEATHFIELD RD
MOLYNEUX RD
POVERTY LA
LEATHERBARROWS LA
M58
Leeds and Liverpool Canal
BEDFORD AVE
ROCK LA
WEAVERS LA
Bradshaw's Farm
Wood Hall Farm
ROCK LA
Melling
Bootle Arms (PH)
New House Farm
Holmes Bridge (swing)
Mill Dam Bridge
CHAPEL LA
CHAPEL LA
1 BEESTON DR
2 ROLETON CL
3 CARDIGAN WAY
4 THE PLANTERS
5 THE SCYTHES
6 THE THRESHERS
7 THE BALES
M58
A5207
NORTHERN PERIMETER RD
ABBERTON PK
St Ambrose Barlow RC High Sch
Prim Sch
SHROPSHIRE CL
WITHAM CL
MOORBRIDGE CL
HOLLINHEY CL
NEWARK CL
GRANTHAM WAY
BRIERLEY CL
CORWEN DR
COPY LA
THE CARTERS
CASTLETON DR
FERNBANK DR
NAVIGATION CL
HARVESTER WAY
BARN CL
REAPERS WAY
Bootle High Sch
BROWN'S LA
CUMBERLAND GATE
M57
A5036
River Alt
Superstore
BREWERY LA
Carr Cottage
Brooklands Farm
DOOLEY DR
DEERBARN DR
OLLERY GN
ORCHARD HEY
MARL RD
HOMESTEAD AVE
PROSPECT WAY
EMERALD CL
WATERWAY AVE
MANOR DR
COPY LA
WHEATFIELD CL
NETHERTON GRANGE
Old Roan Sta
SEFTON RET PK
DUNNINGS BRIDGE RD
A5207
QUNDLE DR
BRADFIELD AVE
KEBLE DR
SEDBERGH AVE
RADLEY DR
Aintree Hall Farm
Holy Rosary RC Prim Sch
WINDSOR PARK RD
HAYDOCK PARK RD
SANDOWN PARK RD
KEMPTON PARK
SPENCER'S LA
SPENCER'S LA
BREWERY LA
M57
Sewage Works
MOLYNEUX WAY
Sch
TOLS AVE
STONEYHURST AVE
WELLINGTON CL
WINCHESTER AVE
ORIEL DR
ROSSALL AVE
ORIEL CL
LINCOLN DR
DENSTONE AVE
TONBRIDGE DR
HAILEYBURY AVE
MARYLAND AVE
LOWTHER AVE
SANDHURST DR
STOWE AVE
ELLESMERE DR
ALTWAY
CLIFTON DR
SHREWSBURY AVE
MOSTYN AVE
CRANWELL CL
DARTMOUTH AVE
ETON DR
Davenhill Cty Prim Sch
Liby
HARROW DR
ATHOLL CRES
Aintree
Bull Bridge
WREKIN DR
VILLAGE NOOK
GREENSIDE AVE
NORTH AVE
BULL BRIDGE LA
CANTERBURY CL
BROOMSGROVE
LANCING DR
SEFTON DR
BLEASDALE AVE
MILL SQ
CHARTERHOUSE DR
UPPINGHAM AVE
FELSTED DR
RYDAL CL
TAUNTON DR
RUGBY DR
SCHOOL LA
VALENTINE GR
WANGO LA
VALLEY CL
CHELTENHAM CL
EXETER CL
EPSOM CL
BEAUMONT DR
OAKHAM DR
MONMOUTH DR
DOWNSIDE DR
YTHAM CL
AINTREE LA
AINTREE LA
REPTON GR
MALVERN GR
DAVENHILL PK
Leeds and Liverpool Canal
AINTREE RACECOURSE RET PK
AINTREE WAY
AINTREE RACECOURSE RET & BSNS PK
BECHERS DR
VALENTINES WAY
TOPHAM DR
ORMSKIRK RD
ORMSKIRK RD
ORMSKIRK RD
BRENKA AVE
MELLING RD
Aintree Race Course
A59
GRANGE RD
WAKEFIELD RD
LECKWITH RD
HEYSHAM RD
Works
A5036
SANDIWAYS AVE
MEADWAY
MARLBOROUGH AVE
BEECH GR
LUNT AVE
1 DURHAM MEWS W
2 DURHAM MEWS E
3 BRECON AVE
4 PETERSFIELD CL
5 PETERLEE WAY
BRECON WLK
JUBILEE DR
MARINA CRES
DURHAM AVE
DURHAM WAY
PARK LA
SALISBURY AVE
LICHFIELD CL
ABBEYSTEAD AVE
RAYMOND AVE
OLIVE GR
PARKFIELD AVE
QUIGLEY AVE
BRIDLE RD
PO
P

27
39

21
30

A
B
C
D
E
F
8
7
01
6
5
00
4
3
99
2
1
98
39
40
41
Whinny Brook
M58
Whitegates Farm
SPURRIER'S LA
OUTLET LA
A506
PRESCOT RD
Moss Nook Farm
MOSS NOOK LA
Basford Farm
MOSS LA
Melling Mount
Ash Holt Farm
GIDDYGATE LA
Moorfield House
Simonswood Brook
Simonswood Hall
HALL LA
Bank Hall Farm
LEATHERBARROWS LA
Glovers Farm
ANGERS LA
Melling House Farm
Melling House
SANDY LA
SCHOOL LA
TITHEBARN LA
Barnes' Farm
BANK LA
ST ANDREW'S VIEW
SHEVINGTON'S LA
THE MOORFIELD CTR
MOORFIELD
SS. Peter & Paul RC Prim Sch
Tower Hill
MOSSDALE RD
Ravenscroft Cty Prim Sch
Eastcroft Park Prim Sch
TRAVIS DR
SOUTHCROFT
HEADBOLT LA
NATHAN GR
WADDICAR LA
Wadacre Farm
CHAPEL LA
Waddicar
English Martyrs RC Prim Sch
MALVERN CL
PENNINE WAY
CLEVELAND CL
MILL LA
DEERBOLT CL
Overdale Prim Sch
LINSLADE CL
Leeds and Liverpool Canal
Melling Cty Prim Sch
STATION RD
Works
Knowsley Ruffwood Comp Sch
Old Rough
Kirkby Park
Kirkby Brow
MELLING WAY
MELLING DR
CHURCH WAY
MILBROOK DR
Ledsons Bridge
SPENCER'S LA
CANAL VIEW
Kirkby Sta
Millbrook Prim Sch
Holy Angel's Prim Schs
Kirkby CE Prim Sch
OLD HALL LA
HALL LA
A5208
COUNTY RD
OLD ROUGH LA
C Ctr
Mkt Sq
Liby
Westvale Prim Sch
WILLIAM ROBERTS AVE
RICHARD HESKETH DR
Westvale
HOULSTON WLK
Kirkby Municipal Golf Course
HAWGREEN RD
WESTFIELD WLK
Knowsley Comm Coll Kirkby Ctr
KIRKBY
Knowsley All Saints RC High Sch
VALLEY RD
TITHE BARN LA
River Alt
INGOE LA
M57
Kirkby Stadium
Knowsley Comm Coll Bracknell Ctr
BEWLEY DR
Sch
BRACKNELL CL
CLIEVES RD
WELLFIELD AVE
PARK BROW DR

40
30

29
22

A
B
C
D
E
F
8
7
01
6
5
00
4
3
99
2
1
98
42
43
44
Brookfield Farm
Voces Farm
Hesketh's Shroggs
Walkden House Farm
Sewage Works
SINEACRE LA
HALL LA
Grayson's Farm
Barrow Nook Hall
Simonswood Brook
New Bridge Farm
Abram's Farm
High Barn Farm
Wood House Farm
STOPGATE LA
SIDING LA
Hall's Folly
Wild Goose Slack
Gate House Bridge
SIMONSWOOD IND PK
Timber Yard
CALDER CL
MOORFIELD
PINGWOOD LA
Woodwards Plantation
Woods Farm
MOSSCROFT
Southead
Bridge Farm
1 LAPFORD WLK
2 BYTON WLK
3 WHITBURN RD
4 KENBURY CL
HEADBOLT LA
BRAMCOTE CL
BRAMCOTE RD
CARFAX RD
LAPFORD CRES
PENTLAND RD
DALE LA
Spencer's House Farm
Eccleston House
NORTH PERIMETER RD
Simonswood Moss
OAKLEE GR
FALSTONE RD
SHACKLADY RD
TRECASTLE RD
ROUGHWOOD DR
FOSCOTE RD
WARRENHOUSE RD
Ashcroft's Plantation
Works
DEPOT RD
DEYCROFT AVE
DEYCROFT WLK
KENBURY RD
GILESCROFT AVE
WATTS CL
JARRETT WLK
JARRETT RD
CHANGFORD RD
NORTH MERSEY BSNS CTR
MOSS END WAY
WOODWARD RD
BROOK HEY DR
5 CHANGFORD GN
6 QUERNMORE WLK
7 BROOK HEY WLK
8 WINGATE WLK
9 JADE CL
10 BIRBECK WLK
11 FAIRTHORN WLK
12 HARLESTON WLK
13 BURWELL CL
14 KENMAY WAY
BIGDALE DR
QUERNMORE RD
Sch
MARL RD
HAMMOND RD
Northwood
CLORAIN CL
BIRBECK RD
BRADMAN RD
SANDERLING RD
CLORAIN RD
DARMOND RD
HARLESTON RD
MOSS LA
ASHCROFT RD
QUARRYSIDE DR
COLWALL RD
COURTYARD WORKS
NEWSTET RD
RETFORD RD
CYGNET CT
COLWALL CL
SIMONSWOOD LA
1 COLWALL WLK
2 SIMONSWOOD WLK
3 LIFTON RD
Top House Farm
BOUNDARY LA
MINSTEAD AVE
Sch
WYLLIN RD
BIRCHILL RD
Playing Field
KNOWSLEY IND PK
STOCKPIT RD
DRAW WELL RD
ACORNFIELD RD
PERIMETER RD
ORMONDE CRES
MINTOR RD
GLEGSIDE RD
MADRYN AVE
BARN HEY RD
FARRIER RD
ARBOUR LA
KIRKBY BANK RD
Orchard Works
CRANSTON RD
LEES RD
WESTHEAD AVE
ACORN BSNS CTR
WEBBER RD
YARDLEY CTR
YARDLEY RD
Kirkby Moss
4 WESTHEAD WLK
5 WESTHEAD CL
A5208
COUNTY RD
Charley Wood
RUSHDEN RD
DELFBY CRES
DULAS GN
DULAS RD
CROSLAND RD
CHARLEY WOOD RD
BROAD LA
LINKS RD
CUSSON RD
GORES RD
MOSSLAWN RD

23
32

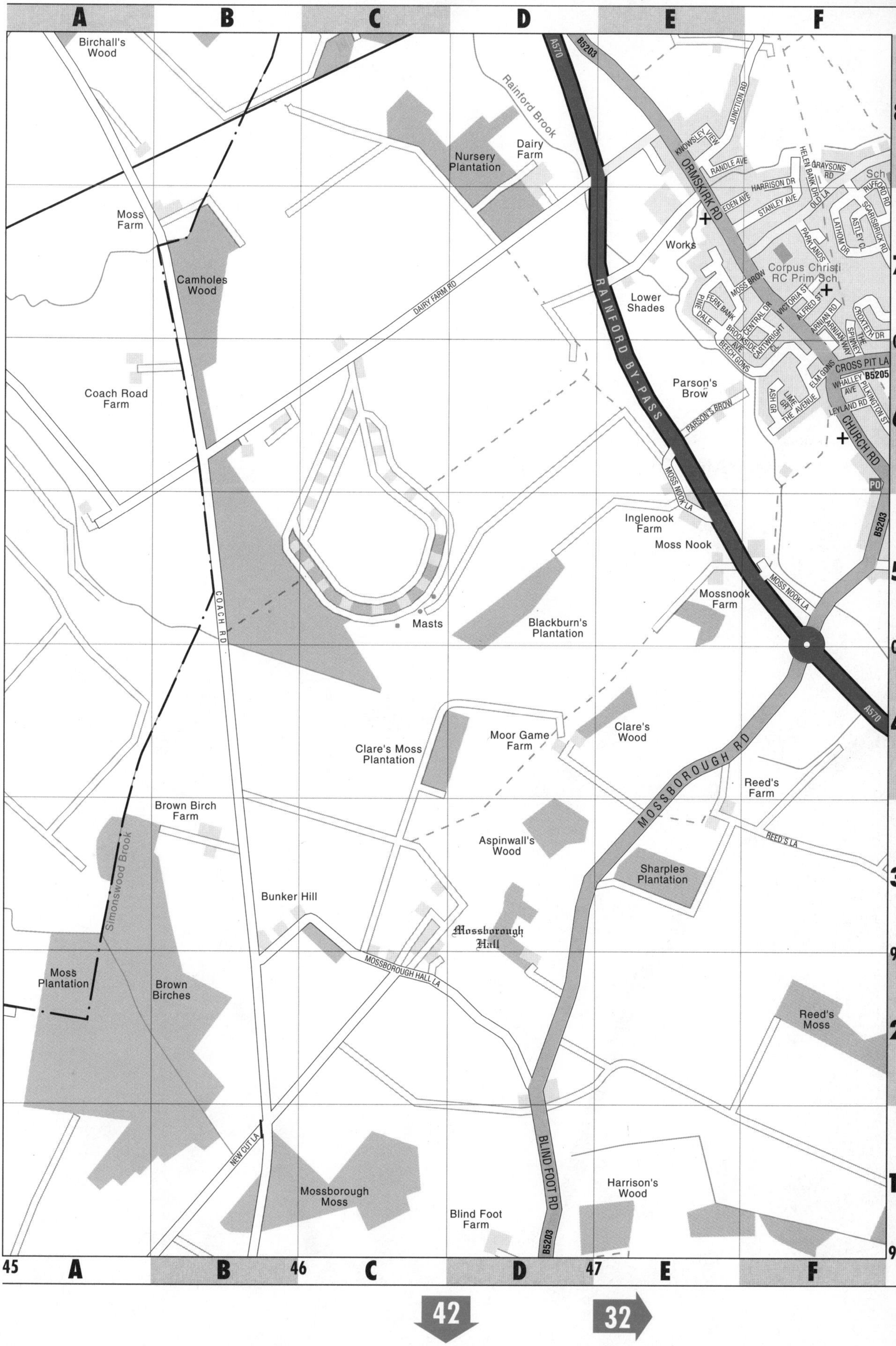
A
B
C
D
E
F
Birchall's Wood
Rainford Brook
Dairy Farm
Nursery Plantation
A570
B5203
JUNCTION RD
KNOWSLEY VIEW
RANDLE AVE
ORMSKIRK RD
HARRISON DR
HELEN BANK DR
GRAYSONS RD
Sch
RUFFORD RD
EDEN AVE
STANLEY AVE
OLD LA
SCARISBRICK RD
LATHOM DR
ASTLEY CL
PARKLANDS
Moss Farm
Works
Camholes Wood
DAIRY FARM RD
Corpus Christi RC Prim Sch
MOSS BROW
VICTORIA ST
ALFRED ST
Lower Shades
RAINFORD BY-PASS
FERN BANK
PINE DALE
CENTRAL DR
BROOKSIDE AVE
CARTWRIGHT CL
BEECH GDNS
ARNIAN RD
ARNIAN WAY
SPINNEY
THE CROXTETH DR
CROSS PIT LA
B5205
ELM GDNS
WHALLEY AVE
PILKINGTON ST
LEYLAND RD
Coach Road Farm
Parson's Brow
PARSON'S BROW
ASH GR
LIME GR
THE AVENUE
CHURCH RD
PO
MOSS NOOK LA
Inglenook Farm
Moss Nook
Mossnook Farm
COACH RD
Masts
Blackburn's Plantation
Clare's Moss Plantation
Moor Game Farm
Clare's Wood
MOSSBOROUGH RD
Reed's Farm
Brown Birch Farm
REED'S LA
Aspinwall's Wood
Simonswood Brook
Bunker Hill
Sharples Plantation
Mossborough Hall
MOSSBOROUGH HALL LA
Moss Plantation
Brown Birches
Reed's Moss
NEW CUT LA
BLIND FOOT RD
Mossborough Moss
Harrison's Wood
Blind Foot Farm
8
7
01
6
5
00
4
3
99
2
1
98
45
46
47

42
32

31
24

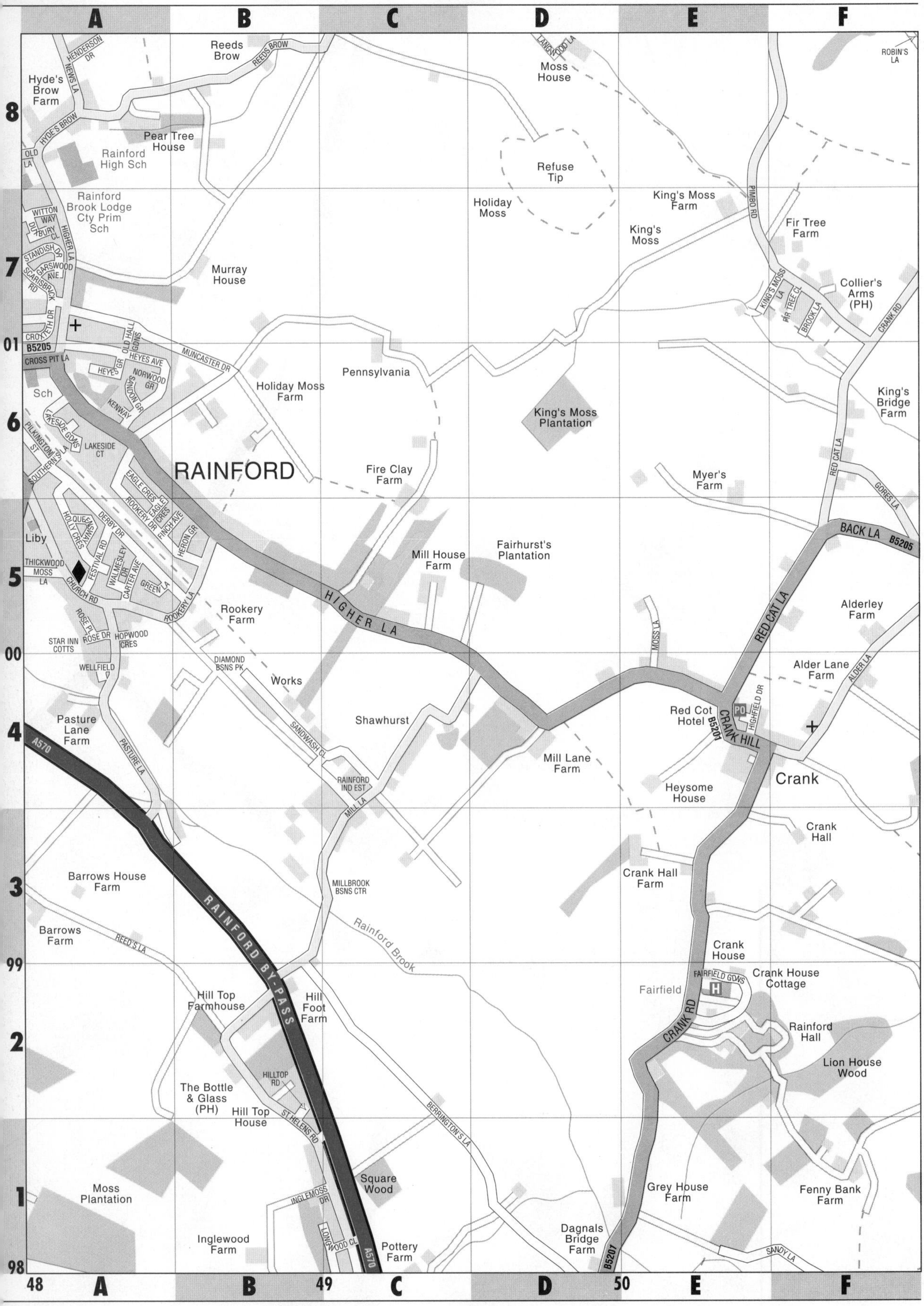
A
B
C
D
E
F
8
7
01
6
5
00
4
3
99
2
1
98
48
49
50
HENDERSON DR
NEWS LA
Hyde's Brow Farm
HYDE'S BROW
Reeds Brow
REEDS BROW
LANGWOOD LA
Moss House
ROBIN'S LA
OLD LA
Pear Tree House
Rainford High Sch
Refuse Tip
Holiday Moss
King's Moss Farm
PIMBO RD
Fir Tree Farm
King's Moss
Rainford Brook Lodge Cty Prim Sch
WITTON WAY
DUXBURY CL
HIGHER LA
STANDISH DR
GARSWOOD AVE
SCARISBRICK RD
Murray House
KING'S MOSS LA
FIR TREE CL
BROOK LA
Collier's Arms (PH)
CRANK RD
CROXTETH DR
CROFT
B5205
OLD HALL GDNS
HEYES AVE
MUNCASTER DR
CROSS PIT LA
HEYES GR
NORWOOD GR
SANDON GR
KENWAY
Holiday Moss Farm
Pennsylvania
King's Moss Plantation
King's Bridge Farm
Sch
LAKESIDE GDNS
LAKESIDE CT
PILKINGTON ST
SOUTHERN'S LA
RAINFORD
Fire Clay Farm
Myer's Farm
RED CAT LA
GORES LA
EAGLE CRES
ROOKERY DR
EAGLE CRES
FINCH AVE
HERON GR
DERBY DR
QUEENSWAY
HOLLY CRES
BACK LA
B5205
Liby
THICKWOOD MOSS LA
FESTIVAL RD
WALMESLEY DR
CARTER AVE
GREEN LA
CHURCH RD
Fairhurst's Plantation
Mill House Farm
Rookery Farm
ROOKERY LA
HIGHER LA
RED CAT LA
Alderley Farm
ROSE PL
ROSE DR
HOPWOOD CRES
STAR INN COTTS
WELLFIELD
MOSS LA
DIAMOND BSNS PK
Works
Alder Lane Farm
ALDER LA
Pasture Lane Farm
Shawhurst
Red Cot Hotel
B5201
CRANK HILL
PO
HIGHFIELD DR
A570
PASTURE LA
SANDWASH CL
Mill Lane Farm
RAINFORD IND EST
MILL LA
Heysome House
Crank
Crank Hall
Barrows House Farm
RAINFORD BY-PASS
MILLBROOK BSNS CTR
Crank Hall Farm
Barrows Farm
REED'S LA
Rainford Brook
Crank House
FAIRFIELD GDNS
Crank House Cottage
Fairfield
H
Hill Top Farmhouse
Hill Foot Farm
CRANK RD
Rainford Hall
Lion House Wood
HILLTOP RD
The Bottle & Glass (PH)
Hill Top House
ST HELENS RD
BERRINGTON'S LA
Square Wood
Moss Plantation
INGLEMOSS DR
Grey House Farm
Fenny Bank Farm
Inglewood Farm
LONGWOOD CL
A570
Pottery Farm
Dagnals Bridge Farm
B5207
SANDY LA

31
43

25
34

A B C D E F
8
7
01
6
5
00
4
3
99
2
1
98
51
52
53
Masts
Beacon Farm
Billinge Plants
Billinge Hall
Shaley Brow Farm
CRANK RD
ROBIN'S LA
Masts
Wiswall's Farm
B5206
PAIGNTON CL
TORQUAY DR
LONGSHAW COMM
Longshaw Common
Chair Wood
UPHOLLAND RD
Moss Vale Farm
Billinge Hill
A571
WIGAN RD
The Old Vicarage
Longshaw House
Maddox House
Rainford Brook Farm
Red Barn Farm
OAKLEY AVE
BEACON RD
COULSHEAD AVE
ST AIDAN'S CL
Great Houghwood
RED BARN RD
Ash Grove Farm
Liby
B5207
NEWTON RD
CROOKHURST AVE
ASH GROVE CRES
NORBURY AVE
WELLS AVE
ROSS CL
STUART CRES
MAPLE CL
LARCH CL
ALDER AVE
ELM DR
Crookhurst Farm
MAIN ST
CONWAY CRES
CONWAY DR
ROYDEN CRES
GREENHILL CRES
GREENHILL RD
ROYDEN RD
WINDSOR RD
ANDREW AVE
LONDON FIELDS
CLAREMONT RD
SCHOOL BROW
RECREATION DR
SCHOOL DR
Sch
BLACKLEYHURST AVE
Guild Hall
GORSEY BROW CL
ROBY WELL WAY
SEFTON GDNS
SEFTON FOLD DR
FAIR VIEW AVE
FAIR VIEW
GORSEY BROW
HAWTHORN CL
BRAESIDE CRES
HILLSIDE CL
PICADILLY
STANDISH AVE
LOSTOCK CL
BARTON CL
STRETTON AVE
MITCHELL RD
TATLOCK CL
GOYT HEY AVE
BROOKS
ASHFIELD CRES
AUGHTON CL
DANESBURY CL
ALDER LA
GORE'S LA
RAINFORD RD
Rainford Delph Farm
PO
B5205
HOLT CRES
HOLT AVE
BEULAH AVE
GARSWOOD CRES
CARR MILL CRES
ALDERLEY CL
CORONATION WLK
MYRTLE GR
LILAC GR
GREENFIELD VIEW
Birchley Hall
Billinge Chapel End Prim Sch
GARSWOOD RD
Blackley Hurst Hall
Fir Wood
ST MARY'S AVE
Sch
CLIFTON RD
ELLIS RD
Nugent House Sch
BILLINGE
Black Brook
BIRCHLEY RD
AVON RD
TRENT RD
SEVERN CL
BIRCHLEY AVE
LINDEN GR
RIBBLE CRES
AVON
ABBOTTS WAY
BROWN HEATH AVE
Brooklands
Clay Wood
DOUGLAS AVE
DEAN CL
POWELL DR
STARTHAM AVE
HOLT CL
Barrows Farm
ARCH LA
High Wood
Moss Bank Bridge
Sewage Works
Chadwick Green
LIME VALE RD
Masons' Arms (PH)
CARR MILL RD
The Goyt
Otter's Swift
Shoot's Delph Farm
BIRCHLEY VIEW
MARTINDALE RD
CHERRY TREE LA
MANOR HOUSE CL
MOSS BANK RD
TROUTBECK GR
MILLBECK GR
BROAD LA
THWAITE GR
DALSTON DR
CROSSDALE WAY
MOSEDALE AVE
GREENBURN AVE
DEEPDALE AVE
CALDBECK GR
Caleb's Wood
Caleb's Rough
Hollin Hey House
Hollin Hey Farm
Winstanley Wood
CLUB ST
PO
INGLETON DR
CRAG GR
BAMPTON AVE
GHYLL GR
LOUGHRIGG AVE
DUNMAIL AVE
Carr Mill
Carr Mill Jun Sch
CARR MILL RD
Carr Mill Dam
GARSWOOD OLD RD
Moss Bank
DEVOKE AVE
HILLBRAE AVE
LORTON AVE
Clinkham Wood
AMBLESIDE PL
ENNERDALE AVE
YEWDALE AVE
MERE GR
KENTMERE AVE
Old Garswood Hall Farm

44
34

33

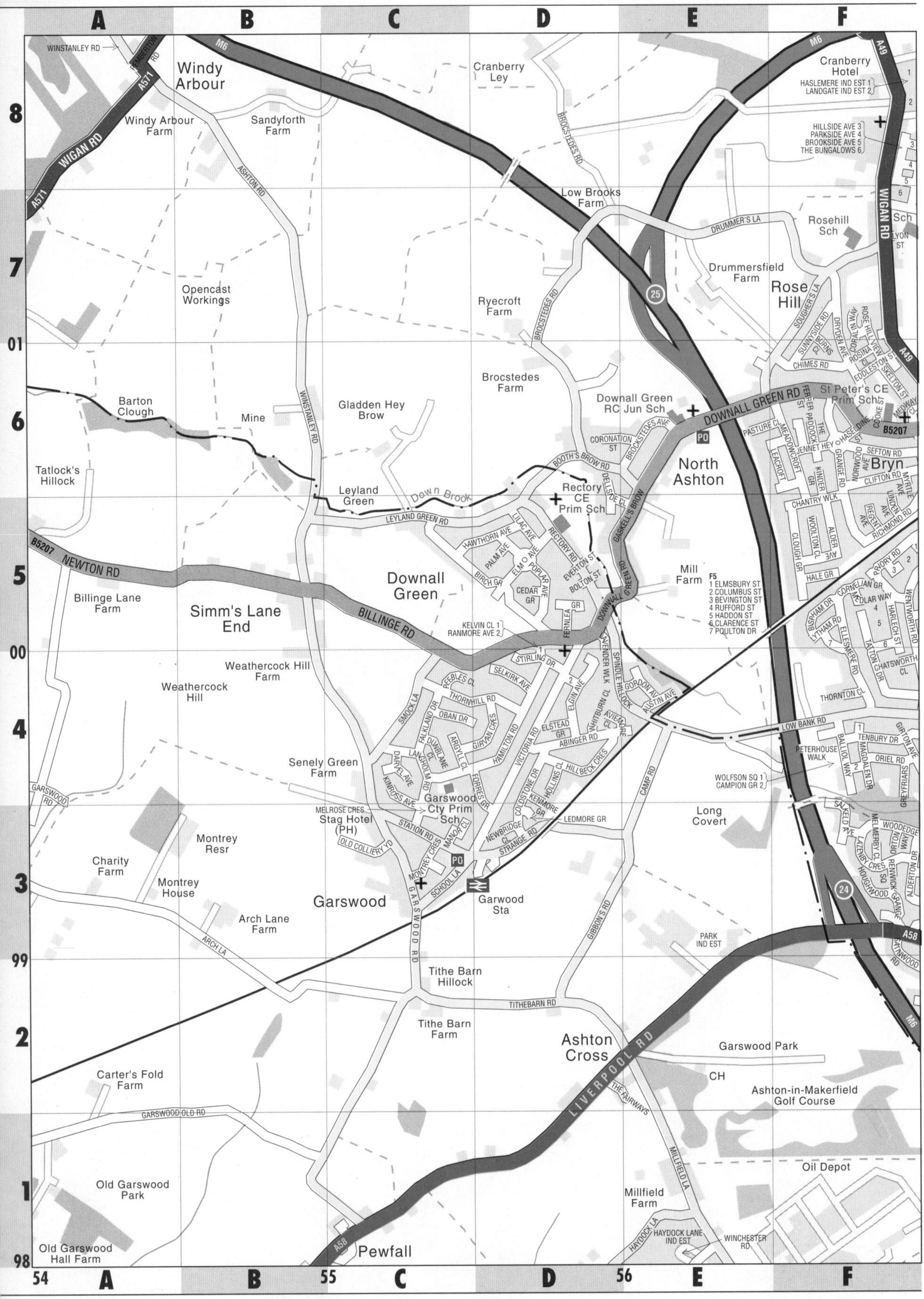

A
B
C
D
E
F
8
7
01
6
5
00
4
3
99
2
1
98
54
55
56
WINSTANLEY RD
PEMBERTON RD
A571
WIGAN RD
M6
Windy Arbour
Windy Arbour Farm
Sandyforth Farm
ASHTON RD
Cranberry Ley
BROCSTEDES RD
Cranberry Hotel
HASLEMERE IND EST 1
LANDGATE IND EST 2
HILLSIDE AVE 3
PARKSIDE AVE 4
BROOKSIDE AVE 5
THE BUNGALOWS 6
A49
Low Brooks Farm
DRUMMER'S LA
Rosehill Sch
Sch
LYON ST
Drummersfield Farm
Rose Hill
Opencast Workings
Ryecroft Farm
25
SOUGHER'S LA
SUNNYSIDE RD
BURNS CL
DRYDEN AVE
ROSINA CL
ROSE HILL VIEW
EDDLESTON ST
SKELTON ST
CHIMES RD
Brocstedes Farm
Barton Clough
Mine
Gladden Hey Brow
WINSTANLEY RD
Downall Green RC Jun Sch
DOWNALL GREEN RD
St Peter's CE Prim Sch
MEDWAY CL
B5207
PO
CORONATION ST
BROCKSTEDES AVE
BOOTH'S BROW RD
PASTURE CL
MEADOWCROFT
FERRER ST
PADDOCK
THE
HASELDINE ST
COOKE ST
LEACROFT
JENNET HEY
SEFTON RD
North Ashton
KINDER GR
GRANGE RD
NORWOOD AVE
Bryn
CLIFTON RD
MYRTLE AVE
Tatlock's Hillock
Leyland Green
Down Brook
Rectory CE Prim Sch
DELLS DE CL
GASKELL'S BROW
CHANTRY WLK
WOOLTON CL
ALDER AVE
REGENT AVE
LINDEN AVE
RICHMOND RD
CLOUGH GR
LEYLAND GREEN RD
LILAC AVE
HAWTHORN AVE
RECTORY RD
B5207
NEWTON RD
PALM AVE
ELM AVE
POPLAR AVE
EVERTON ST
Downall Green
BIRCH GR
CEDAR GR
BOLTON ST
Mill Farm
F5
1 ELMSBURY ST
2 COLUMBUS ST
3 BEVINGTON ST
4 RUFFORD ST
5 HADDON ST
6 CLARENCE ST
7 POULTON DR
PRIORY RD
HALE GR
Billinge Lane Farm
Simm's Lane End
BILLINGE RD
FERNLEA
GR
DOWNALL GREEN RD
CORNELIAN GR
BISPHAM DR
MEDLAR WAY
WENTWORTH RD
HARLECH ST
LYTHAM RD
ELLESMERE RD
TALTON DR
KELVIN CL 1
RANMORE AVE 2
STIRLING DR
LAVENDER WLK
SPINDLE HILLOCK
CHATSWORTH CL
Weathercock Hill Farm
Weathercock Hill
PEEBLES CL
SELKIRK AVE
ELGIN AVE
GORDON AV
AUSTIN AVE
THORNTON CL
THORNHILL RD
SMOCK LA
FALKLAND DR
OBAN DR
GIRVAN CRES
WHITBURN CL
AVIEMORE CL
ELSTEAD GR
ABINGER RD
LOW BANK RD
TENBURY DR
GIRTON AVE
DUMBLANE CL
ARGYLL CL
HAMILTON RD
VICTORIA RD
LANGHOLM RD
HILLBECK CRES
BALLIOL WAY
MAGDALEN DR
PETERHOUSE WALK
ORIEL RD
Senely Green Farm
DARVEL AVE
HOLLINS CL
CAMP RD
KINROSS AVE
FORRES GR
COLDSTONE DR
WOLFSON SQ 1
CAMPION GR 2
GREYFRIARS
GARSWOOD RD
Garswood Cty Prim Sch
MELROSE CRES
Stag Hotel (PH)
KENMORE GR
LEDMORE GR
SALKELD AVE
WOODEDGE
STATION RD
NEWBRIDGE CL
STRANGE RD
Long Covert
Montrey Resr
OLD COLLIERY YD
MANOR CL
MONTREY CRES
MELMERBY CL
LAZENBY CRES
ORTON WAY
ALDERTON DR
Charity Farm
SCHOOL LA
Garwood Sta
RENWICK SQ
HOUGHWOOD GRANGE
Montrey House
Garswood
24
Arch Lane Farm
GIBBON'S RD
PARK IND EST
A58
ARCH LA
GARSWOOD RD
Tithe Barn Hillock
TITHEBARN RD
M6
Tithe Barn Farm
Ashton Cross
LIVERPOOL RD
Garswood Park
Carter's Fold Farm
CH
Ashton-in-Makerfield Golf Course
THE FAIRWAYS
GARSWOOD OLD RD
MILLFIELD LA
Oil Depot
Old Garswood Park
Millfield Farm
HAYDOCK LA
HAYDOCK LANE IND EST
WINCHESTER RD
Old Garswood Hall Farm
A58
Pewfall

33

45

36

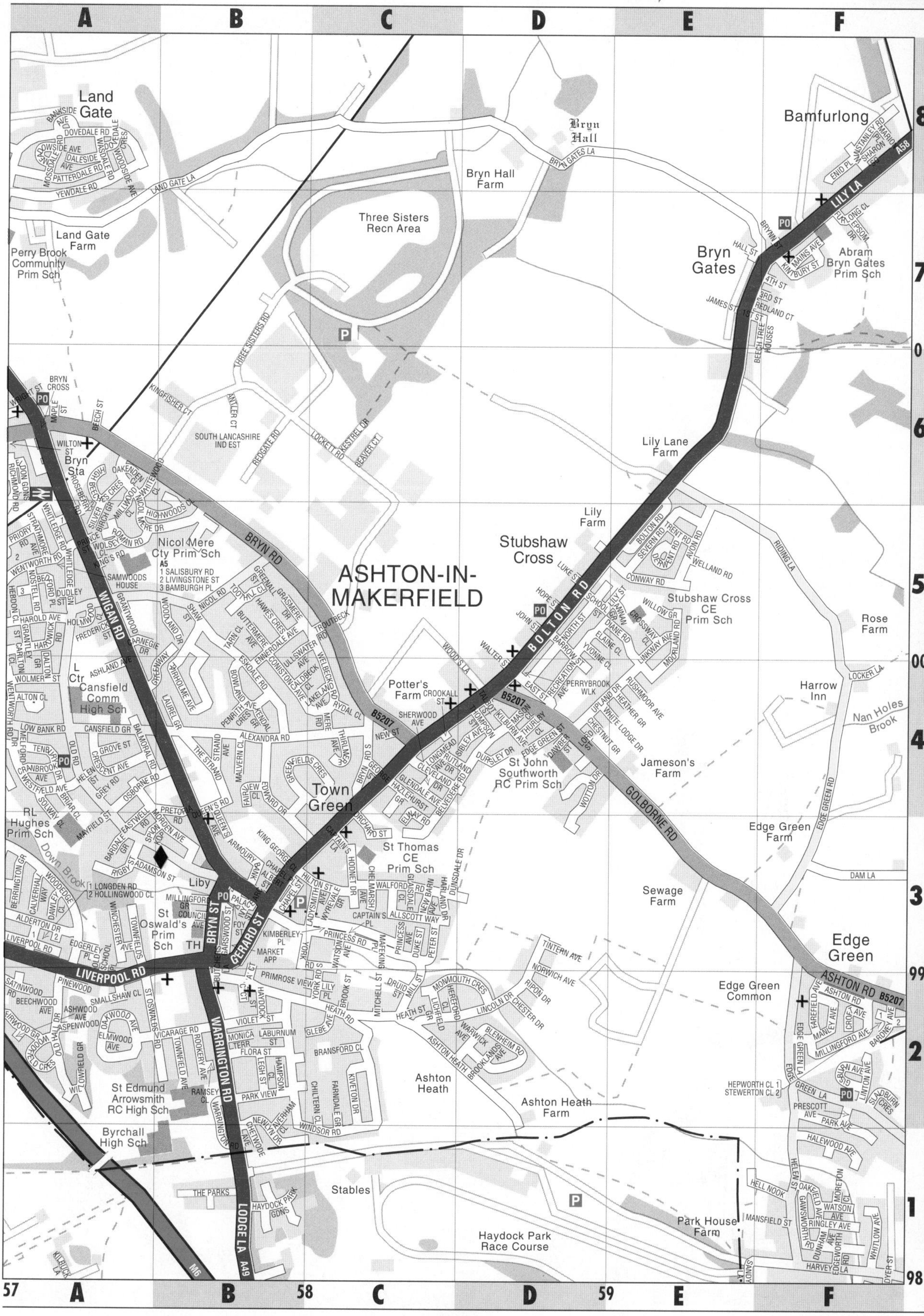
A
B
C
D
E
F
Land Gate
Bryn Hall
Bamfurlong
Bryn Hall Farm
Three Sisters Recn Area
Land Gate Farm
Perry Brook Community Prim Sch
Bryn Gates
Abram Bryn Gates Prim Sch
BANKSIDE AVE
DOVEDALE RD
DALESIDE AVE
PATTERDALE RD
WOODSIDE AVE
YEWDALE RD
LAND GATE LA
BRYN GATES LA
LILY LA
A58
MAINS AVE
KINTBURY ST
HALL ST
JAMES ST
1ST ST
3RD ST
4TH ST
REDLAND CT
BEECH TREE HOUSES
THREE SISTERS RD
KINGFISHER CT
ANTLER CT
REDGATE RD
LOCKETT RD
KESTREL DR
BEAVER CT
SOUTH LANCASHIRE IND EST
BRYN CROSS
WRIGHT ST
MAPLE ST
BEECH ST
WILTON ST
Bryn Sta
Lily Lane Farm
Lily Farm
Stubshaw Cross
ASHTON-IN-MAKERFIELD
Nicol Mere Cty Prim Sch
A5
1 SALISBURY RD
2 LIVINGSTONE ST
3 BAMBURGH PL
SAMWOODS HOUSE
WIGAN RD
BRYN RD
BOLTON RD
GOLBORNE RD
LUKE ST
HOPE ST
JOHN ST
WALTER ST
WOOD'S LA
Stubshaw Cross CE Prim Sch
Rose Farm
RIDING LA
WELLAND RD
CONWAY RD
BOLTON RD
SEVERN RD
TRENT RD
AVON RD
DERWENT RD
WILLOW GR
CROSSWAY
LINKWAY AVE
MOORLAND RD
Harrow Inn
LOCKER LA
Nan Holes Brook
Potter's Farm
CROOKALL ST
SHERWOOD AVE
NEW ST
B5207
PERRYBROOK WLK
RUSHMOOR AVE
HEATHER GR
UPLAND DR
WHITE LODGE DR
Jameson's Farm
St John Southworth RC Prim Sch
WOTTON DR
EDGE GREEN ST
CHESTNUT GR
Cansfield Comm High Sch
L Ctr
ALTON CL
WOLMER ST
LOW BANK RD
CANSFIELD GR
ALEXANDRA RD
Town Green
RL Hughes Prim Sch
Down Brook
1 LONGDEN RD
2 HOLLINGWOOD CL
Liby
St Oswald's Prim Sch
TH
BRYN ST
GERARD ST
St Thomas CE Prim Sch
CAPTAIN'S PL
KIMBERLEY PL
MARKET APP
PRINCESS RD
ALLSCOTT WAY
Sewage Farm
EDGE GREEN RD
Edge Green Farm
DAM LA
Edge Green
ASHTON RD
Edge Green Common
LIVERPOOL RD
WARRINGTON RD
PRIMROSE VIEW
HEATH RD
HEATH ST
MONMOUTH CRES
TINTERN AVE
NORWICH AVE
RIPON DR
CHESTER DR
LINCOLN DR
ASHTON HEATH
BLENHEIM RD
BROOKLANDS AVE
Ashton Heath
Ashton Heath Farm
St Edmund Arrowsmith RC High Sch
Byrchall High Sch
VICARAGE RD
PARK VIEW
WINDSOR RD
BRANSFORD CL
KIVETON DR
MILLINGFORD AVE
HEPWORTH CL 1
STEWERTON CL 2
GREEN LA
PRESCOTT AVE
PARK AVE
HALEWOOD AVE
Stables
THE PARKS
HAYDOCK PARK GDNS
LODGE LA
A49
M6
Haydock Park Race Course
Park House Farm
HELL NOOK
MANSFIELD ST
WATSON AVE
RINGLEY AVE
HARVEY LA
WHITLOW AVE
DYER ST
SANDY LA
KILBUCK LA
8
7
01
6
5
00
4
3
99
2
1
98
57
58
59

46

36

35

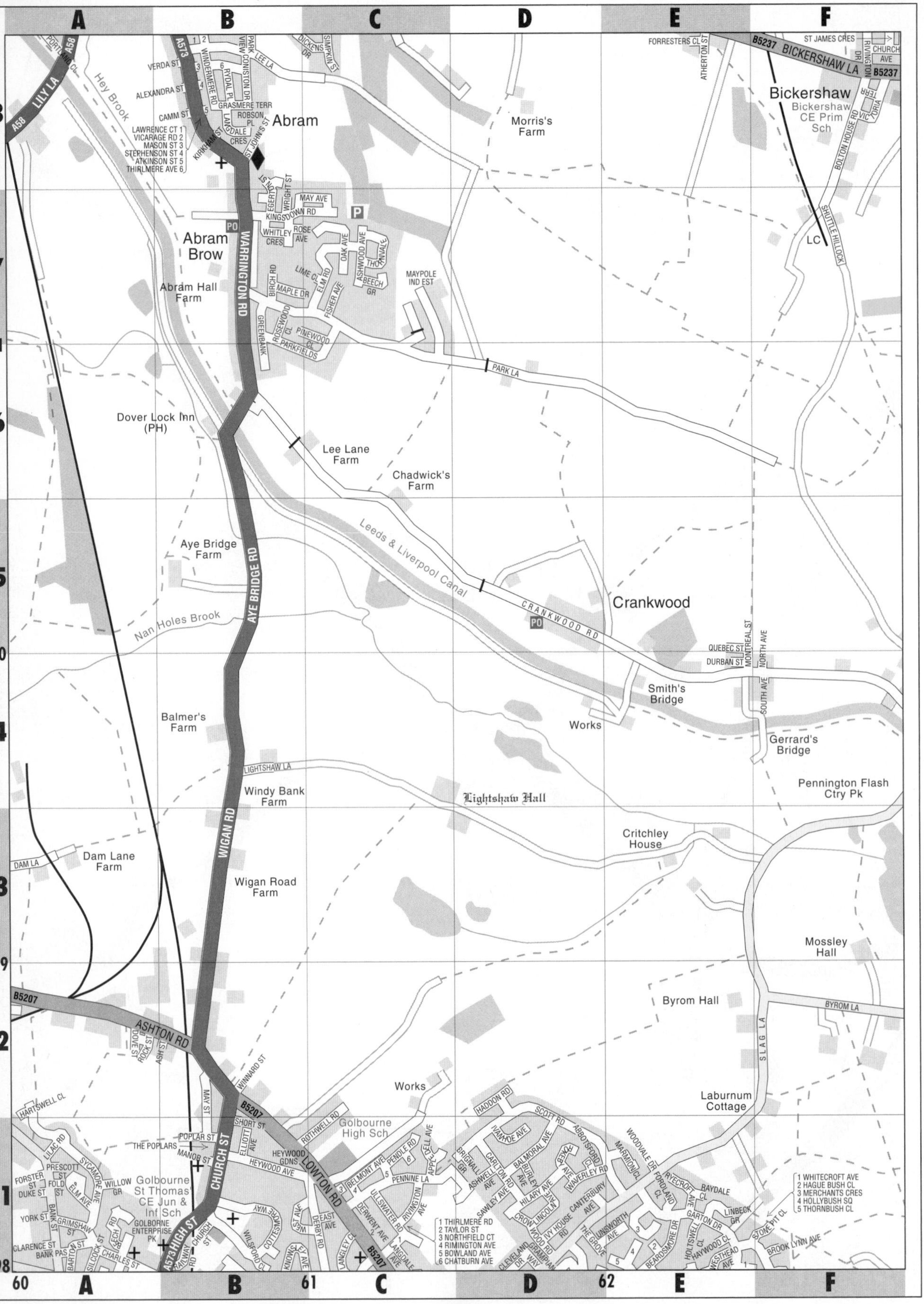

A
B
C
D
E
F
8
7
01
6
5
00
4
3
99
2
1
98
60
61
62
A58
LILY LA
PORTLAND CL
A573
Hey Brook
VERDA ST
ALEXANDRA ST
CAMM ST
LAWRENCE CT 1
VICARAGE RD 2
MASON ST 3
STEPHENSON ST 4
ATKINSON ST 5
THIRLMERE AVE 6
KIRKHAM ST
WINDERMERE RD
RYDAL PL
GRASMERE TERR
ROBSON PL
LANGDALE CRES
PARK VIEW
CONISTON DR
LEE LA
DICKENS DR
SIMPKIN ST
ST JOHN'S ST
Abram
Morris's Farm
FORRESTERS CL
ATHERTON ST
B5237
BICKERSHAW LA
ST JAMES CRES
CHURCH AVE
RIVINGTON DR
Bickershaw
Bickershaw CE Prim Sch
BOLTON HOUSE RD
VICTORIA TERR
SHUTTLE HILLOCK
LC
EGERTON ST
WRIGHT ST
MAY AVE
KINGSDOWN RD
WHITLEY CRES
ROSE AVE
PO
P
Abram Brow
WARRINGTON RD
OAK AVE
ASHWOOD AVE
THORNVALE
BEECH GR
LIME CL
ELM RD
BIRCH RD
MAPLE DR
FISHER AVE
MAYPOLE IND EST
Abram Hall Farm
GREENBANK
ROSEWOOD CL
PINEWOOD CL
PARKFIELDS
PARK LA
Dover Lock Inn (PH)
Lee Lane Farm
Chadwick's Farm
Leeds & Liverpool Canal
Aye Bridge Farm
AYE BRIDGE RD
CRANKWOOD RD
Crankwood
Nan Holes Brook
MONTREAL ST
NORTH AVE
QUEBEC ST
DURBAN ST
SOUTH AVE
Smith's Bridge
Works
Gerrard's Bridge
Balmer's Farm
LIGHTSHAW LA
Windy Bank Farm
Lightshaw Hall
Pennington Flash Ctry Pk
Critchley House
DAM LA
Dam Lane Farm
WIGAN RD
Wigan Road Farm
Mossley Hall
B5207
Byrom Hall
BYROM LA
ASHTON RD
DOVE ST
ROCK ST
ASH ST
SLAG LA
WINNARD ST
Works
Laburnum Cottage
HARTSWELL CL
MAY ST
SHORT ST
ROTHWELL RD
Golbourne High Sch
HADDON RD
SCOTT RD
ABBOTSFORD CL
WOODVALE DR
MARMION CL
THE POPLARS
POPLAR ST
MANOR ST
CHURCH ST
ELLIOTT AVE
HEYWOOD GDNS
HEYWOOD AVE
LOWTON RD
PENDLE RD
APPLEDELL AVE
BELMONT AVE
PENNINE LA
BRIGNALL GR
ASHWELL AVE
CARLTON RD
IVANHOE AVE
BALMORAL AVE
BURLEY AVE
HILARY AVE
WAVERLEY RD
LILAC RD
PRESCOTT ST
SYCAMORE AVE
FORSTER ST
FOLD ST
DUKE ST
ELM AVE
WILLOW GR
Golbourne St Thomas' CE Jun & Inf Sch
BANK ST
YORK ST
GRIMSHAW ST
GOLBORNE ENTERPRISE PK
CLARENCE ST
BANK PAS
BARTON ST
SILCOCK ST
CHARLES ST
A573 HIGH ST
RAILWAY RD
COTTESMORE WAY
WILSFORD CL
WEST AVE
KNOWSLEY AVE
EAST AVE
DERBY RD
ULLSWATER RD
DERWENT AVE
RIVINGTON AVE
LANGDALE AVE
LANGLEY CL
1 THIRLMERE RD
2 TAYLOR ST
3 NORTHFIELD CT
4 RIMINGTON AVE
5 BOWLAND AVE
6 CHATBURN AVE
SAWLEY AVE
CROW WOOD RD
LINCOLN AVE
CLEVELAND DR
GRAMPIAN WAY
IVY HOUSE RD
CANTERBURY AVE
THE GROVE
UNSWORTH AVE
BEARDSMORE DR
FORDLAND CL
RYECROFT AVE
RAYDALE CL
GARTON DR
HOLTSWELL CL
HAYWOOD CL
WESTHEAD AVE
LINBECK GR
STONE PIT CL
BROOK LYNN AVE
1 WHITECROFT AVE
2 HAGUE BUSH CL
3 MERCHANTS CRES
4 HOLLYBUSH SQ
5 THORNBUSH CL

35

47

26
38

A
B
C
D
E
F
8
7
97
6
5
96
4
3
95
2
1
94
30
31
32
Sefton Coastal Path
Marine Lake
ALBERT RD 1
DEACON CL 2
E8
1 WATER ST
2 SANDRINGHAM AVE
BOSSOM CT
Seaforth
CROSBY RD N
A565
B5421
SANDRINGHAM RD
ST ANDREWS CT
ALEXANDRA RD
VICTORIA RD
MARINE TERR
WATERLOO RD
GREAT GEORGE'S RD
SOUTH VIEW
WALMER RD
GREENBANK
BROOKLANDS AVE
BROOKFIELD AVE
BROOKSIDE AVE
BROOK VALE
PARK TERR
BRAMHALL RD
SANDY RD
CROSBY RD S
Radar Sta
Port of Liverpool
Euro Rail Terminal
F7
1 BEDFORD PL
2 GLADSTONE AVE
3 RIVERSDALE RD
4 BELGRAVE RD
LC
A5036 PRINCESS WAY
GORDON RD
HARROWBY RD
CECIL RD
Sch
ELM DR
BARKELEY DR
CHURCH RD
CHURCH GR
Royal Seaforth
Container Terminal
F6
1 LATHOM CL
2 LATHOM AVE
3 CLARENDON RD
Royal Seaforth Dock
A565
A5036
REGENT RD
SHORE RD
Gladstone Dock
Alexandra Dock
Rock Lighthouse
Perch Rock
1 MARINE PARK MANSIONS
2 BECKENHAM RD
KING'S PAR
Marine Lake
UNION TERR
MARINE PROM
A554
KING'S PAR
LB Sta
ROWSON ST A554
1 TIVOLI VILLA'S
2 VICTORIA RD
3 WATERS EDGE APARTMENTS
PORTLAND ST
ATHERTON ST
WELLINGTON RD
CAVENDISH
BURLINGTON RD
WATERLOO RD
WINDSOR ST
RICHMOND ST
VIRGINIA RD
BELMONT RD
BALMORAL RD
VICTORIA PAR
ALBERT ST
TOLLEMACHE ST
TOWER PROM

51
38

A6
1 GLADSTONE CT
2 WOOLFALL TERR
3 HOGARTH ST

37
27

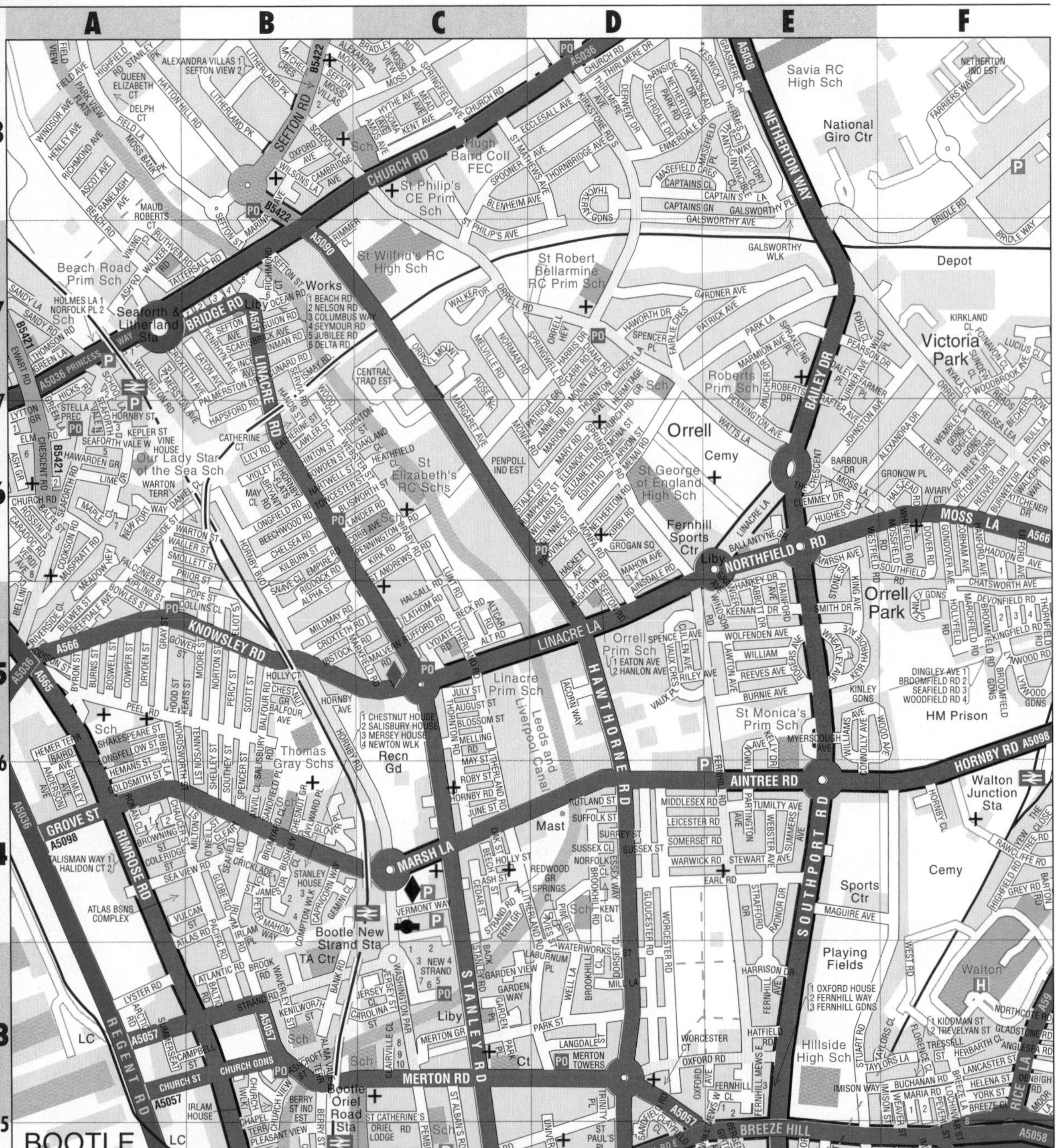

37
52

C3
1 THE HEXAGON
2 MEDWAY
3 MARINERS WAY
4 THE ESPLANADE
5 MANS SQ
6 THE PALATINE

F1
1 LINTON ST
2 ASKEW ST
3 ESPIN ST
F2
1 KNOWSLEY ST
2 PENNINGTON ST
3 WYNDHAM ST
4 BRIDE ST
5 BROADBELT ST
6 CROMWELL RD
7 GROSVENOR RD
8 NORTH BREEZE HILL
9 BREEZE HILL
10 PENUEL RD

28
40

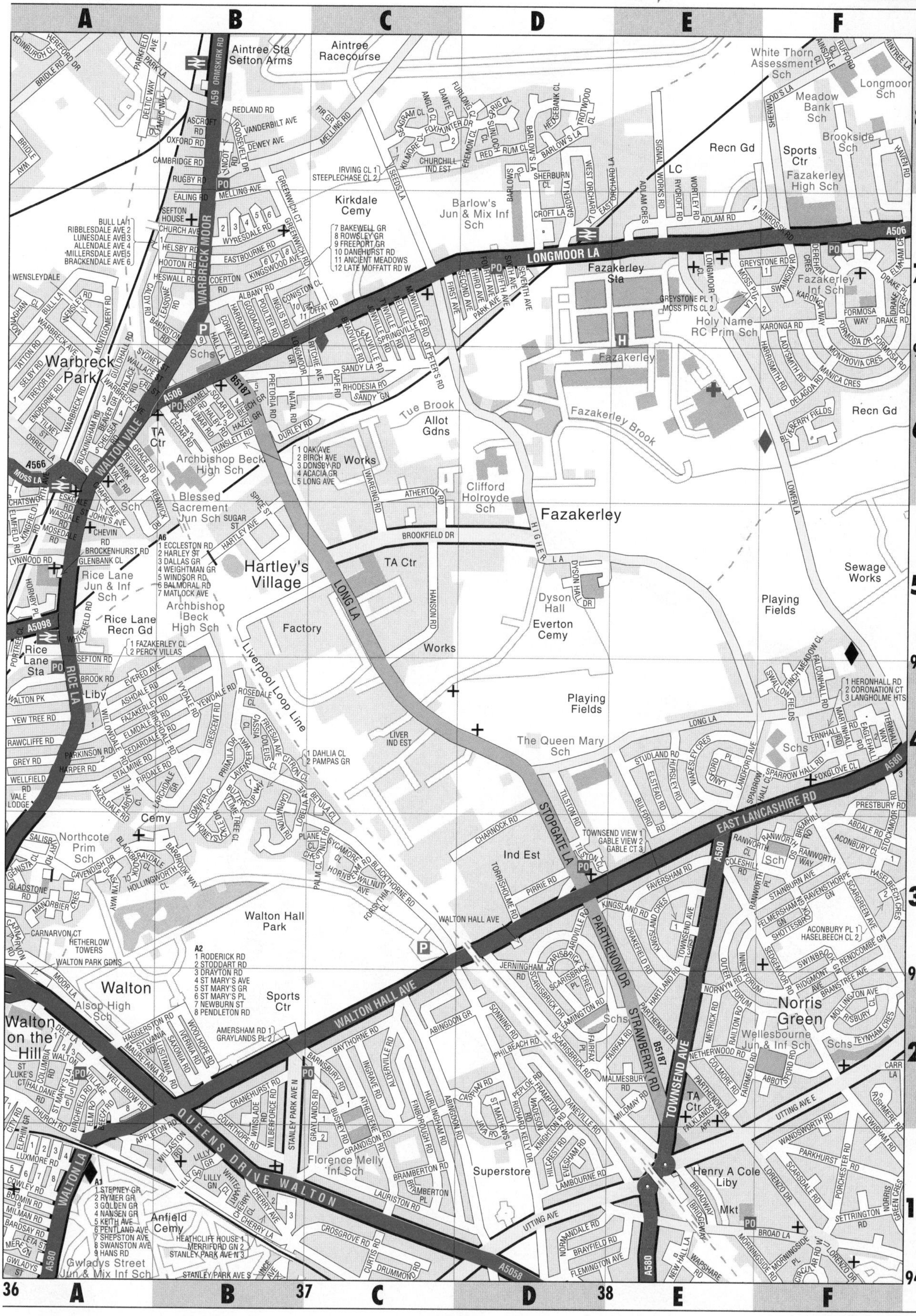
A
B
C
D
E
F
Aintree Sta
Sefton Arms
Aintree Racecourse
White Thorn Assessment Sch
Longmoor Sch
Meadow Bank Sch
Brookside Sch
Sports Ctr
Fazakerley High Sch
Recn Gd
LC
Kirkdale Cemy
Barlow's Jun & Mix Inf Sch
ORMSKIRK RD
WARBRECK MOOR
LONGMOOR LA
A506
A59
Fazakerley Sta
Fazakerley Inf Sch
Holy Name RC Prim Sch
Fazakerley
Fazakerley Brook
Tue Brook
Allot Gdns
Works
Clifford Holroyde Sch
Fazakerley
Warbreck Park
Schs
TA Ctr
Archbishop Beck High Sch
Blessed Sacrement Jun Sch
Hartley's Village
Rice Lane Jun & Inf Sch
Rice Lane Recn Gd
Archbishop Beck High Sch
Factory
LONG LA
BROOKFIELD DR
HIGHER LA
Dyson Hall
Everton Cemy
Sewage Works
Playing Fields
Rice Lane Sta
Liby
WALTON VALE
RICE LA
A5098
A566
Liverpool Loop Line
LIVER IND EST
The Queen Mary Sch
Playing Fields
LONG LA
STOPGATE LA
EAST LANCASHIRE RD
A580
Cemy
Northcote Prim Sch
Ind Est
Walton Hall Park
WALTON HALL AVE
PARTHENON DR
STRAWBERRY RD
B5187
TOWNSEND AVE
Norris Green
Wellesbourne Jun & Inf Sch
Walton
Alsop High Sch
Walton on the Hill
Sports Ctr
Schs
TA Ctr
QUEENS DRIVE WALTON
Florence Melly Inf Sch
Superstore
Henry A Cole Liby
Mkt
Anfield Cemy
Gwladys Street Jun & Mix Inf Sch
WALTON LA
A5058
8
7
6
5
4
3
2
1
97
96
95
94
36
37
38

53
40

39
29

A1
1 BRANTHWAITE CL
2 HELMDON CL
3 GLASSONBY WAY
4 BRANTHWAITE GR
5 BLAISDON CL
6 NORRIS GREEN WAY

39
54

30
42

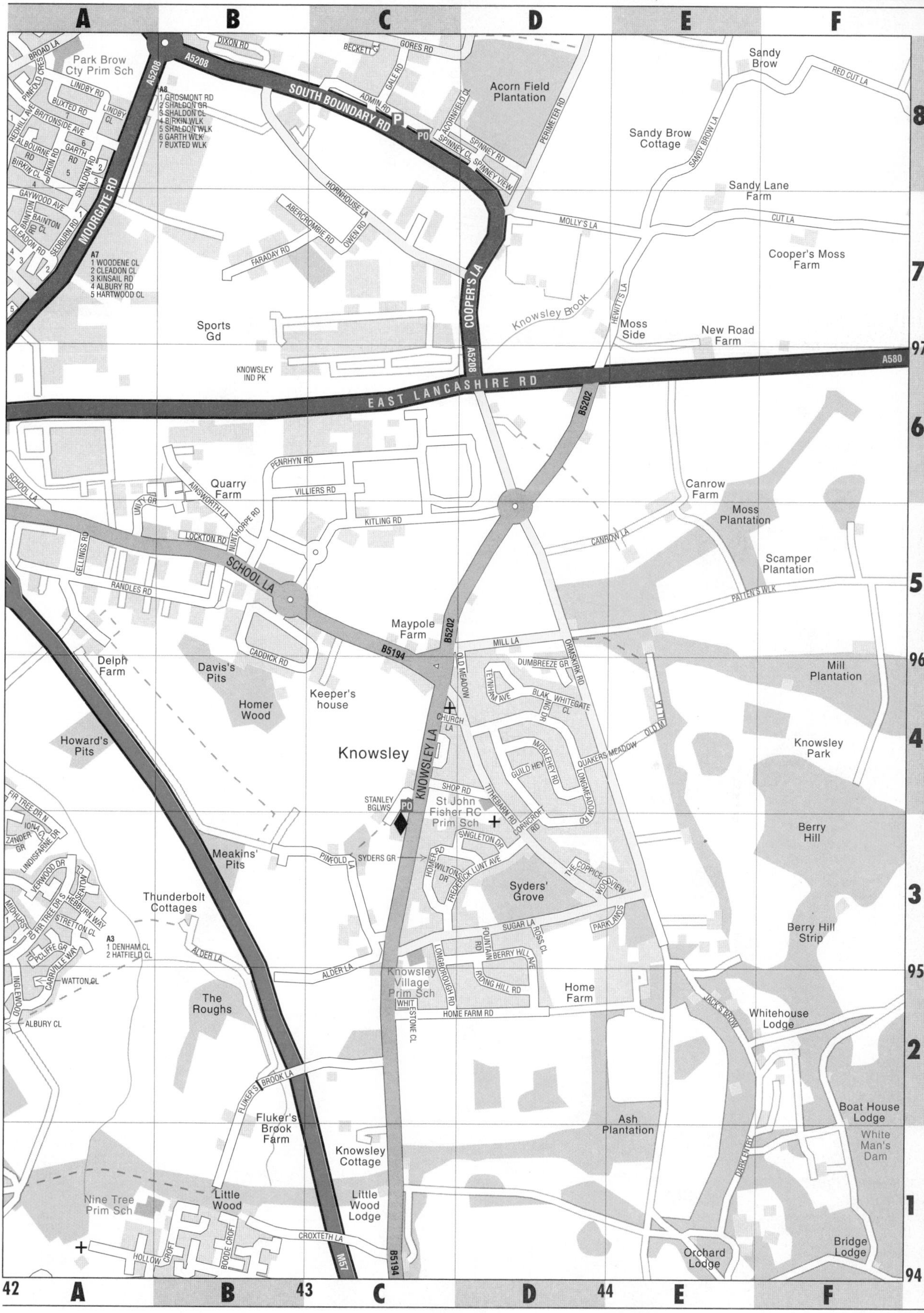
A
B
C
D
E
F
8
7
97
6
5
96
4
3
95
2
1
94
42
43
44
Park Brow Cty Prim Sch
BROAD LA
PINFOLD CRES
LINDBY RD
LINDBY CL
BUXTED RD
BRITONSIDE AVE
REDHILL AVE
ALBOURNE RD
GARTH RD
BIRKIN CL
SHALDON RD
GAYWOOD AVE
BAINTON CL
BAINTON RD
SEDBURN RD
CLEADON RD
MOORGATE RD
A5208
DIXON RD
BECKETT CL
GORES RD
A8
1 GROSMONT RD
2 SHALDON GR
3 SHALDON CL
4 BIRKIN WLK
5 SHALDON WLK
6 GARTH WLK
7 BUXTED WLK
SOUTH BOUNDARY RD
ADMIN RD
GALE RD
P
PO
ACORNFIELD CL
SPINNEY CL
SPINNEY RD
SPINNEY VIEW
Acorn Field Plantation
PERIMETER RD
Sandy Brow
RED CUT LA
Sandy Brow Cottage
SANDY BROW LA
Sandy Lane Farm
HORNHOUSE LA
ABERCROMBIE RD
OWEN RD
FARADAY RD
MOLLY'S LA
CUT LA
Cooper's Moss Farm
A7
1 WOODENE CL
2 CLEADON CL
3 KINSAIL RD
4 ALBURY RD
5 HARTWOOD CL
COOPER'S LA
Knowsley Brook
HEWITT'S LA
Moss Side
New Road Farm
Sports Gd
KNOWSLEY IND PK
A580
EAST LANCASHIRE RD
B5202
SCHOOL LA
Quarry Farm
PENRHYN RD
VILLIERS RD
AINSWORTH LA
UNITY GR
NUNTHORPE RD
KITLING RD
Canrow Farm
Moss Plantation
CANROW LA
LOCKTON RD
GELLINGS RD
RANDLES RD
Scamper Plantation
PATTEN'S WLK
Maypole Farm
MILL LA
CADDICK RD
B5194
Delph Farm
Davis's Pits
Homer Wood
Keeper's house
OLD MEADOW
DUMBREEZE GR
ORMSKIRK RD
TEYNHAM AVE
BLAKING DR
WHITEGATE CL
Mill Plantation
CHURCH LA
MIDDLEHEY RD
QUAKERS MEADOW
OLD MILL LA
Howard's Pits
Knowsley
KNOWSLEY LA
GUILD HEY
LONGMEADOW RD
Knowsley Park
SHOP RD
TITHEBARN RD
STANLEY BGLWS
St John Fisher RC Prim Sch
CORNCROFT RD
Berry Hill
FIR TREE DR N
IONA CL
ZANDER GR
LINDISFARNE DR
VERWOOD DR
Meakins' Pits
PINFOLD LA
SYDERS GR
HOMER RD
SWGLETON DR
WILTON DR
FREDERICK LUNT AVE
THE COPPICE
WOODVIEW
Thunderbolt Cottages
Syders' Grove
MIDHURST RD
FIR TREE DR S
HEBBURN WAY
SEATON CL
STRETTON CL
PARKLANDS
SUGAR LA
FOUNTAIN RD
ROSS CL
Berry Hill Strip
A3
1 DENHAM CL
2 HATFIELD CL
ALDER LA
BERRY HILL AVE
WATTON CL
CARRVILLE WAY
INGLEWOOD
LONGBOROUGH RD
RIDING HILL RD
Knowsley Village Prim Sch
WHITESTONE CL
HOME FARM RD
Home Farm
JACK'S BROW
The Roughs
ALBURY CL
Whitehouse Lodge
BROOK LA
FLUKER'S LA
Fluker's Brook Farm
Ash Plantation
DARK ENTRY
Boat House Lodge
White Man's Dam
Knowsley Cottage
Nine Tree Prim Sch
Little Wood
Little Wood Lodge
HOLLOW CROFT
BOODE CROFT
CROXTETH LA
M57
B5194
Orchard Lodge
Bridge Lodge

55
42

41
31

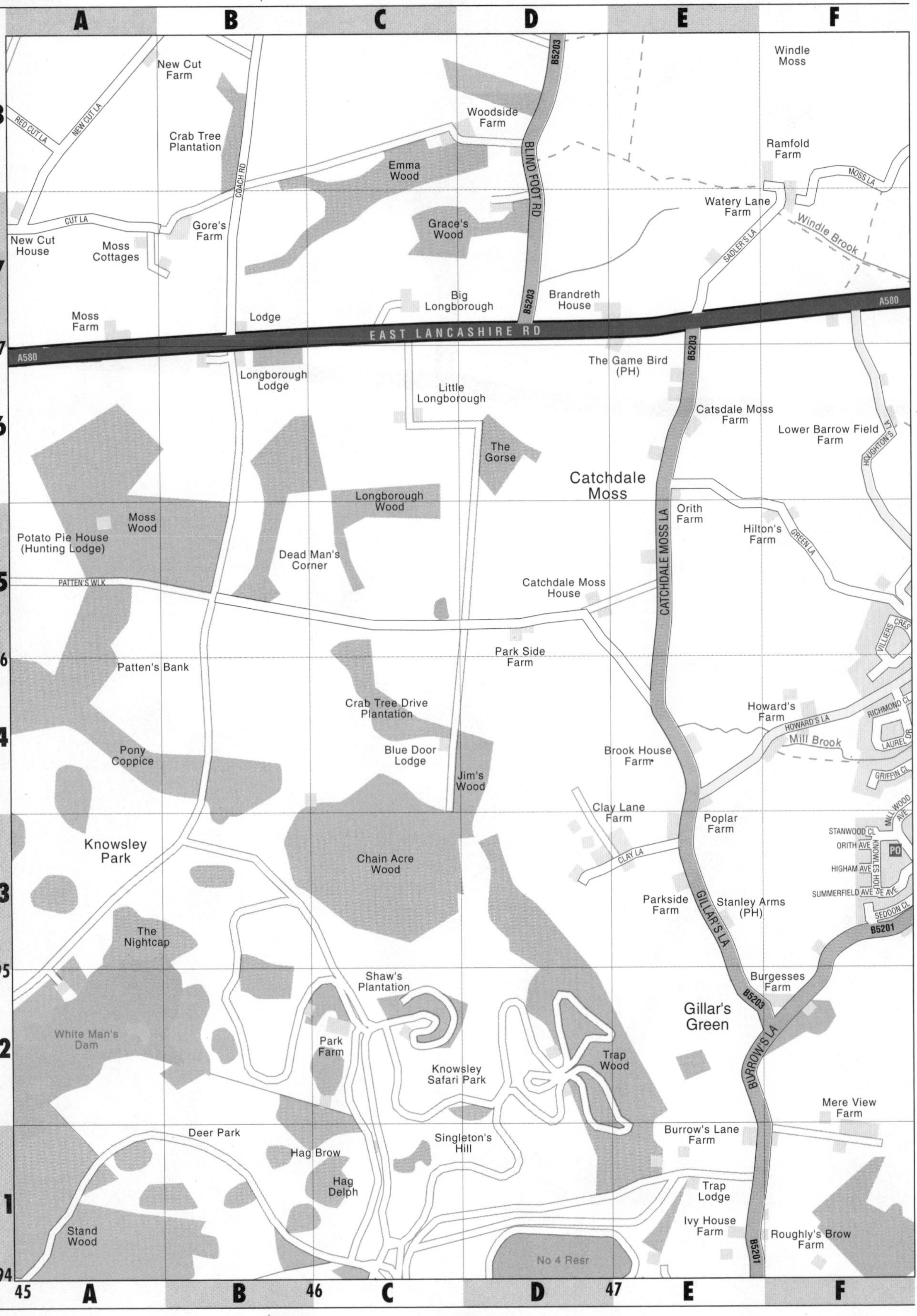
A
B
C
D
E
F
8
7
97
6
5
96
4
3
95
2
1
94
45
46
47
New Cut Farm
Crab Tree Plantation
RED CUT LA
NEW CUT LA
COACH RD
CUT LA
New Cut House
Moss Cottages
Gore's Farm
Moss Farm
Lodge
Woodside Farm
Emma Wood
Grace's Wood
Big Longborough
B5203
BLIND FOOT RD
Brandreth House
Windle Moss
Ramfold Farm
MOSS LA
Watery Lane Farm
SADLER'S LA
Windle Brook
A580
EAST LANCASHIRE RD
Longborough Lodge
Little Longborough
The Game Bird (PH)
Catsdale Moss Farm
Lower Barrow Field Farm
HOUGHTON'S LA
The Gorse
Catchdale Moss
Longborough Wood
Moss Wood
Potato Pie House (Hunting Lodge)
Dead Man's Corner
Orith Farm
Hilton's Farm
GREEN LA
CATCHDALE MOSS LA
PATTEN'S WLK
Catchdale Moss House
VILLIERS CRES
Park Side Farm
Patten's Bank
Crab Tree Drive Plantation
Howard's Farm
HOWARD'S LA
RICHMOND CL
Mill Brook
LAUREL DR
Pony Coppice
Blue Door Lodge
Jim's Wood
Brook House Farm
GRIFFIN CL
Clay Lane Farm
Poplar Farm
MILL WOOD AVE
STANWOOD CL
ORITH AVE
KNOWLES HOUSE AVE
PO
HIGHAM AVE
Knowsley Park
Chain Acre Wood
CLAY LA
Parkside Farm
GILLAR'S LA
Stanley Arms (PH)
SUMMERFIELD AVE
SEDDON CL
The Nightcap
B5201
Shaw's Plantation
Burgesses Farm
Gillar's Green
White Man's Dam
Park Farm
Trap Wood
BURROW'S LA
Knowsley Safari Park
Mere View Farm
Deer Park
Singleton's Hill
Burrow's Lane Farm
Hag Brow
Hag Delph
Trap Lodge
Ivy House Farm
Stand Wood
Roughly's Brow Farm
No 4 Resr

41
56

32
44

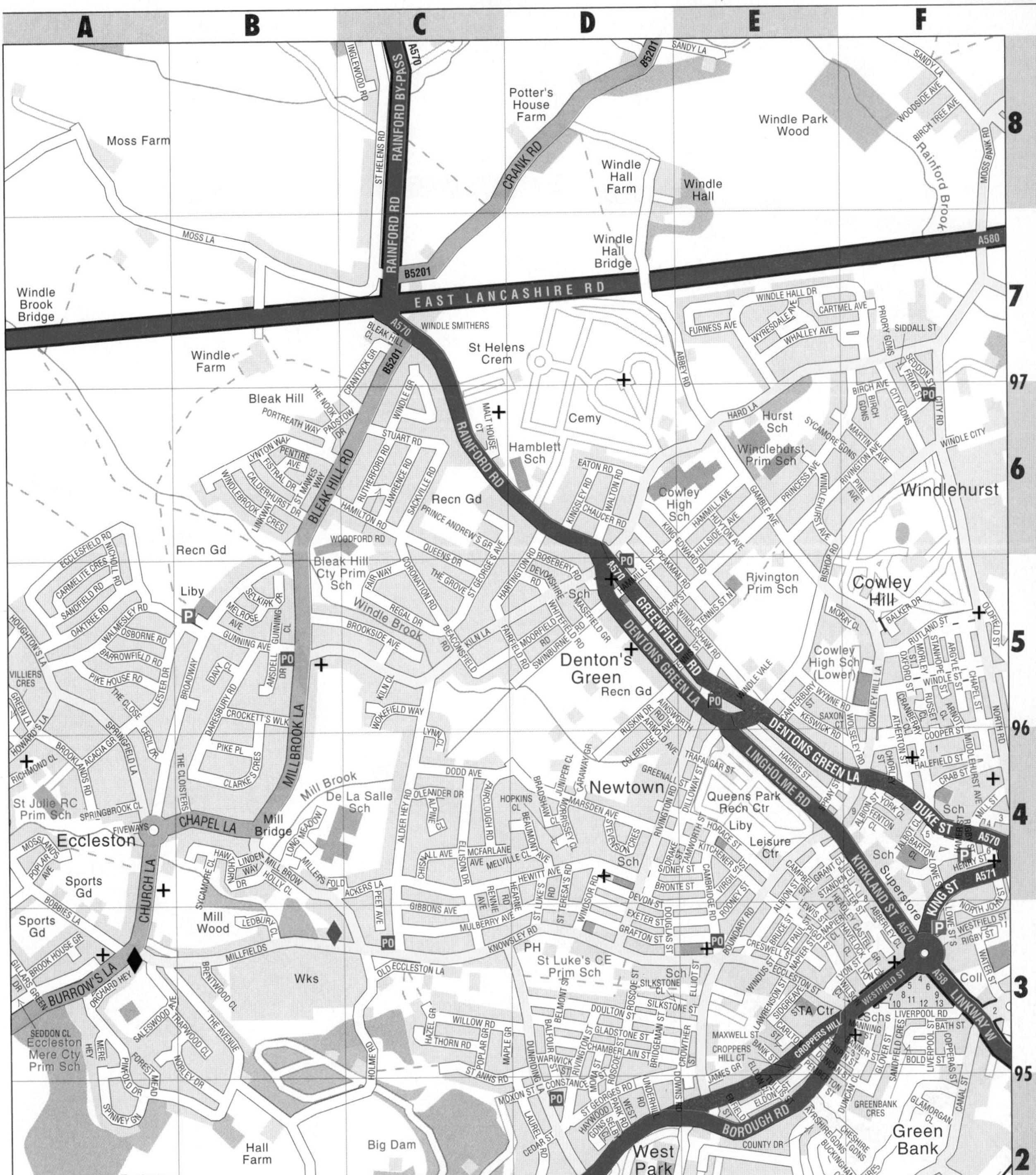

F3
1 NEW CROSS ST
2 CHALON WAY W
3 BANNER WLK

F4
1 MORLEY WAY
2 OXFORD ST
3 VOLUNTEER ST
4 LEACH ST
5 RANDON GR
6 NEW CROSS ST
7 PALMER CL
8 BURNELL CL

57
44

43
33

A B C D E F

A B C D E F

A3
1 COTHAM ST
2 VICTORIA SQ
3 WATERLOO ST
4 CROSS ST
5 MILK ST
6 EXCHANGE ST
7 LAGRANGE ARC
8 PALATINE ARC
9 MARKET ST
10 CHURCH SQ
11 ST MARY'S ARC
12 BROWNLOW ARC

43
58

34
46

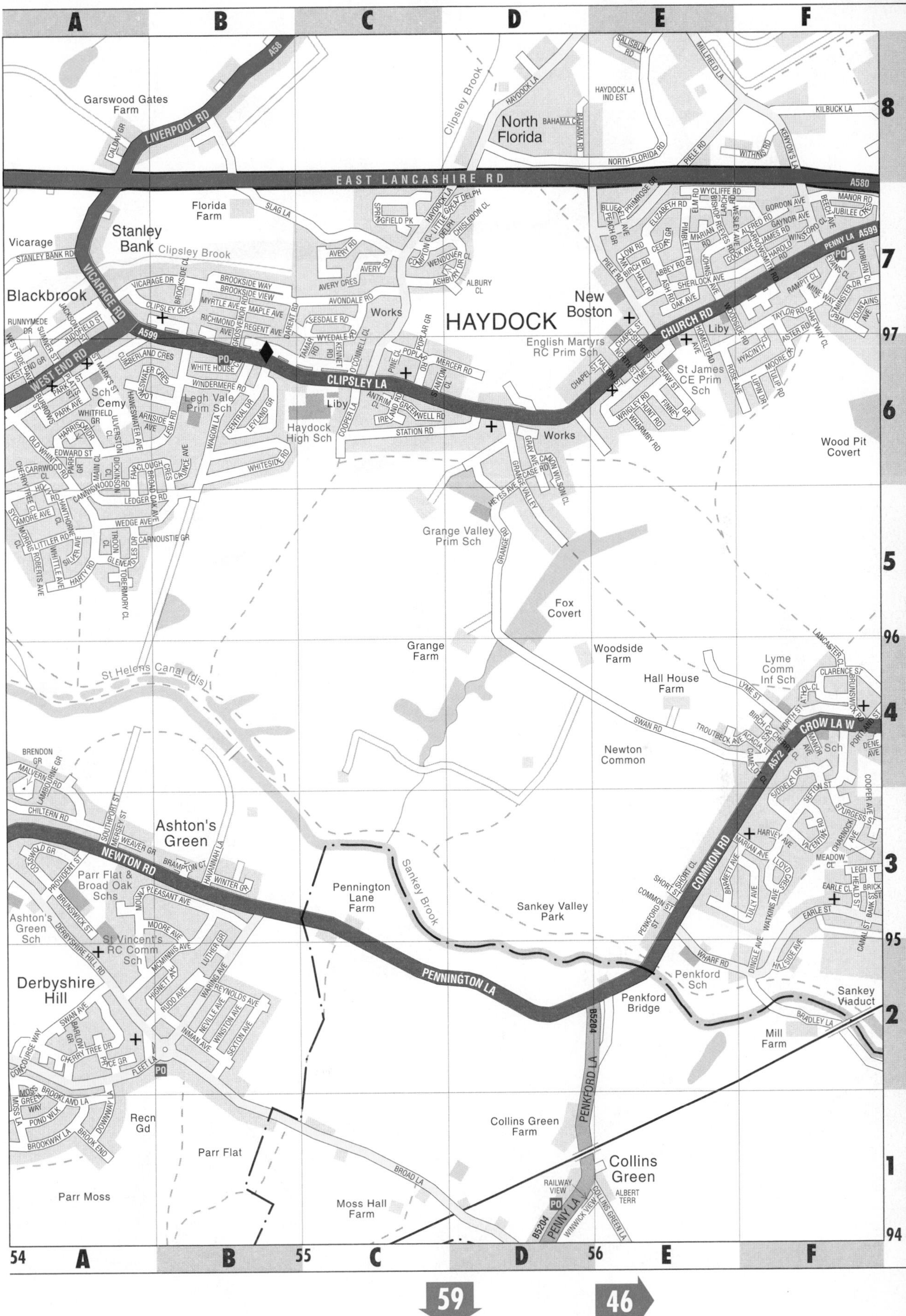
A
B
C
D
E
F
8
7
97
6
5
96
4
3
95
2
1
94
54
55
56
Garswood Gates Farm
LIVERPOOL RD
A58
CALDAY GR
North Florida
BAHAMA CL
BAHAMA RD
HAYDOCK LA
HAYDOCK LA IND EST
SALISBURY RD
MILLFIELD LA
KILBUCK LA
NORTH FLORIDA RD
PIELE RD
WITHINS RD
KENYON'S LA
Clipsley Brook
EAST LANCASHIRE RD
A580
Florida Farm
SLAG LA
Stanley Bank
Clipsley Brook
Vicarage
STANLEY BANK RD
VICARAGE RD
Blackbrook
VICARAGE DR
BROOKSIDE CL
BROOKSIDE WAY
BROOKSIDE VIEW
CLIPSLEY CRES
MYRTLE AVE
MAPLE AVE
RICHMOND AVE
REGENT AVE
GROSVENOR RD
DARENT RD
AVERY RD
AVERY SQ
AVERY CRES
AVONDALE RD
ESDALE RD
WYEDALE RD
SPRINGFIELD PK
HAYDOCK LA
LITTLE DELPH
GREAT DELPH
CHISLEDON CL
WENDOVER CL
ASHBURY DR
ALBURY CL
Works
HAYDOCK
New Boston
English Martyrs RC Prim Sch
RUNNYMEDE DR
JACKSON ST
SUMMER ST
JUDDFIELD ST
WEST END RD
WEST SIDE AVE
WEST END GR
A599
PO
WHITE HOUSE
WINDERMERE RD
CLIPSLEY LA
Sch
Cemy
Legh Vale Prim Sch
Liby
Haydock High Sch
WHITFIELD GR
PARK AVE
PARK ST
ST MARY'S ST
BURROWS
HARRISON DR
ARNSIDE AVE
LEGH RD
HAWESWATER AVE
ULVERSTON AVE
WAGON LA
CENTRAL DR
LEYLAND GR
COOPER LA
O'CONNELL CL
KENNET
TAMAR RD
PINE CL
POPLAR GR
POPLAR RD
MERCER RD
STANTON CL
ANTRIM CL
GREENWELL RD
IRELAND RD
STATION RD
OLD WHINT RD
EDWARD ST
CARRWOOD CL
CHERRY TREE CL
HOLLY RD
SYCAMORE AVE
MORRIS CL
LITTLER RD
ROBERTS AVE
SILVER AVE
WHITTLE AVE
HARTY RD
HAWTHORNE
CANNISWOOD RD
DICKINSON
FAIRCLOUGH
BROAD OAK AVE
LEDGER RD
WEDGE AVE
CARNOUSTIE GR
TROON CL
GLENEAGLES DR
TOBERMORY CL
WHITESIDE RD
MAIN CL
CALUNCE AVE
CRES
BLUEBELL AVE
PEACH GR
PRIMROSE GR
ELIZABETH RD
WYCLIFFE RD
ELM RD
BISHOP REEVES RD
WESLEY AVE
ARROWSMITH RD
GORDON AVE
GAYNOR AVE
MANOR RD
JUBILEE CRES
BEECH AVE
LOW RD
CEDAR GR
PIMBLETT RD
MARIAN RD
ALFRED RD
JAMES RD
HAROLD RD
WINSFORD CL
COOK AVE
PENNY LA
A599
PO
WOBURN CL
EVANS CL
HALL RD
ABBEY RD
ASH RD
BIRCH RD
SHERLOCK AVE
OAK AVE
JOHNS AVE
RAMPIT CL
MINE WAY
WESTMINSTER DR
FOUNTAINS AVE
CHURCH RD
WOODSIDE RD
Liby
TAYLOR RD
SHAFTWAY CL
ASTER RD
HYACINTH
MOORE DR
LUPIN DR
TULIP RD
St James CE Prim Sch
HOMESTEAD AVE
ROSE AVE
CHAPEL ST
NORTH ST
LYME ST
SHAW ST
WRIGLEY RD
HUNT RD
FINNEY GR
WHARMBY RD
Works
GRAY AVE
CASE RD
CANON WILSON CL
GRANGE VALLEY
HEYES AVE
Grange Valley Prim Sch
GRANGE RD
Wood Pit Covert
Fox Covert
Grange Farm
Woodside Farm
Hall House Farm
Lyme Comm Inf Sch
LANCASTER CL
CLARENCE ST
BRUNSWICK ST
ATHOL CL
LYME ST
SWAN RD
TROUTBECK AVE
BIRCH ST
NORTH ST
ACACIA ST
CAMELOT CL
CROW LA W
A572
MANOR AVE
Sch
PORTLAND ST
DENE AVE
Newton Common
St Helens Canal (dis)
BRENDON GR
MALVERN RD
LAMBOURNE GR
CHILTERN RD
SOUTHPORT ST
MERSEY ST
WEAVER GR
Ashton's Green
BRAMPTON CT
HAVANNAH LA
WINTER GR
NEWTON RD
COTSWOLD GR
PROVIDENT ST
Parr Flat & Broad Oak Schs
MOUNT PLEASANT AVE
BRUNSWICK ST
Ashton's Green Sch
DERBYSHIRE HILL RD
St Vincent's RC Comm Sch
MOORE AVE
McMINNIS AVE
LUTHER GR
Pennington Lane Farm
Sankey Brook
Sankey Valley Park
SIDDELEY DR
SEFTON ST
COOPER AVE
HARVEY AVE
MARIAN AVE
BARNETT AVE
LLOYD CRES
VALENTINE RD
BURGESS ST
CHARNOCK AVE
MEADOW CL
LEGH ST
EARLE CL
HEALD ST
BRICK ST
BANK ST
EARLE ST
CANAL ST
COMMON RD
SHORT CL
SHORT ST
COMMON ST
PENKFORD ST
TULLY AVE
WATKINS AVE
DINGLE AVE
HILLSIDE AVE
WHARF RD
Penkford Sch
PENNINGTON LA
Penkford Bridge
Sankey Viaduct
BRADLEY LA
Mill Farm
Derbyshire Hill
HIGNETT AVE
WARING AVE
REYNOLDS AVE
RUDD AVE
NEVILLE AVE
WINSTON AVE
SEXTON AVE
INMAN AVE
SWAN AVE
BARLOW GR
CHERRY TREE DR
PRICE GR
FLEET LA
PO
CONCOURSE WAY
MOSS GREEN WAY
BROOKLAND LA
POND WLK
MOSS LA
DOWNWAY LA
BROOKWAY LA
BROOK END
Recn Gd
Parr Flat
Parr Moss
B5204
PENKFORD LA
Collins Green Farm
Collins Green
RAILWAY VIEW
PO
ALBERT TERR
BROAD LA
Moss Hall Farm
B5204
PENNY LA
WINWICK VIEW
COLLINS GREEN LA

59
46

45
35

A
B
C
D
E
F
8
7
97
6
5
96
4
3
95
2
1
94
57
58
59
YEW TREE FARM TRAD EST
KILBUCK LA
Old Boston
OLD BOSTON TRAD EST
WILCOCK RD
DIXON CL
PYE CL
OLD BOSTON
PENNY LA
A599
M6
A49
LODGE LA
Haydock Park
White Door Covert
White Door Dam
Lady Hill Plantation
SPRINGFIELD AVE 1
HIGHFIELD AVE 2
CLIFTONMILL MEADOWS 3
SANDY LA
BARN LA
A580
MANOR RD
A599
23
EAST LANCASHIRE RD
B5209
CORONATION DR
PLANE TREE GR
KING GEORGE RD
PRINCESS AVE
NORMAN AVE
QUEENS RD
SOUTHWARD RD
WINDSOR DR
BUCKFAST AVE
ABBEYWAY N
ST ALBANS CL
ABBEYWAY S
Haydock Park Farm
Fox Covert
Dean Dam
Dean Dam Farm
LADYBARN AVE
WILMOT DR
PARK RD
WEARHEAD CL
A580
Ellam's Brook
Ellam's Rough
Newton- Haydock Bridge
NEWTON LA
WOODLANDS IND EST
Lawson's Farm
VISTA RD
Hollows Bridge
Haydock Park Golf Course
CH
ASHTON RD
Newton-le-Willows Community Sch
ROB LA
BILLINGTON AVE
URMSTON AVE
JOHNSON AVE
MARTIN AVE
ELSTON AVE
DIXON AVE
PORTER AVE
WEEDON AVE
CUNLIFFE AVE
WILLIAMS AVE
WIGHTMAN AVE
MULLINS AVE
HORRIDGE AVE
WALSH CL
WETHERBY
SPEAKMAN AVE
WHEATLEY AVE
MARITIME CL
KEMPTON CL
BELVEDERE RD
CROWN PARK DR
CROWN FIELDS CL
BORRON RD
FRAWLEY AVE
DUNCAN AVE
QUEENS DR
CHELTENHAM DR
DAMIAN DR
ANNETTE AVE
CROWN GDNS
DAVIES AVE
KERSHAW WAY
RIPON CL
GEORGE ST
VISTA AVE
REDMAYNE CL
RUSKIN AVE
LATHAM AVE
BEECHWOOD AVE
THE ROOKERY
Ct
THE PARCHMENTS
Newton Bank Sch
SILVERDALE RD
St Mary's RC Inf Sch
GREENSHANK CL
THE AVENUE
A572
COBDEN ST
RYKEDEN
DALE VIEW
CASTLE HILL
B5209
RUSHTON AVE
COLE AVE
HIGH ST
CLARENCE ST
Liby
WATER ST
PO
CROW LA E
PLEASANCE WAY
WALMSLEY ST
MERCER ST
PO
GOLBORNE ST
Newton Lake
MIERE RD
A572
CROW LA W
CHURCH ST
1 NORTHWOOD AVE
2 WOODLAND AVE
M6
BERTRAM ST
HEATHER BRAE
YEW TREE AVE
THE COPSE
The District Prim Sch
CROSS LA
St Helen's Coll Newton Campus
SANDPIPER CL
DUNLIN AVE
DEAN MEADOW
HARRISON WAY
SUNNYBANK
MANSE GDNS
BIRLEY ST
St Aelred's RC High Sch
St Peter's CE Prim Sch
SOUTHWORTH RD
A572
BACK MARKET ST
NEVILLE ST
NELSON ST
MARKET ST
PATTERSON ST
BARN WAY
St Mary's Jun Sch
GREENFIELD CL
Newton Cty Prim Sch
WILLOW AVE
PARK RD N
WILLOW RD
WILLOWDALE
A572
HOLFORD WAY
EASTWOOD AVE
ST JOHN ST
CROWN ST
HAYDOCK ST
FOUNDRY ST
SCHOOL ST
DERBY ST
DERBY CL
MILTON AVE
WINSTON AVE
VICTORIA RD
WHIMBREL AVE
PIPIT AVE
ROSEMARY DR
TH
P
CHAPEL ST
HOTEL ST
HOPE ST
SERIN CL
PLOVER CL
Newton-le-Willows Sta
P
SCEPTRE CL
TAMWORTH ST
STANLEY ST
OXFORD ST
FAIRCLOUGH ST
HOUGHTON ST
COLLINGWOOD RD
SISKIN CL
Stones Crossing
LEGH ST
SANKEY ST
LEGH ST
BROOKFIELD ST
WARGRAVE RD
ACORN ST
ALFRED ST
Mill House Sch
VIADUCT ST
BACK LEGH ST
WELLINGTON ST
BRIDGE ST
PRINCES ST
KING ST
P
P
THE CROSSINGS
GLOVER ST
SYCAMORE AVE
POPLAR AVE
HOLLY AVE
TRACY DR
CHESHIRE CL
CONWAY DR
ROSCOE AVE
BANASTRE DR
BRICK ST
REGENT ST
WOODS CT
GABLE ST
QUEEN ST
RAILWAY ST
SUNBEAM ST
RYDAL ST
OAK AVE
HAWTHORN AVE
MILL LA
BURKHARDT DR
EARLE ST
SUEZ ST
JUNCTION LA
CHEMICAL ST
HOUGHTON ST
Earlestown Sta
OLD WARGRAVE RD
ALDER ST
Wargrave
ALDER AVE
NORMAN AVE
SANDRA DR
PARK VIEW
Newton Park Farm
DEACON TRAD EST
NEWTON-LE-WILLOWS
LAUREL AVE
CEDAR CRES
SHERI DR
WAYFARERS DR
NEWTON PARK DR
GRANT ST 1
BACK BOOTH ST 2
BOOTH ST 3
BACK LAWRENCE ST 4
LAWRENCE ST 5
WELLINGTON GDNS 6
WELLINGTON CL 7
MARKET ST 8
GRAFTON ST 9
BACK BRIDGE ST 10
JUNCTION LA
GROSVENOR GDNS
CEDAR AVE
PARK AVE N
ELM AVE
ASH AVE
LARCH AVE
ROMAN CL
MAPLE AVE
PINE AVE
FERN AVE
PARK RD S
WINDSOR AVE
WOBURN AVE
WARWICK AVE
WHITEFIELD AVE
Earlestown
KINGSWAY
DEVONSHIRE GDNS
IVY AVE
LILY AVE
WELBECK AVE
CONNAUGHT DR
WARGRAVE RD
DAISY AVE
PARK AVE S
MYRTLE AVE
WOODSTOCK AVE
SANKEY VALLEY IND EST
CATHERINE WAY
FINDLAY CL
FINDLAY CL
RICHMOND GDNS
GOOCH DR
STEPHENSON RD
GRENWOOD CL
BORRENDEL RD
ADAMS CL
Newton Brook
CENTRAL WAY
Cemy
Newton Community
VALLEY VIEW
H
P
KENILWORTH GDNS
LEAMINGTON AVE
CHURCH DR
St Helen's Canal (dis)
BRADLEGH RD
Sch
Wargrave House Sch
CORONATION DR
BUNGALOW RD
WINWICK RD
BRADLEY LA
Sankey Brook
WARGRAVE MEWS
Red Bank
FARM WAY
HOVERTY PREC 1
NOON CT 2
COUNCE AVE 3
LANGLEY AVE 4
SCOTT WLK 5
THOMPSON CL 6
INGHAM AVE 7
FEARNLEY WAY 8
KENT WAY 9
OLD HEY WLK 10
TYRER RD
VULCAN CL
LINEAR VIEW
CONROY WAY
VULCAN IND EST
Works
RED BANK AVE
New Hey Farm
NEWTON RD
A49
HERMITAGE GREEN LA

45
60

36

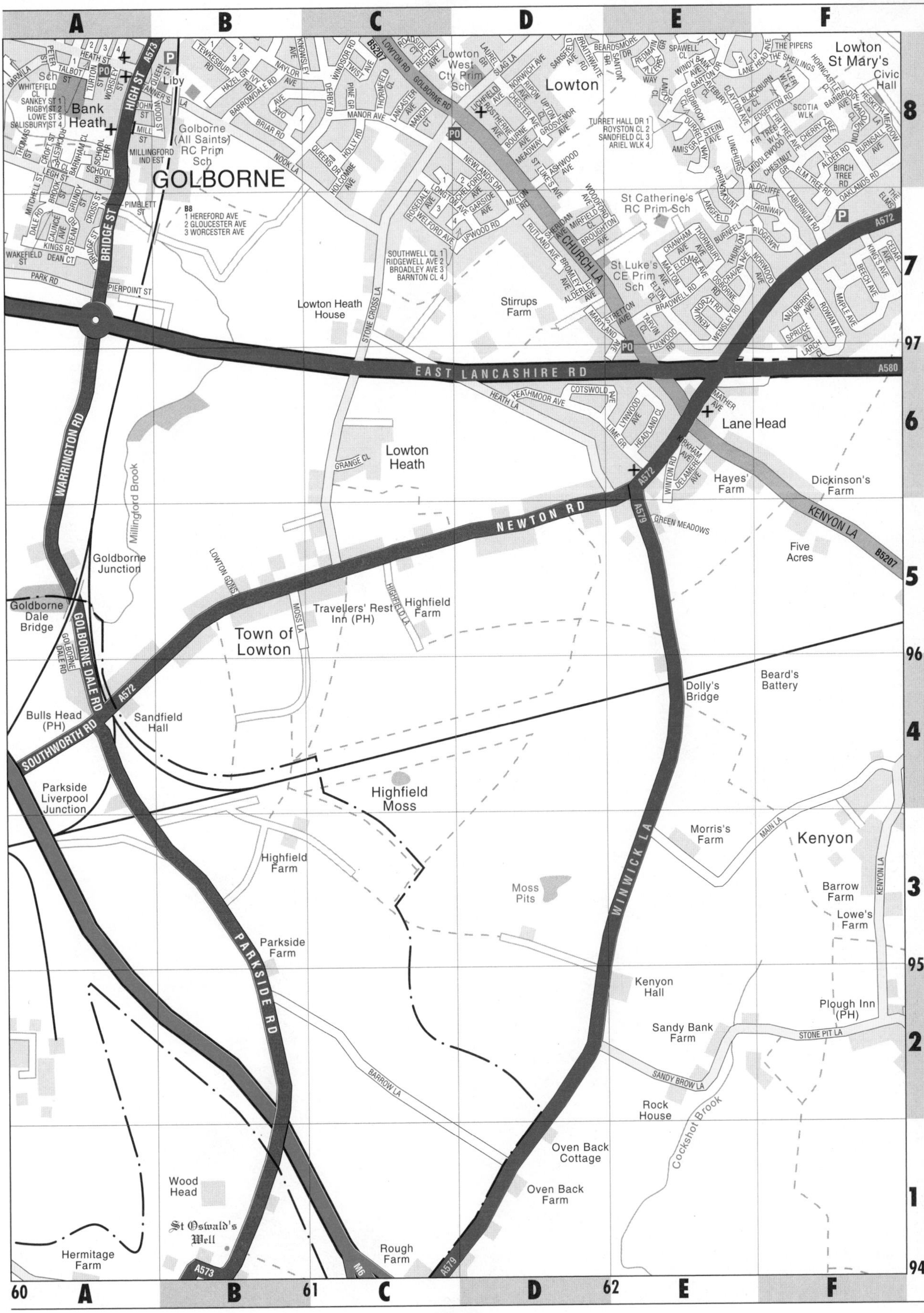
A
B
C
D
E
F
8
7
97
6
5
96
4
3
95
2
1
94
60
61
62
GOLBORNE
Bank Heath
Golborne (All Saints) RC Prim Sch
Lowton
Lowton West Cty Prim Sch
Lowton St Mary's
Civic Hall
St Catherine's RC Prim Sch
St Luke's CE Prim Sch
Stirrups Farm
Lowton Heath House
Lowton Heath
Lane Head
Hayes' Farm
Dickinson's Farm
Five Acres
Goldborne Junction
Goldborne Dale Bridge
Travellers' Rest Inn (PH)
Highfield Farm
Town of Lowton
Bulls Head (PH)
Sandfield Hall
Parkside Liverpool Junction
Highfield Moss
Dolly's Bridge
Beard's Battery
Morris's Farm
Kenyon
Barrow Farm
Lowe's Farm
Moss Pits
Parkside Farm
Kenyon Hall
Plough Inn (PH)
Sandy Bank Farm
Rock House
Oven Back Cottage
Oven Back Farm
Wood Head
St Oswald's Well
Hermitage Farm
Rough Farm
Millingford Brook
Cockshot Brook
EAST LANCASHIRE RD
NEWTON RD
WARRINGTON RD
GOLBORNE DALE RD
SOUTHWORTH RD
PARKSIDE RD
WINWICK LA
KENYON LA
CHURCH LA
BRIDGE ST
HIGH ST
HEATH LA
MAIN LA
STONE PIT LA
SANDY BROW LA
BARROW LA
KENYON LA
STONE CROSS LA
MOSS LA
HIGHFIELD LA
LOWTON GDNS
GRANGE CL
GREEN MEADOWS
PARK RD
PIERPOINT ST
A572
A573
A579
A580
B5207
M6
B8
1 HEREFORD AVE
2 GLOUCESTER AVE
3 WORCESTER AVE
SOUTHWELL CL 1
RIDGEWELL AVE 2
BROADLEY AVE 3
BARNTON CL 4
TURRET HALL DR 1
ROYSTON CL 2
SANDFIELD CL 3
ARIEL WLK 4
SANKEY ST 1
RIGBY ST 2
LOWE ST 3
SALISBURY ST 4
MILLINGFORD IND EST
PO
P
Liby
Sch

61

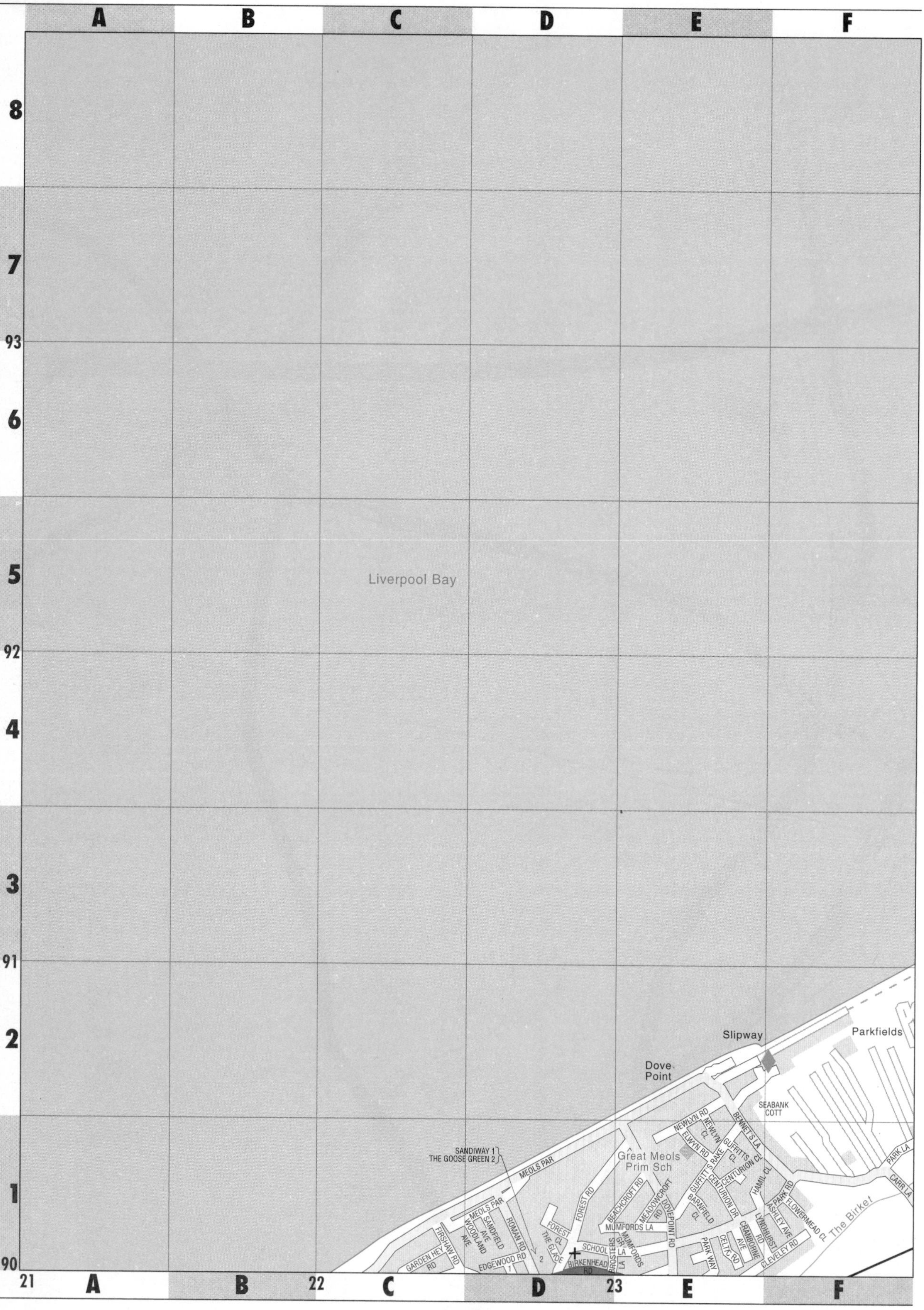
A
B
C
D
E
F
8
7
93
6
5
92
4
3
91
2
1
90
21
22
23
Liverpool Bay
Slipway
Parkfields
Dove Point
SEABANK COTT
NEWLYN RD
NEWLYN CL
ELWYN RD
BENNET'S LA
GUFFITTS CL
GUFFITT'S RAKE
CENTURION CL
CENTURION DR
HAMIL CL
PARK LA
CARR LA
SANDIWAY 1
THE GOOSE GREEN 2
MEOLS PAR
Great Meols Prim Sch
FOREST RD
BEACHCROFT RD
MEADOWCROFT RD
DOVEPOINT RD
BARNFIELD CL
PARK RD
FLOWERMEAD CL
ASHLEY AVE
LYNDHURST RD
CRANBORNE AVE
The Birket
MEOLS PAR
SANDFIELD AVE
WOODLAND AVE
ROMAN RD
FOREST CL
THE GLADE
MUMFORDS LA
MUMFORDS GR
MUMFORDS LA
BROSTERS LA
SCHOOL LA
PARK WAY
CELTIC RD
CLEVELEY RD
FIRSHAW RD
GARDEN HEY RD
EDGEWOOD RD
BIRKENHEAD RD

63

50

A
B
C
D
E
F
8
7
93
6
5
92
4
3
91
2
1
90
24
25
26
Liverpool Bay
North Wirral Coastal Park
CH
Leasowe Castle Hotel
Golf Course
CASTLE FIELDS EST
A551
Wallasey Embankment
LEASOWE RD
LEASOWE GDNS
MEREHEATH GDNS
MARSHFIELD CT
HEATH CASTLEHEATH CL
THE SANDHILLS
THE BEECHES
THE STAKES
CASTLEGRANGE CL
THE HEATHLANDS
THE LAURELS
CASTLEFORD RISE
GARSWOOD CL
FARNWORTH AVE
CRONTON AVE
FINDLEY DR
DITTON LA
WAKEFIELD DR
MURRAYFIELD DR
RAVENHILL CRES
BLACKHEATH DR
GREENHEATH WAY
WHITEHEATH WAY
TWICKENHAM DR
FARMSIDE
REEDS AVE E
REEDS AVE W
REEDS LA
BIRKET AVE
BIRKET SQ
PO
Leasowe Common
P
Lighthouse (dis)
LINGHAM LA
The Birket
Parkfield House
Lingham Farm
TARRAN WAY N
TARRAN WAY W
TARRAN WAY E
TARRAN DR
TARRAN RD
TARRAN WAY S
SUNNYSIDE
PASTURE RD
Works
Leasowe Hotel (PH)
REEDVILLE GR
Moreton Sta
STATION APP
Arrowe Brook
FB
WASTDALE CT 1
WASTDALE MEWS 2
PARK LA
CURLEW CT
CURLEW WAY
LINGHAM CL
BRADMAN RD
BERRYLANDS RD
BRAMBLE WAY
MEADFOOT RD
PASTURE AVE
PASTURE CRES
SCHOOL CL
SUNFIELD RD
LOMBARD RD
KINGSMEAD RD
YEW TREE RD
SAXON RD
WEST WAY
WEST WAY SQ
FURZE WAY
IVY LA
EAST WAY
OUNDLE RD
ROSSALL RD
DANGER LA
DANESWELL DR
Eastway Prim Sch
AVONDALE AVE
KERN WAY
WASTDALE DR
MALLARD WAY
GLASIER RD
LINGHAM LA
ELEANOR RD
HARVEST LA
HEATHMOOR RD
FLAXHILL
BERRYLANDS CL
Moreton
WITLEY AVE
WITLEY CL
LYONS CL
LYONS RD
BLUNDELLS DR
Sacred Heart RC Prim Sch
A553
HOYLAKE RD
ASHBY CL
MILLHOUSE LA
MILLHOUSE CL
DESFORD CL
LC
GLENFIELD CL
BRADGATE CL
FOXTON CL
ANSTEY CL
OAKHAM DR
CARNOUSTIE CL
TURNBERRY CL
BELFRY CL
ST AUSTELL CL
TANWORTH GR
CARR LA
ESKDALE AVE
BERMUDA RD
SMILIE AVE
HARDIE AVE
TOWN MEADOW LA
LINEAR PK
BURDEN RD
KESTREL RD
E1
1 GARDEN LA
2 OAKENHOLT RD
Lingham Prim Sch
EDGEHILL RD
DIGG LA
FELICITY GR
OVERGREEN GR
WILLASTON RD
MARYLAND LA
OLD MARYLAND LA
BARNSTON LA
LITHERLAND AVE
Liby
SILVERBURN AVE
KNUTSFORD RD
ORCHARD RD
KNUTSFORD GN
FAIRMEAD RD
BURNLEY RD
STUART AVE

64

50

49

A
B
C
D
E
F
8
7
6
5
4
3
2
1
93
92
91
90
27
28
29
Liverpool Bay
KING'S PAR
A554
WELLINGTON RD
THE CLIFF
COASTAL DR
Slipway
P
THE CHANNEL
THE BANKS
MOCKBEGGAR WHARF
Warren Park
(Municipal Golf
Course)
Harrison
Park
B5477 HARRISON DR
Wallasey
Sta
CH
BAYSWATER CT
BAYSWATER RD
E6
1 MARSHLANDS RD
2 TOWN FIELDS
Golf Links
Dunes
Picnic
Area
GREEN LA
Golf
Course
Greenleas
Prim Sch
WALLASEY VILLAGE
St
Mary's
Coll
St George's
Prim Sch
Clare
Mount
Sch
Wallasey
Village
Sta
LEASOWE RD
A551
St Mary's
Coll
Our Lady of
Lourdes
RC Prim Sch
Leasowe
Castleway
Prim Sch
Lby
Leasowe
Prim Schs
The Mosslands
Sch
WALLASEY
Recn Gd
ST HILARY BROW
WALLASEY RD
B5145
BRECK RD
A5139
M53
F4
1 BLETCHLEY AVE
2 BRYNMOSS AVE
3 CROMARTY RD
4 MILLTHWAITE CT
Mosslands
Lower
Sch
Bidston
Golf Course
Bidston
Ind Est
Bidston
Moss
Bidston
Dock
Wallasey
Sch
The Birket
Factory
Bidston
Sta
LC
Leasowe
Sta
A554
Superstore
Sports
Ctr
Works
WALLASEY BRIDGE RD
A5088
Claremount
Sch
FENDER LA
A553
Fender
Farm
Fender
Bridge
Bidston
Village
CE Sch
Vyner
Prim Sch
Bidston
CH
Bidston
Hall
B5151
BOUNDARY RD
HOYLAKE RD
Holy Cross RC
Prim & Mid
Schs
Birkenhead
North
Sta
A5030 BEAUFORT RD
STANLEY RD
M53

49
65

B7
1 CURZON AVE
2 STANFORD AVE
3 GREENBANK AVE
4 FOUNTAIN RD
5 SOUTH VILLAS
6 CYPRUS TERR
7 STANLEY TERR
8 OSBORNE VALE

B8
1 BROCKLEY RD
2 CRESSINGHAM RD
3 CAVENDISH RD
4 SEYMOUR PL W
5 FERN HILL
6 ONSLOW RD

37
52

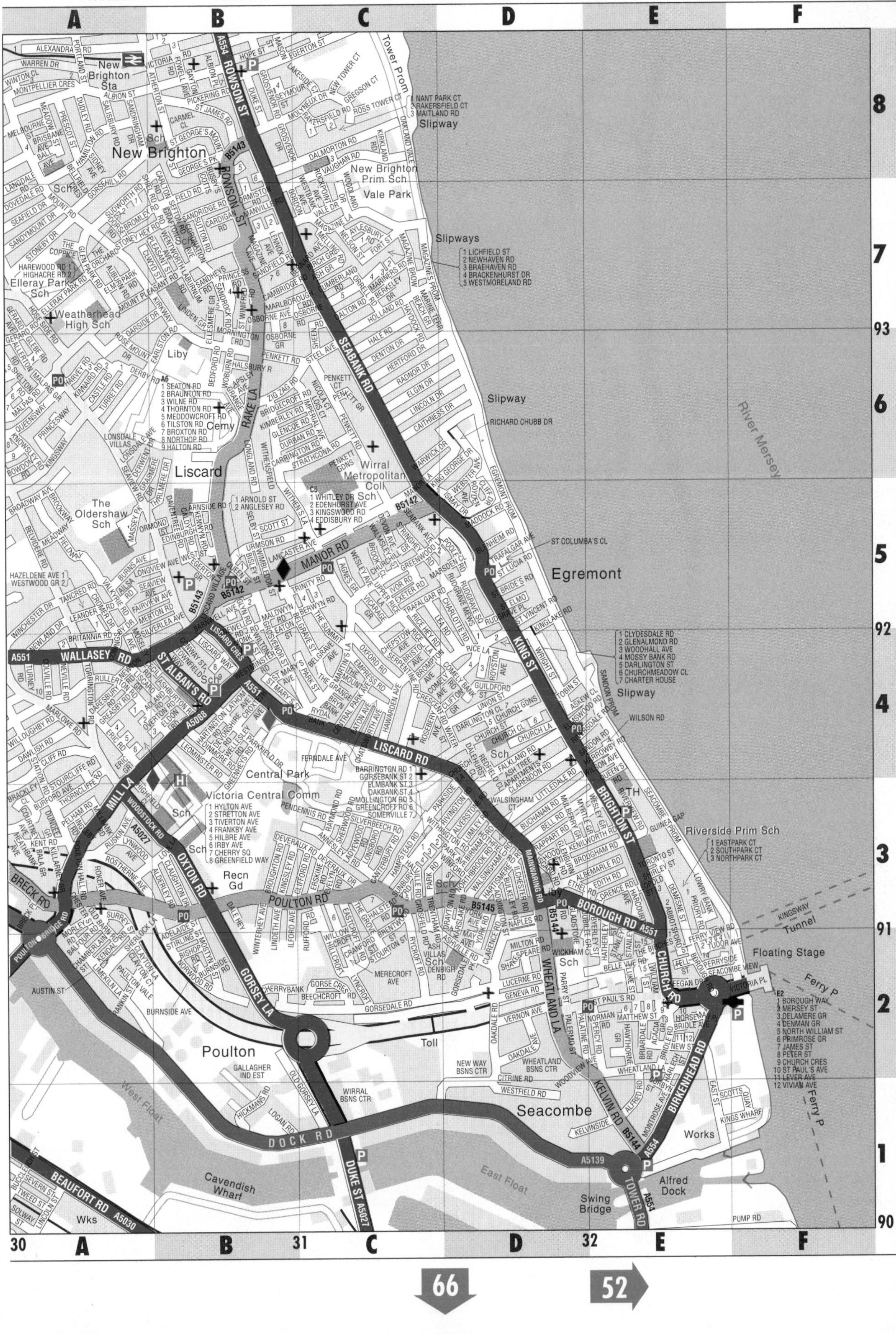

66
52

51
38

E8
1 DELAMORE ST
2 CHIRKDALE ST
3 BACK WESTMINSTER RD
4 BRUNSWICK CL
5 DRYBURGH WAY
6 WARDEN ST
7 BRADEWELL CL
8 ROCKLEY ST
9 ST HILDA ST
10 LONGRIDGE WLK
11 MILNTHORPE CL

F7
1 TEULON CL
2 LUTYENS CL
3 COCKERELL CL
4 HARTLEY CL
5 WYRE RD
6 GOSCHEN ST
7 ELM BANK
8 YORK VILLAS
9 PULFORD ST
10 BALFOUR ST
11 GORST ST
12 RANDOLPH ST
13 GURNALL ST
14 HAYFIELD ST
15 ATTWOOD ST
16 NORGATE ST
17 SAKER ST

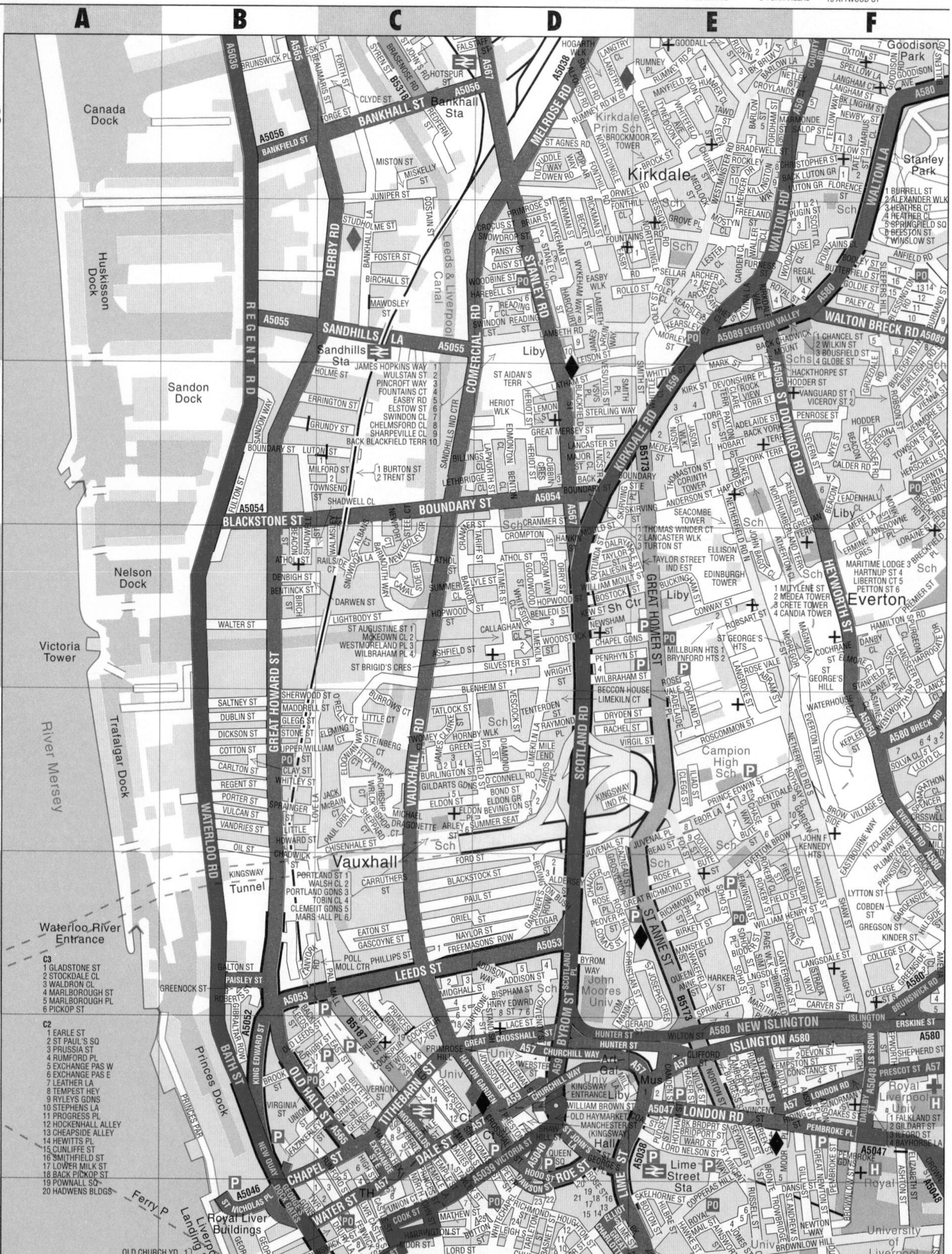

D1
1 GRADWELL ST
2 COLLEGE LA
3 OLD POST OFFICE PL
4 BROOKS ALLEY
5 LYCEUM PL
6 FAIRCLOUGH ST
7 CASES ST
8 CLAYTON SQ
9 LEIGH PL
10 LEIGH ST
11 TYRER ST
12 HOUGHTON LA
13 ST JOHN'S WAY
14 CHARLOTTE WAY
15 HOUGHTON WAY
16 MARKET WAY
17 MARKET SQ
18 ST JOHN'S SQ
19 ST GEORGE'S WAY
20 GREAT CHARLOTTE ST
21 DAWSON WAY
22 BRYTHEN ST
23 WILLIAMSON SQ
24 WILLIAMSON ST
25 RAINFORD GDNS
26 BACK LORD ST

D3
1 LIMEKILN LA
2 WELLINGTON ST

51

3 NICHOLAS ST
4 ST STEPHENS PL
5 HOLY CROSS CL

D4
1 BURROUGHS GDNS
2 BEVINGTON HILL
3 ENNERDALE ST

E1
1 LAWTON ST
2 BACK RENSHAW ST

67

3 PLEASANT ST
4 EDWARD ST
5 RUSSELL PL
6 WARREN ST

E2
1 COMMUTATION ROW
2 BACK COMMUTATION ROW
3 LAMBERT WAY
4 MARQUIS ST
5 ST ANDREWS GDNS

E3
1 BICKERSTAFFE ST
2 DRINKWATER GDNS
3 RODERICK ST
4 TRINITY WLK

E4
1 ST MARTIN'S MEWS
2 CLIFTON GR
3 SHERIFF CL
4 HIGHAM SQ
5 UPPER BUTE ST
6 WATMOUGH ST
7 BERESFORD ST
8 BACK BEAU ST
9 UPPER BEAU ST

F3
1 CANTERBURY WAY
2 TICHBOURNE WAY
3 MELDA CL
4 TRAFALGAR WAY
5 ERSKINE IND EST

F4
1 NORTHCOTE CL
2 LETTERSTONE WLK
3 LETTERSTONE CL
4 CADMUS WLK
5 FISHGUARD CL
6 BLYTHE WAY
7 GLENVALE WLK
8 GLEAVE SQ

A5
1 FRIAR ST
2 PREMIER ST
3 DOWNING ST
4 RUTLAND CL
5 HANDFIELD PL
6 STOCKBRIDGE PL
7 BULWER ST
8 RISHTON ST
9 TYNEMOUTH CL
10 RISHTON CL
11 QUEENS MEWS

A6
1 VYRNWY ST
2 VIENNA ST
3 ADKINS ST
4 TENBY ST
5 BACK GRANTON RD
6 HOULDING ST
7 HAWKESWORTH ST
8 BOYCOTT ST
9 CROUCH ST

A7
1 BAGNALL ST
2 BALTIC ST
3 GILMAN ST
4 TINSLEY ST
5 LAKE ST
6 VARTHEN ST

B5
1 LARCH LEA
2 SPRING BANK RD
3 AVON ST
4 FRANKLIN PL
5 PARLE CT

39

B6
1 LUDWIG RD
2 OLD BARN RD
3 STONEHILL AVE
4 ST DAVID'S RD
5 TAPLOW ST
6 TWICKENHAM ST

54

E8
1 GARSFIELD RD
2 SANDYVILLE GR
3 DURRANT RD
4 PARLOW RD
5 MILNE RD

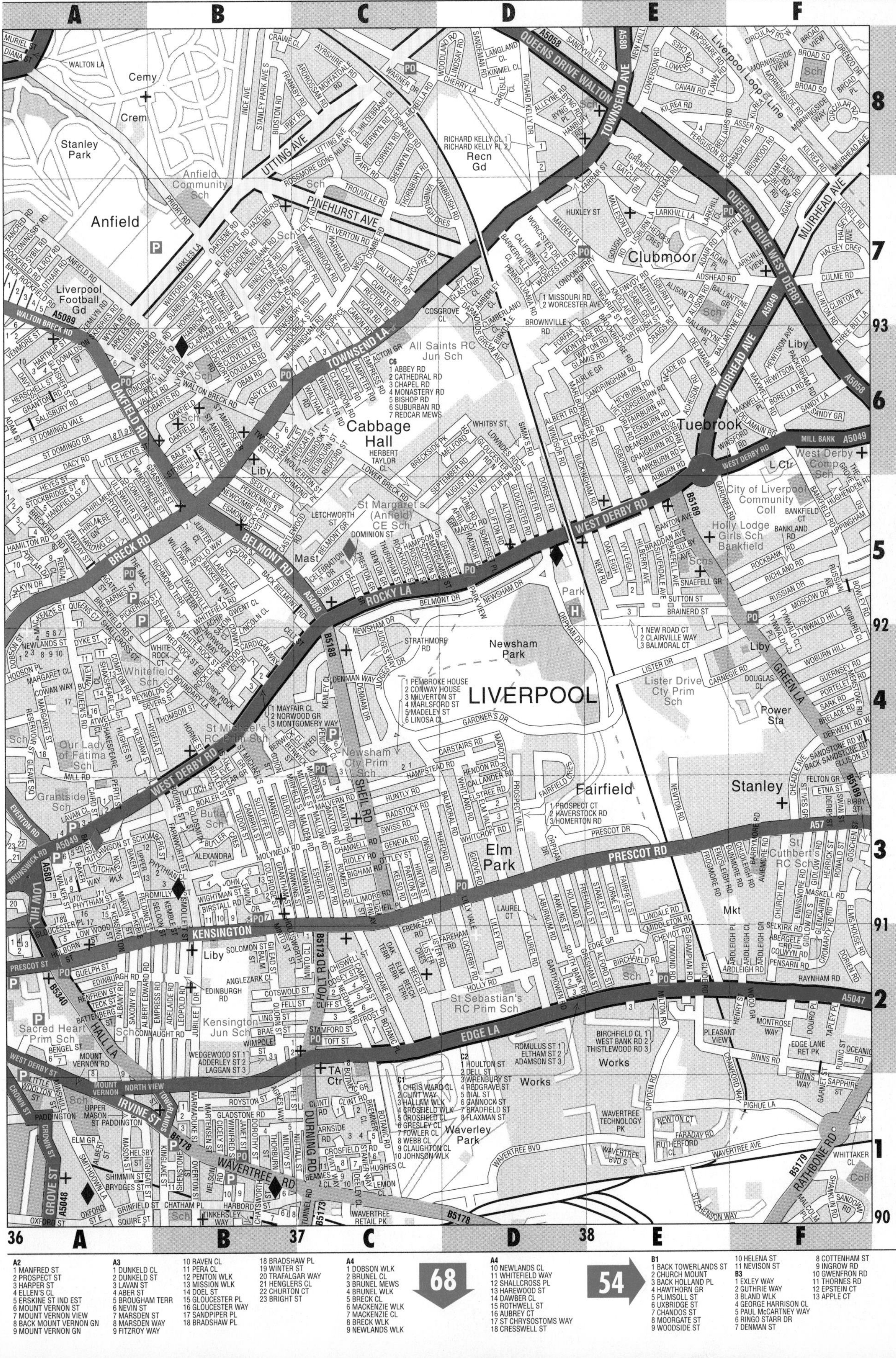

A2
1 MANFRED ST
2 PROSPECT ST
3 HARPER ST
4 ELLEN'S CL
5 ERSKINE ST IND EST
6 MOUNT VERNON ST
7 MOUNT VERNON VIEW
8 BACK MOUNT VERNON GN
9 MOUNT VERNON GN

A3
1 DUNKELD CL
2 DUNKELD ST
3 LAVAN ST
4 ABER ST
5 BROUGHAM TERR
6 NEVIN ST
7 MARSDEN ST
8 MARSDEN WAY
9 FITZROY WAY
10 RAVEN CL
11 PERA CL
12 PENTON WLK
13 MISSION WLK
14 DOEL ST
15 GLOUCESTER PL
16 GLOUCESTER WAY
17 SANDPIPER PL
18 BRADSHAW PL
18 BRADSHAW PL
19 WINTER ST
20 TRAFALGAR WAY
21 HENGLERS CL
22 CHURTON CT
23 BRIGHT ST

A4
1 DOBSON WLK
2 BRUNEL CL
3 BRUNEL MEWS
4 BRUNEL WLK
5 BRECK CL
6 MACKENZIE WLK
7 MACKENZIE CL
8 BRECK WLK
9 NEWLANDS WLK

68

A4
10 NEWLANDS CL
11 WHITEFIELD WAY
12 SHALLCROSS PL
13 HAREWOOD ST
14 DAWBER CL
15 ROTHWELL ST
16 AUBREY CT
17 ST CHRYSOSTOMS WAY
18 CRESSWELL ST

54

B1
1 BACK TOWERLANDS ST
2 CHURCH MOUNT
3 BACK HOLLAND PL
4 HAWTHORN GR
5 PLIMSOLL ST
6 UXBRIDGE ST
7 CHANDOS ST
8 MOORGATE ST
9 WOODSIDE ST
10 HELENA ST
11 NEVISON ST

B3
1 EXLEY WAY
2 GUTHRIE WAY
3 BLAND WLK
4 GEORGE HARRISON CL
5 PAUL McCARTNEY WAY
6 RINGO STARR DR
7 DENMAN ST
8 COTTENHAM ST
9 INGROW RD
10 GWENFRON RD
11 THORNES RD
12 EPSTEIN CT
13 APPLE CT

53
40

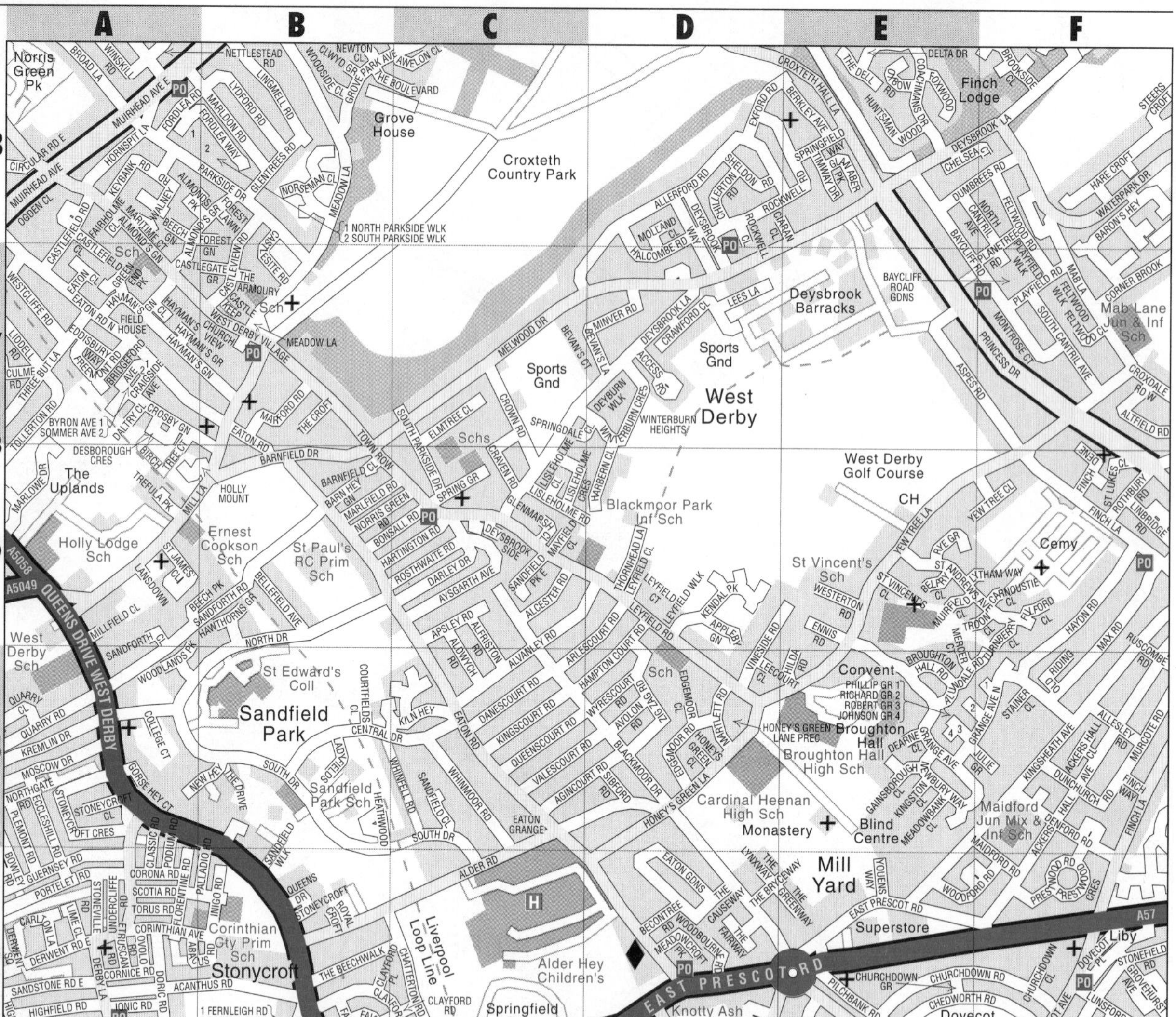

53
69

A3
1 CHILDERS ST
2 MACFARREN ST
3 BELL ST
4 BATLEY ST
5 BOOTH ST
6 ST OSWALD HOUSE
7 RAVENSWOOD RD
8 BEATTY RD

41
56

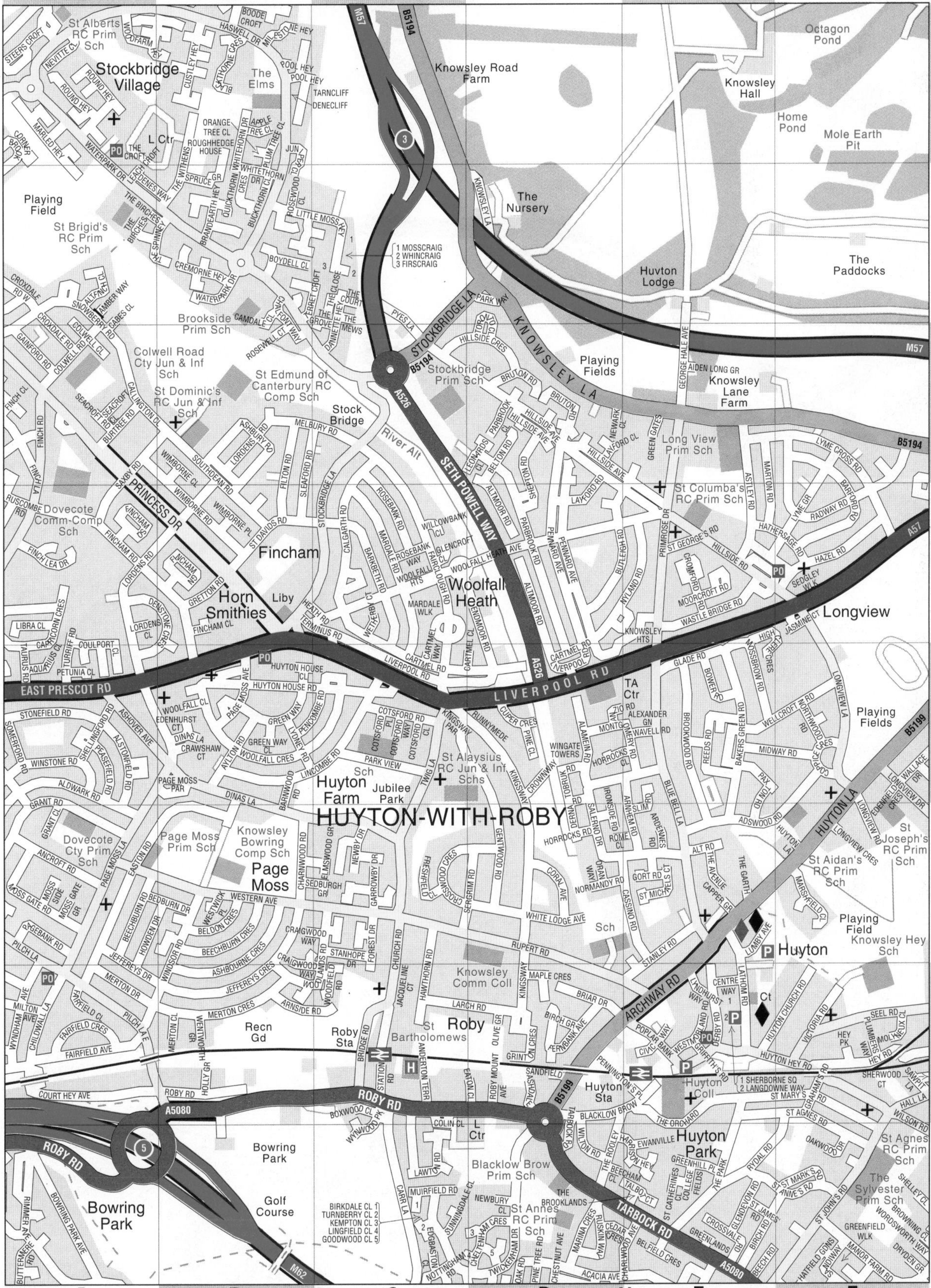
Stockbridge Village
St Alberts RC Prim Sch
The Elms
Playing Field
St Brigid's RC Prim Sch
Brookside Prim Sch
Colwell Road Cty Jun & Inf Sch
St Edmund of Canterbury RC Comp Sch
St Dominic's RC Jun & Inf Sch
Stock Bridge
Knowsley Road Farm
The Nursery
Octagon Pond
Knowsley Hall
Home Pond
Mole Earth Pit
The Paddocks
Huyton Lodge
Playing Fields
Knowsley Lane Farm
Stockbridge Prim Sch
Long View Prim Sch
St Columba's RC Prim Sch
Dovecote Comm Comp Sch
Fincham
Horn Smithies
Liby
Woolfall Heath
Longview
SETH POWELL WAY
KNOWSLEY LA
STOCKBRIDGE LA
PRINCESS DR
EAST PRESCOT RD
LIVERPOOL RD
HUYTON LA
ARCHWAY RD
ROBY RD
TARBOCK RD
TA Ctr
Playing Fields
St Alaysius RC Jun & Inf Schs
Huyton Farm
Jubilee Park
HUYTON-WITH-ROBY
Dovecote Cty Prim Sch
Page Moss Prim Sch
Knowsley Bowring Comp Sch
Page Moss
St Joseph's RC Prim Sch
St Aidan's RC Prim Sch
Playing Field
Knowsley Hey Sch
Huyton
Knowsley Comm Coll
Recn Gd
Roby Sta
St Bartholomews
Roby
Huyton Sta
Huyton Coll
Huyton Park
Bowring Park
Golf Course
Blacklow Brow Prim Sch
St Annes RC Prim Sch
The Sylvester Prim Sch
St Agnes RC Prim Sch
M57
M62
A5080
B5194
A526
A57
B5199
A B C D E F
8 7 93 6 5 92 4 3 91 2 1 90
42 43 44

70
56

55
42

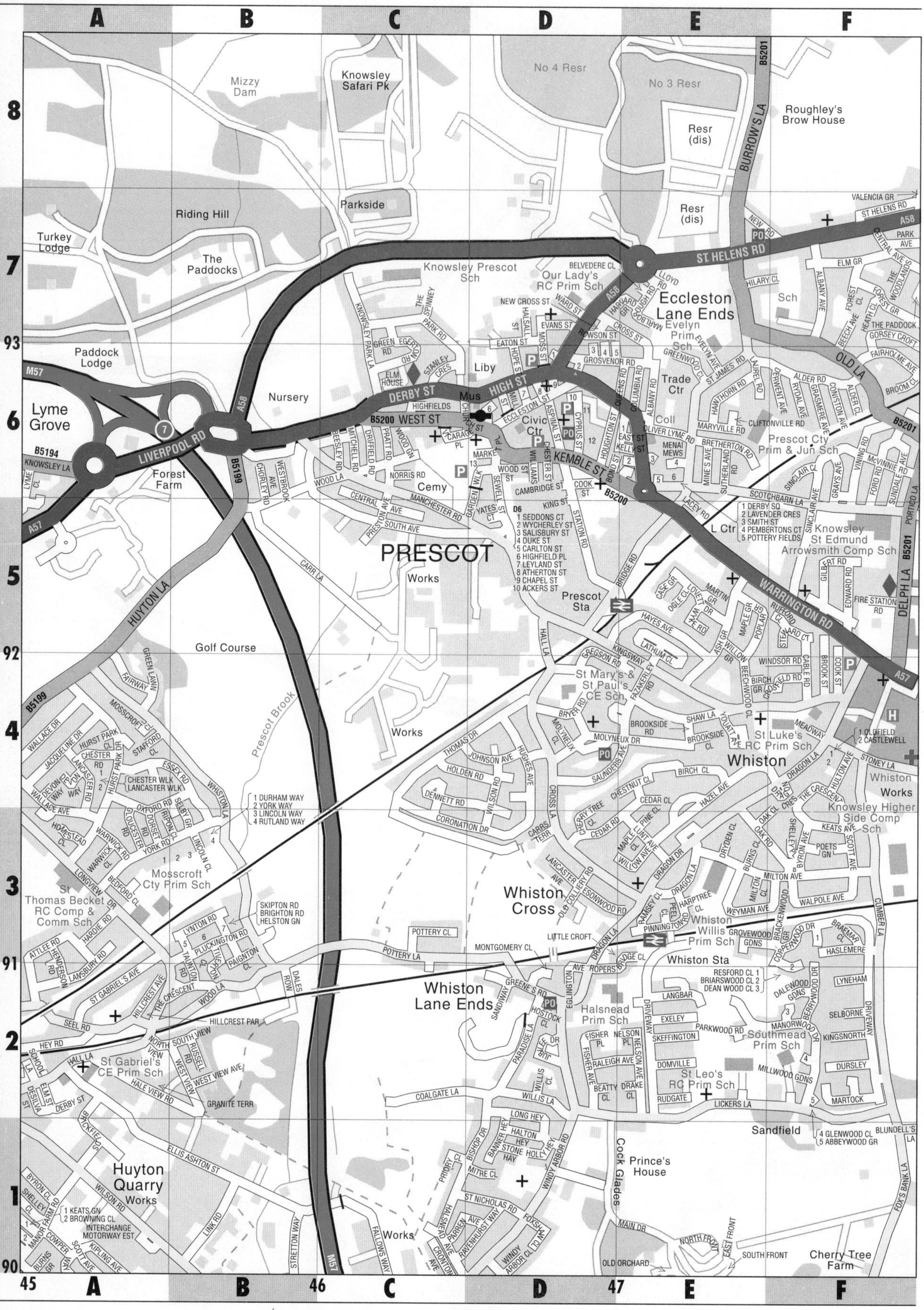
A
B
C
D
E
F
8
7
93
6
5
92
4
3
91
2
1
90
45
46
47
Mizzy Dam
Knowsley Safari Pk
No 4 Resr
No 3 Resr
Roughley's Brow House
Resr (dis)
Resr (dis)
BURROW'S LA
B5201
Riding Hill
Parkside
Turkey Lodge
The Paddocks
Knowsley Prescot Sch
Our Lady's RC Prim Sch
BELVEDERE CL
ST HELENS RD
A58
VALENCIA GR
ST HELENS RD
PARK AVE
ELM GR
HILARY CL
Sch
Eccleston Lane Ends
Evelyn Prim Sch
NEW CROSS ST
WARD ST
EVANS ST
ROWSON ST
CROSS ST
Paddock Lodge
M57
Lyme Grove
Nursery
DERBY ST
HIGH ST
Liby
Mus
HIGHFIELDS
B5200 WEST ST
ECCLESTON ST
Civic Ctr
PO
GROSVENOR RD
Trade Ctr
Coll
OLIVER LYME RD
MARYVILLE RD
CLIFTONVILLE RD
Prescot Cty Prim & Jun Sch
OLD LA
B5201
THE PADDOCK
GORSEY CROFT
FAIRHOLME AVE
BROOM CL
ALDER RD
LIVERPOOL RD
B5194
KNOWSLEY LA
Forest Farm
B5199
CHORLEY RD
WESTBROOK AVE
WOOD LA
NORRIS RD
Cemy
CENTRAL AVE
MANCHESTER RD
SOUTH AVE
PRESCOT
KEMBLE ST
B5200
CAMBRIDGE ST
KING ST
COOK ST
STATION RD
D6
1 SEDDONS CT
2 WYCHERLEY ST
3 SALISBURY ST
4 DUKE ST
5 CARLTON ST
6 HIGHFIELD PL
7 LEYLAND ST
8 ATHERTON ST
9 CHAPEL ST
10 ACKERS ST
SCOTCHBARN LA
LACEY RD
1 DERBY SQ
2 LAVENDER CRES
3 SMITH ST
4 PEMBERTONS CT
5 POTTERY FIELDS
L Ctr
Knowsley St Edmund Arrowsmith Comp Sch
A57
Works
CARR LA
HUYTON LA
Prescot Sta
WARRINGTON RD
DELPH LA
FIRE STATION RD
BRIDGE RD
HAYES AVE
KINGSWAY
Golf Course
GREGSON RD
St Mary's & St Paul's CE Sch
WINDSOR RD
CABLE RD
BROOK ST
COOK ST
B5199
FAIRWAY
GREEN LAWN
MOSSCROFT CL
WALLACE DR
HURST PARK
STAFFORD
Prescot Brook
Works
THOMAS DR
JOHNSON AVE
HOLDEN RD
BROOKSIDE RD
MOLYNEUX DR
SHAW LA
St Luke's RC Prim Sch
Whiston
1 OLDFIELD
2 CASTLEWELL
STONEY LA
Whiston Works
Knowsley Higher Side Comp Sch
H
CHESTER WLK
LANCASTER WLK
ESSEX RD
1 DURHAM WAY
2 YORK WAY
3 LINCOLN WAY
4 RUTLAND WAY
DENNETT RD
CORONATION DR
SAUNDERS AVE
BIRCH CL
CHESTNUT CL
CEDAR CL
HAZEL AVE
CEDAR RD
KEATS AVE
POETS GN
SCOTT AVE
Mosscroft Cty Prim Sch
St Thomas Becket RC Comp & Comm Sch
Whiston Cross
MILTON AVE
WALPOLE AVE
WEYMAN AVE
CUMBER LA
SKIPTON RD
BRIGHTON RD
HELSTON GN
POTTERY CL
LITTLE CROFT
Whiston Willis Prim Sch
BRAEMAR CL
HASLEMERE
LYNTON RD
PLUCKINGTON RD
PAIGNTON CL
ATTLEE RD
LANSBURY RD
POTTERY LA
MONTGOMERY CL
Whiston Sta
ROPERS BRIDGE CL
RESFORD CL 1
BRIARSWOOD CL 2
DEAN WOOD CL 3
LYNEHAM
DALES ROW
ST GABRIEL'S AVE
HILLCREST AVE
THE CRESCENT
WOOD LA
Whiston Lane Ends
GREENE'S RD
HOSTOCK CL
LANGBAR
SELBORNE
SEEL RD
HILLCREST PAR
Halsnead Prim Sch
EXELEY
PARKWOOD RD
Southmead Prim Sch
KINGSNORTH
HEY RD
SOUTH VIEW
FISHER PL
NELSON PL
SKEFFINGTON
St Gabriel's CE Prim Sch
WEST VIEW AVE
RALEIGH AVE
DOMVILLE
DURSLEY
HALE VIEW RD
GRANITE TERR
COALGATE LA
WILLIS LA
BEATTY CL
DRAKE CL
St Leo's RC Prim Sch
RUDGATE
LICKERS LA
MARTOCK
DERBY ST
LONG HEY
HALTON HEY
STONE HEY
HOLLY HEY
Sandfield
4 GLENWOOD CL
5 ABBEYWOOD GR
BLUNDELL'S LA
ELLIS ASHTON ST
Huyton Quarry Works
Cock Glades
Prince's House
MITRE CL
ST NICHOLAS RD
1 KEATS GN
2 BROWNING CL
INTERCHANGE MOTORWAY EST
LINK RD
STRETTON WAY
M57
Works
FALLOWS WAY
RAVENHURST WAY
WINDY ARBOR CL
MAIN DR
NORTH FRONT
EAST FRONT
SOUTH FRONT
OLD ORCHARD
Cherry Tree Farm
FOX'S BANK LA
KIPLING AVE
SCOTT AVE
BURNS GR
COWPER WAY

55
71

43
58

A
B
C
D
E
F
8
7
93
6
5
92
4
3
91
2
1
90
48
49
50
Valencia Farm
Eccleston Park
Portico
Grange Park
Broadway Comm High Sch
Thatto Heath
Thatto Heath Sta
Thatto Heath Comm Prim Sch
Liby
St Matthews CE Prim Sch
St Austin's RC Prim Sch
Nutgrove Meth Prim Sch
Brown Edge
Playing Fields
The Meads
Eccleston Park Sta
Portico Lodge
Rainhill Neuro-Psychiatric Unit
Nut Grove
Sutton Heath
Depot
Farm Annexe
Rainhill
Elton
Two Butt La
St John Vianney RC Prim Sch
PH
Lea Green
Elton Head Hall Farm
LOWFIELD IND EST
Glasshouse Farm
FB
Longton Lane Comm Prim Sch
Holt
Pendlebury Brook
ST HELENS LINKWAY
Micklehead Farm
Micklehead Green Farm
Rainhill Sta
Sports Ground
Rainhill Park Prim Sch
Rainhill St Ann's CE Prim Sch
Brookhouse Bridge
Rainhill High Sch
Home Farm
Blundell's Hill
Loyola Hall
Chapel House Farm
Wood's House Farm
Oakdene Prim Sch
Dean's House Farm
Blundell's Hill Golf Club
Rainhill Stoops
St Bartholomew's RC Prim Sch
Fairchild Farm
Rainhill Hall Farm
Tower Coll
Golf Course
PRESCOT RD
ST HELENS RD
THATTO HEATH RD
NUTGROVE RD
ELTON HEAD RD
RAINHILL RD
WARRINGTON RD
TWO BUTT LA
BLUNDELL'S LA
MILL LA
CHAPEL LA
SCHOOL LA
A58
B5413
B5204
B5201
A570
A57
M62
1 CROWN ST
2 COMMON ST
3 GORSEFIELD
4 OAKFIELD CL
5 BILLINGHAM RD
1 HOLLEY CT
2 BRAITHWAITE CL
3 STATION ST
1 WIDDALE AVE
2 KINGSDALE AVE
TOFTWOOD GDNS 1
ANDERSON CL 2
72
58

57
44

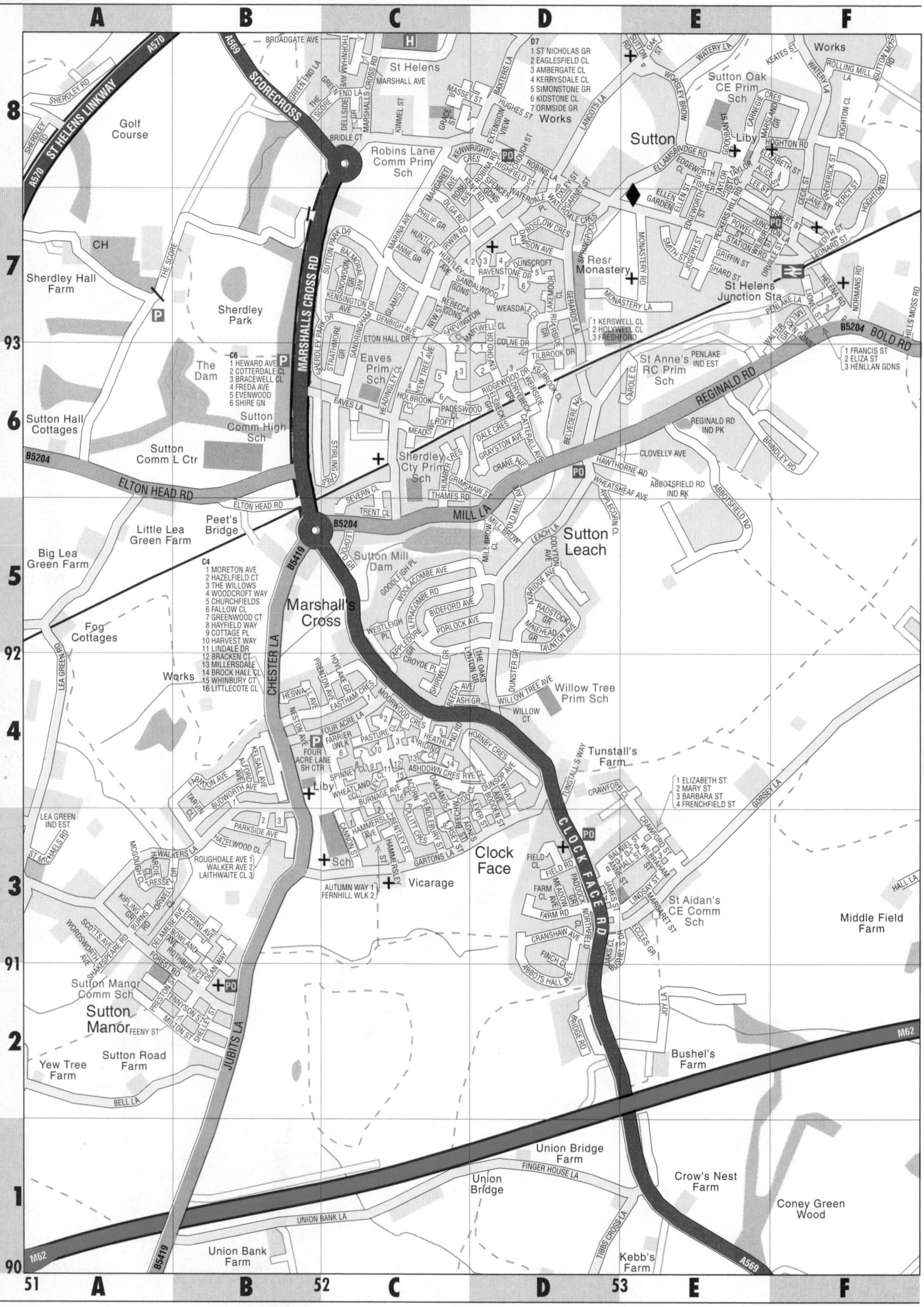
A
B
C
D
E
F
8
7
93
6
5
92
4
3
91
2
1
90
51
52
53
St Helens
Works
Sutton Oak CE Prim Sch
Sutton
Liby
Golf Course
ST HELENS LINKWAY
A570
SHERDLEY RD
SCORECROSS
A569
BROADGATE AVE
THORNHAM AVE
MARSHALLS CROSS RD
MARSHALL AVE
KIMMEL ST
BRIDLE CT
Robins Lane Comm Prim Sch
D7
1 ST NICHOLAS GR
2 EAGLESFIELD CL
3 AMBERGATE CL
4 KERRYSDALE CL
5 SIMONSTONE GR
6 KIDSTONE CL
7 ORMSIDE GR
BAXTERS LA
HUGHES ST
EXTENSION VIEW
LANCOTS LA
WATERY LA
WORSLEY BROW
ELLAMSBRIDGE RD
HOGHTON RD
ELIZABETH ST
FREDERICK ST
PERCY ST
HOGHTON CL
ROLLING MILL LA
KEATES ST
CARNEGIE CRES
GOODBAN ST
ROBINS LA
HIGHFIELD ST
KENWRIGHT CRES
OXLEY ST
GARNET ST
WATERDALE CRES
ELLEN ST
EDGEWORTH ST
PECKERS HILL RD
JUNCTION LA
HERBERT ST
LEONARD ST
STATION RD
GRIFFIN ST
SHARD ST
SMITH ST
JOSEPH ST
MONASTERY RD
MONASTERY LA
Resr
Monastery
St Helens Junction Sta
CH
Sherdley Hall Farm
THE SCORE
Sherdley Park
MARSHALLS CROSS RD
SUTTON PARK DR
BALMORAL AVE
SNOWDON GR
KENSINGTON AVE
SANDRINGHAM DR
DENBIGH AVE
GLAMIS GR
MARINA AVE
PHILIP GR
ANNE GR
HUNTLEY GR
IRWIN RD
OLGA RD
SANDALWOOD GDNS
REBECCA GDNS
BOSCOW CRES
DUNSCROFT
RAVENSTONE DR
WEASDALE CL
LAKEMOOR CL
GERARDS LA
SPRINGPOOL
1 KERSWELL CL
2 HOLYWELL CL
3 FRESHFORD
ETON HALL DR
SHERDLEY PARK DR
STRATHMORE GR
Eaves Prim Sch
The Dam
C6
1 HEWARD AVE
2 COTTERDALE CL
3 BRACEWELL CL
4 FREDA AVE
5 EVENWOOD
6 SHIRE GN
MARYWELL CL
COLNE DR
TILBROOK DR
RIDGEWOOD DR
KELBROOK CL
PENLAKE IND EST
St Anne's RC Prim Sch
REGINALD RD
B5204
BOLD RD
1 FRANCIS ST
2 ELIZA ST
3 HENLLAN GDNS
PENLAKE LA
HELENA RD
NORMANS RD
HILLS MOSS RD
LIONEL ST
Sutton Hall Cottages
Sutton Comm High Sch
Sutton Comm L Ctr
EAVES LA
HOLBROOK
PADESWOOD
MEADOWCROFT
DALE CRES
GRAYSTON AVE
CRANE AVE
CATTERALL AVE
BELVEDERE AVE
CLOVELLY AVE
HAWTHORNE RD
REGINALD RD IND PK
BRINDLEY RD
ABBOTSFIELD RD IND PK
ABBOTSFIELD RD
WHEATSHEAF AVE
KIPLECORN CL
Sherdley Cty Prim Sch
HUMBER CRES
GRIMSHAW ST
THAMES RD
STIRLING CRES
ELTON HEAD RD
SEVERN CL
TRENT CL
MILL LA
Peet's Bridge
Little Lea Green Farm
Big Lea Green Farm
LEOPOLD GR
Sutton Mill Dam
MILL BROW CL
OLD MILL AVE
LEACH LA
Sutton Leach
COLYTON AVE
AXBRIDGE AVE
RADSTOCK GR
MINEHEAD GR
TAUNTON AVE
WOOLACOMBE AVE
GOODLEIGH PL
ILFRACOMBE RD
BIDEFORD AVE
PORLOCK AVE
WESTLEIGH PL
APPLEDORE GR
CROYDE PL
SHIRWELL GR
LYNTON GR
THE OAKS
DUNSTER GR
Marshall's Cross
C4
1 MORETON AVE
2 HAZELFIELD CT
3 THE WILLOWS
4 WOODCROFT WAY
5 CHURCHFIELDS
6 FALLOW CL
7 GREENWOOD CT
8 HAYFIELD WAY
9 COTTAGE PL
10 HARVEST WAY
11 LINDALE DR
12 BRACKEN CT
13 MILLERSDALE
14 BROCK HALL CL
15 WHINBURY CT
16 LITTLECOTE CL
B5419
CHESTER LA
Fog Cottages
LEA GREEN RD
Works
Willow Tree Prim Sch
WILLOW TREE AVE
BEECH AVE
ASH GR
WILLOW CT
HESWALL AVE
PRENTON AVE
HOYLAKE GR
EASTHAM CRES
MOORWOOD CRES
NESTON AVE
FOUR ACRE LA
FARRIER WLK
PASTURE CL
RIDING CL
HEATHLAND RD
HORNBY CRES
Four Acre Lane Sh Ctr
ASHDOWN CRES
RYE CL
DUNSOP AVE
WRAY AVE
BODDEN ST
LEVER ST
Tunstall's Farm
TUNSTALL'S WAY
CRAWFORD AVE
1 ELIZABETH ST
2 MARY ST
3 BARBARA ST
4 FRENCHFIELD ST
GORSEY LA
FARNDON AVE
ALFORD AVE
KELSALL AVE
BUDWORTH AVE
TARVIN CL
WHEATLAND LA
BURNAGE AVE
OAKLANDS
PENDLEBURY ST
POLLITT CRES
LEA GREEN IND EST
ST MICHAELS RD
PARKSIDE AVE
HAZELWOOD CL
WALKERS LA
ROUGHDALE AVE 1
WALKER AVE 2
LAITHWAITE CL 3
HAMMERSLEY AVE
CANNON ST
GARTONS LA
Sch
Clock Face
CLOCK FACE RD
FIELD CL
FIELD RD
FARM CL
MEADOW AVE
PADDOCK RD
NORTHFIELD
FARM RD
JAMES ST
BALNIEL ST
MARSHALL ST
WILBRAHAM ST
CRAWFORD ST
LINDSAY ST
MARGARET ST
St Aidan's CE Comm Sch
ECCLES GR
HALL LA
Middle Field Farm
McGOUGH CL
HARDIE CL
RESSEY CL
ORWELL CL
KIPLING GR
BURNS GR
DELAMERE AVE
EPPING AVE
BOWLAND AVE
SCOTTS AVE
WORDSWORTH AVE
SHAKESPEARE RD
ROTHBURY CL
DEAN WAY
FOREST RD
AUTUMN WAY 1
FERNHILL WLK 2
Vicarage
CRANSHAW AVE
FINCH CL
ABBOTS HALL AVE
OAKS CL
BUSHEL'S DR
Sutton Manor Comm Sch
Sutton Manor
PRESTON ST
TENNYSON ST
SHELLEY ST
MILTON ST
FEENY ST
PO
JUBITS LA
JOY LA
BRIDGE RD
Bushel's Farm
M62
Yew Tree Farm
Sutton Road Farm
BELL LA
Union Bridge Farm
FINGER HOUSE LA
Union Bridge
Crow's Nest Farm
Coney Green Wood
UNION BANK LA
Union Bank Farm
TIBBS CROSS LA
Kebb's Farm
A569

57
73

45
60

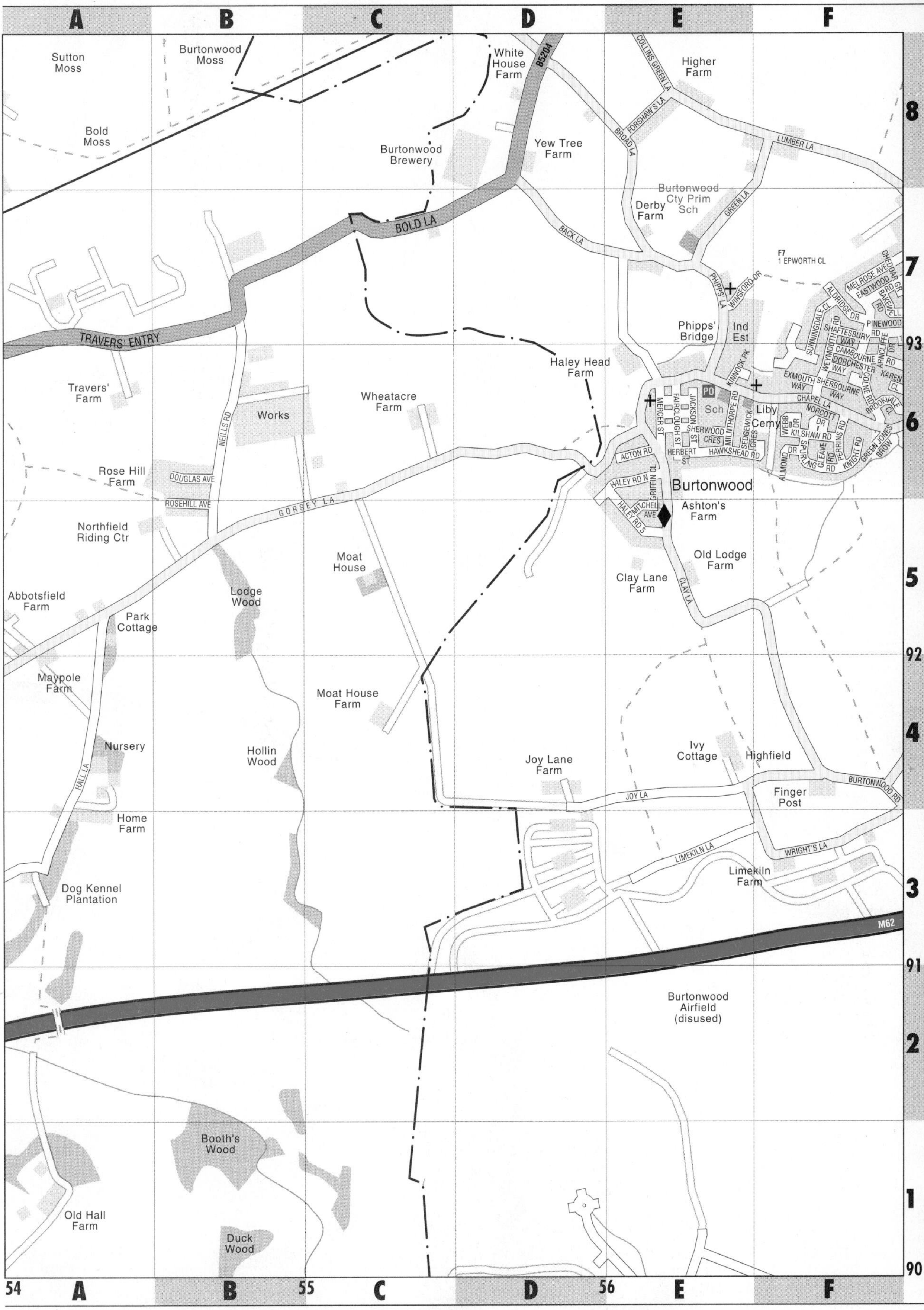
A
B
C
D
E
F
Sutton Moss
Burtonwood Moss
White House Farm
B5204
Higher Farm
COLLINS GREEN LA
FORSHAW'S LA
BROAD LA
LUMBER LA
Bold Moss
Burtonwood Brewery
Yew Tree Farm
Burtonwood Cty Prim Sch
Derby Farm
GREEN LA
BACK LA
BOLD LA
F7
1 EPWORTH CL
PHIPPS LA
WINSFORD DR
TRAVERS' ENTRY
Phipps' Bridge
Ind Est
KINNOCK PK
Haley Head Farm
Travers' Farm
Wheatacre Farm
Works
NEILLS RD
MERCER ST
FAIRCLOUGH ST
JACKSON ST
PO
Sch
MILNTHORPE RD
SEDGEWICK CRES
Liby
Cemy
SHERWOOD CRES
HAWKSHEAD RD
HERBERT ST
ACTON RD
CHAPEL LA
NORCOTT DR
KILSHAW RD
WEBB DR
PERRINS RD
KNIGHT RD
GREEN JONES BROW
ALMOND DR
GLEAVE RD
SPURLING RD
EXMOUTH WAY
SHERBOURNE WAY
DORCHESTER WAY
CAMBOURNE RD
WEYMOUTH RD
SHAFTESBURY WAY
SUNNINGDALE CL
ALDRIDGE DR
MELROSE AVE
EASTWOOD
CHEDDAR GR
PINEWOOD
ARNCLIFFE DR
KAREN CL
COLNE RD
BROOKVALE CL
Rose Hill Farm
DOUGLAS AVE
ROSEHILL AVE
GORSEY LA
HALEY RD N
GRIFFIN CL
MITCHELL AVE
HALEY RD S
Burtonwood
Ashton's Farm
Northfield Riding Ctr
Moat House
Old Lodge Farm
Clay Lane Farm
CLAY LA
Abbotsfield Farm
Lodge Wood
Park Cottage
Maypole Farm
Moat House Farm
Nursery
Hollin Wood
Joy Lane Farm
Ivy Cottage
Highfield
BURTONWOOD RD
Finger Post
JOY LA
HALL LA
Home Farm
LIMEKILN LA
WRIGHT'S LA
Limekiln Farm
Dog Kennel Plantation
M62
Burtonwood Airfield (disused)
Booth's Wood
Old Hall Farm
Duck Wood
8
7
93
6
5
92
4
3
91
2
1
90
54
55
56

74
60

59
46

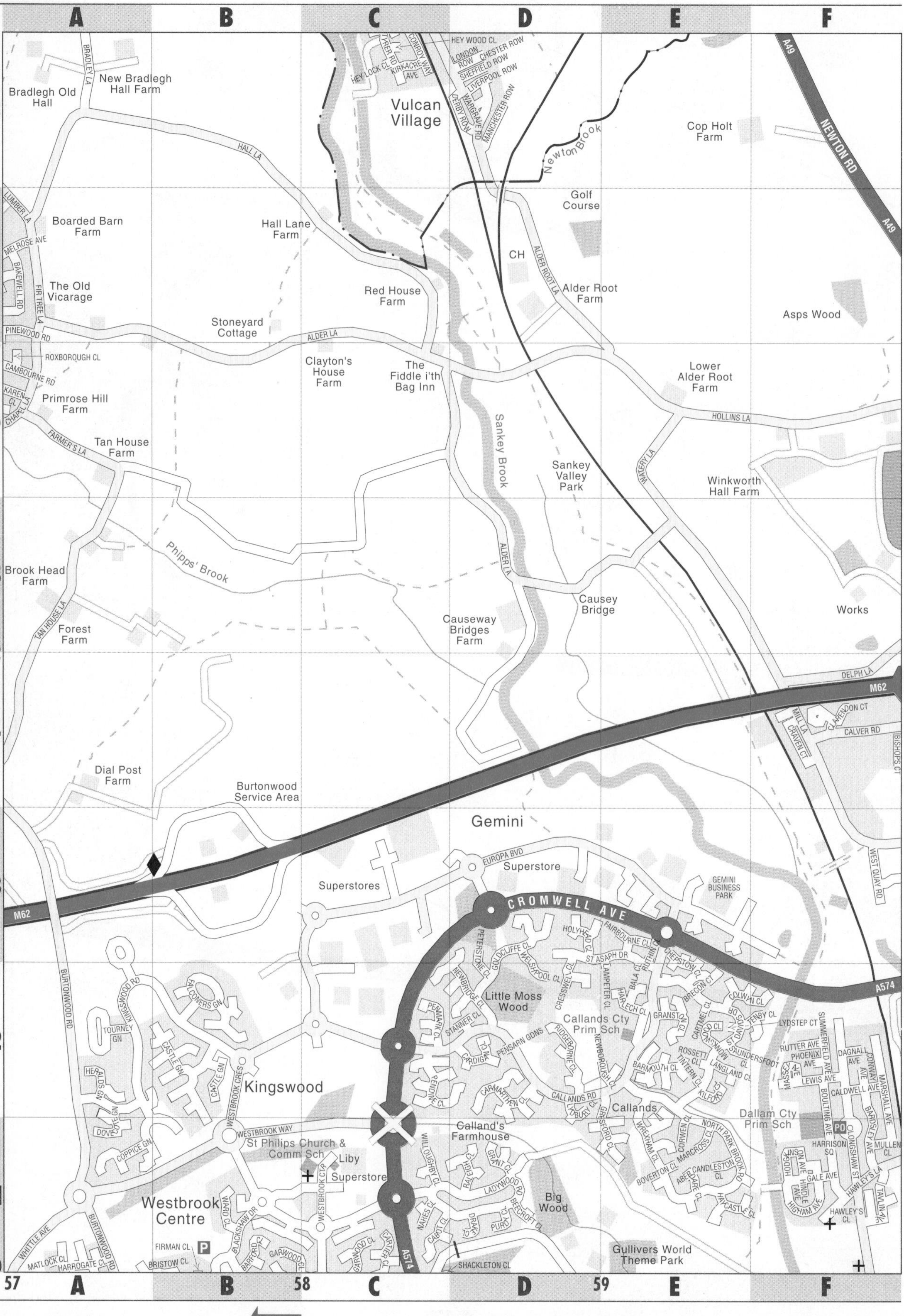
A
B
C
D
E
F
8
7
93
6
5
92
4
3
91
2
1
90
57
58
59
Bradlegh Old Hall
New Bradlegh Hall Farm
BRADLEY LA
HALL LA
Vulcan Village
HEY WOOD CL
LONDON ROW
CHESTER ROW
SHEFFIELD ROW
LIVERPOOL ROW
DERBY ROW
WARGRAVE RD
MANCHESTER ROW
CONROY WAY
KIRKACRE AVE
HEY LOCK CL
TYRER RD
Cop Holt Farm
NEWTON RD
A49
Newton Brook
LUMBER LA
Boarded Barn Farm
Hall Lane Farm
Golf Course
MELROSE AVE
BAKEWELL RD
FIR TREE LA
The Old Vicarage
CH
ALDER ROOT LA
Alder Root Farm
Red House Farm
Asps Wood
PINEWOOD RD
Stoneyard Cottage
ALDER LA
ROXBOROUGH CL
CAMBOURNE RD
Clayton's House Farm
The Fiddle i'th Bag Inn
Lower Alder Root Farm
KAREN CL
CHAPEL LA
Primrose Hill Farm
HOLLINS LA
FARMER'S LA
Tan House Farm
Sankey Brook
Sankey Valley Park
WATERY LA
Winkworth Hall Farm
Phipps' Brook
ALDER LA
Brook Head Farm
Causey Bridge
Works
TAN HOUSE LA
Forest Farm
Causeway Bridges Farm
DELPH LA
M62
MILL LA
CLARENDON CT
CRAVEN CT
CALVER RD
BISHOPS CT
Dial Post Farm
Burtonwood Service Area
Gemini
EUROPA BVD
Superstore
GEMINI BUSINESS PARK
WEST QUAY RD
Superstores
CROMWELL AVE
M62
HOLYHEAD CL
FAIRBOURNE CL
RUTHIN CL
CHEPSTOW CL
ST ASAPH DR
PETERSTONE CL
GOLDCLIFFE CL
WELSHPOOL CL
BURTONWOOD RD
NEWBRIDGE CL
Little Moss Wood
CRESSWELL CL
LAMPETER CL
BALA CL
HARLECH CL
BRECON CT
COLWYN CL
A574
KINGSWOOD RD
FALCONERS GN
PENMARK CL
STANNER CL
Callands Cty Prim Sch
GRANSTON CL
CARMEL CL
TENBY CL
LYDSTEP CT
SUMMERFIELD AVE
TOURNEY GN
CASTLE GN
PENSARN GDNS
RIDGEBORNE CL
NEWBOROUGH CL
ROSSETTI CL
SAUNDERSFOOT CL
RUTTER AVE
PHOENIX AVE
DAGNALL AVE
CONWAY AVE
MARSHALL AVE
CARDIGAN CL
TINTERN CL
LANGLAND CL
HERALDS GN
CAXTON GN
WESTBROOK CRES
Kingswood
PENDINE CL
CARMARTHEN CL
BARMOUTH CL
LEWIS AVE
CALDWELL AVE
DOVE CL
COPPICE GN
WESTBROOK WAY
CALLANDS RD
GRESFORD CL
Callands
WREXHAM CL
CORWEN CL
NORTH PARK BROOK RD
KILFORD CL
Dallam Cty Prim Sch
BOULTING AVE
BARDSLEY AVE
MULLEN CL
St Philips Church & Comm Sch
Liby
Calland's Farmhouse
WILLOUGHBY CL
MARCROSS CL
CANDLESTON CL
HARRISON SQ
LONGSHAW ST
PO
Superstore
GRANT CL
LADYWOOD RD
Big Wood
BOVERTON CL
ABERDARE CL
HAYCASTLE CL
HODGKINSON AVE
HINDLE AVE
GALE AVE
HIGHAM AVE
HAWLEY'S LA
TAYLOR ST
HAWLEY'S CL
WHITTLE AVE
Westbrook Centre
WARD CL
BLACKSHAW DR
WESTBROOK CTR
NAHES CL
CABOT CL
DRAKE CL
PURDY CL
BEECROFT CL
FIRMAN CL
P
GARWOOD CL
CARTER CL
MATLOCK CL
HARROGATE CL
BRISTOW CL
BARFORD CL
GARWOOD CL
SHACKLETON CL
Gullivers World Theme Park

59

47

A
B
C
D
E
F
8
7
93
6
5
92
4
3
91
2
1
90
60
61
62
HERMITAGE GREEN LA
The Hermit Inn (PH)
Hermitage Green
GEROSA AVE
A573
M6
WINWICK LA
A579
22
A49
Sand Pit
Island Plantation
Southworth Hall
Cockshot Farm
SMITHY BROW
Smithy Brow
Cockshot Brook
Cockshot Bridge
DAM LA
SOUTHWORTH LA
Highfields
HIGHFIELD LA
WATERWORKS LA
GOLBORNE RD
OLD SCHOOL HOUSE LA
GREEN LANE CL
GREEN LA
THE PRIORY
Mill House Brow
HORNBY LA
PILGRIM CL
ILEX AVE
ST OSWALDS CL
MYDDLETON LA
WINWICK LINK RD
Arbury
ARBURY LA
Winwick
HOLLINS LA
CHURCH WLK
PO
ASH RD
MAPLE RD
Winwick CE Prim Sch
Leisure Ctr
PH
HOLLINS DR
RECTORY LA
RECTORY CL
FARINGDON RD
FALCONDALE RD
LINKSIDE AVE
Delph Farm
DELPH LA
H
Winwick Psychiatric
Mainfield
Spa Well Farm
NEWTON RD
Delph Farm
DELPH LA
Midhops Farm
M62
10
9
Houghton Green
PH
MILL LA
Peel Hall
WOBURN RD
ELM RD
BIRCH AVE
BISHOPS CT
Radley Plantation
RADLEY LA
Recn Gd
P
BALLATER DR
WARRINGTON
NEWHAVEN RD
HASTINGS AVE
BEXHILL AVE
POPLARS AVE
COTSWOLD PL
COTSWOLD RD
ULVERSTON AVE
GRISEDALE AVE
ENNERDALE AVE
CAMERON CT
SEAFORD PL
CRAWLEY AVE
CHILTERN RD
KENTMERE PL
WANSFELL PL
CHEVIOT AVE
MILL LA
CALVER RD
TOLL BAR RD
OXENHAM RD
PENTLAND AVE
CLEVELAND RD
PETWORTH AVE
ESKDALE AVE 1
BUTTERMERE CRES 2
ESWATER CL
WINDERMERE AVE
THIRLMERE AVE
ULLSWATER AVE
BUTTERMERE AVE
HORSESHOE CRES
St Andrew's CE Prim Sch
Hulme
Winwick Quay
St Stephen's RC Prim Sch
CARTMEL AVE
SCAFELL AVE
BENTHAM AVE
ST STEPHEN'S AVE
HUNTER AVE
SANDY LA W
CANBERRA AVE
QUAIL CL
MALLARD CL
LINNET CL
OSPREY CL
GRASMERE AVE
DUNNOCK CL
FOXFIELD CL
P
MORVEN CL
St Bridget's RC Prim Sch
Cinnamon Brow
CINNAMON LA N
GABLES CL
PERTH CL
P
BRIERS CL
Sch
WASLEY CL
ENFIELD PARK RD
ACKERLEY CL
Blackbrook
CROMWELL AVE
A574
Leisure Ctr
AJAX AVE
CROWE AVE
ACHILLES AVE
POOLE AVE
POOLE CRES
COOPER AVE
LOCKER AVE
MARRON AVE
DEAN CRES
ARMOUR AVE
DENSHAM AVE
CURRANS RD
PO
PATTERDALE AVE
KESWICK AVE
KIRKSTONE AVE
BOWNESS AVE
STATHAM AVE
SANDY LA
THE COPPINS
BYRON CT
SMALL CRES
SMALL AVE
HUGHES PL
HUGHES AVE
FESTIVAL AVE
FESTIVAL CRES
POPLARS PL
Liby
PO
CAPESTHORNE RD
Orford
NORTHWAY
CLOUGH AVE
FISHER AVE
SHAKESPEARE GR
KEATS GR
BURNS GR
TENNYSON DR
DRYDEN PL
RUSKIN AVE
Sch
KIPLING AVE
CLIVE AVE
MILVAIN DR
BEATTY AVE
MARINA DR
FIELDVIEW DR
SCHOOL RD
POVEY RD
PRIMROSE CL
CALDBECK AVE
NEVILLE AVE
Dallam Brook
ANTRIM RD
ALBAN RET PK
HAWLEY'S LA
Long Lane Cty Prim Sch
Longford
A50
LONG LA
Warrington Collegiate Inst
WINSTANLEY IND EST
LONGFIELD RD
William Beamont Cty High Sch
WARRINGTON BSNS PK
ST MARGARET'S AVE 1
VALE OWEN RD 2
PO
ORFORD GN
HALLOWS AVE
WARREN RD
BURTON RD
PARK RD
BIRTLES RD
BRUCE AVE
OSBORNE AVE
MARTIN AVE
BOYLE AVE
DEREK AVE
DARWEN GDNS
Brook Acre Cty Prim Sch
HARDING AVE
SEALAND CL
WOODVALE CL
MALCOLM AVE
FERGUSON DR
HILDEN PL
ATHLONE RD
WINWICK RD
A49
ANDOVER CL
BAWTRY CT
DUXFORD CT
CATFOSS CL
BIGGIN CT
HILDEN RD
FINNINGLEY CT
RUDLOE CT
VALLEY CT
RUISLIP CT
WADDINGTON CL
ST MAWGAN CT
ANSON CL
BLENHEIM CL
BLACKBROOK AVE
VALIANT CL
INSALL RD
Liby
FEARNHEAD CROSS
Padgate Cty High Sch
A574
BIRCHWOOD WAY
1 POCKLINGTON CT
2 UNSWORTH CT
Padgate
Recn Gd
WEST VIEW
P
WAYWELL CL
SOLWAY CL
KINROSS CL
DUNDEE CL
SHETLAND CL
GAIRLOCH CL
KILSYTH CL
MONTROSE CL
LOCKERBIE CL
COLDSTREAM CL
MILL FARM CL
TEAL CL
MEDWAY CL
SEVERN CL
THAMES CL
GREENWOOD CRES
HALIFAX CL
METEOR CRES
BITTERN CL
AVOCET CL
CANBERRA SQ
WHITTAKER AVE
FAIRBROTHER CRES
TRUMPER AVE
NUMBER RD
TYNE CL
TROSSACH CL
LANGDALE CL
REDESDALE CL
MERRICK CL
GRANTHAM CT
ORANGE GR
AVERY CL
LYNDALE AVE
APPLETREE GR
GAYHURST AVE
PARKFIELDS LA
VULCAN CL
BROMLEY CL
BICKLEY CL
CINNAMON LA
NEWTON GR
DELAFIELD CL
WELBY CL
ST BRIDGETS CL
CROPPERS RD
SHERWOOD CL

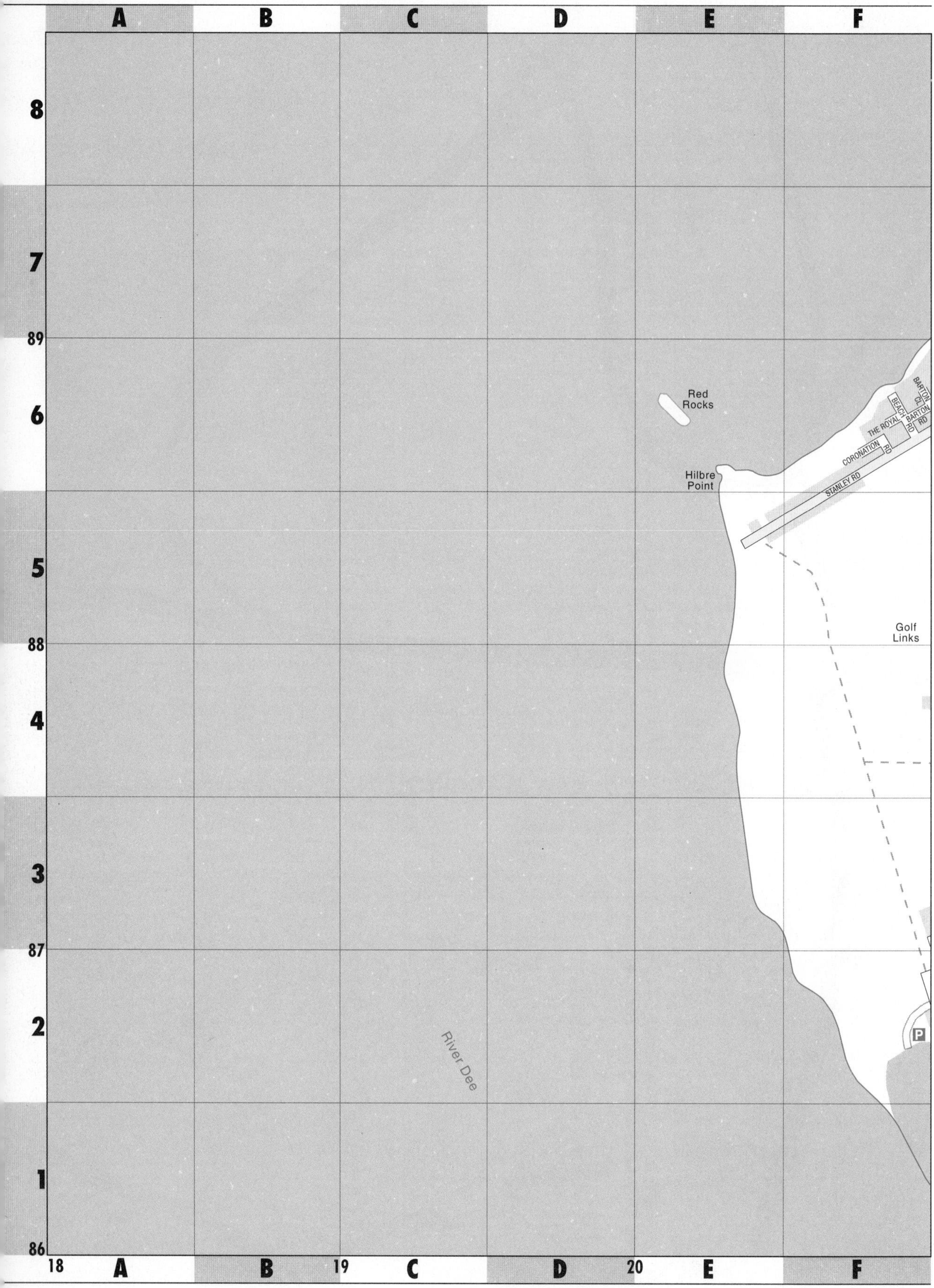
A
B
C
D
E
F
8
7
89
6
5
88
4
3
87
2
1
86
18
19
20
Red Rocks
Hilbre Point
BARTON CL
BEACH RD
BARTON RD
THE ROYAL
CORONATION RD
STANLEY RD
Golf Links
P
River Dee

48
64

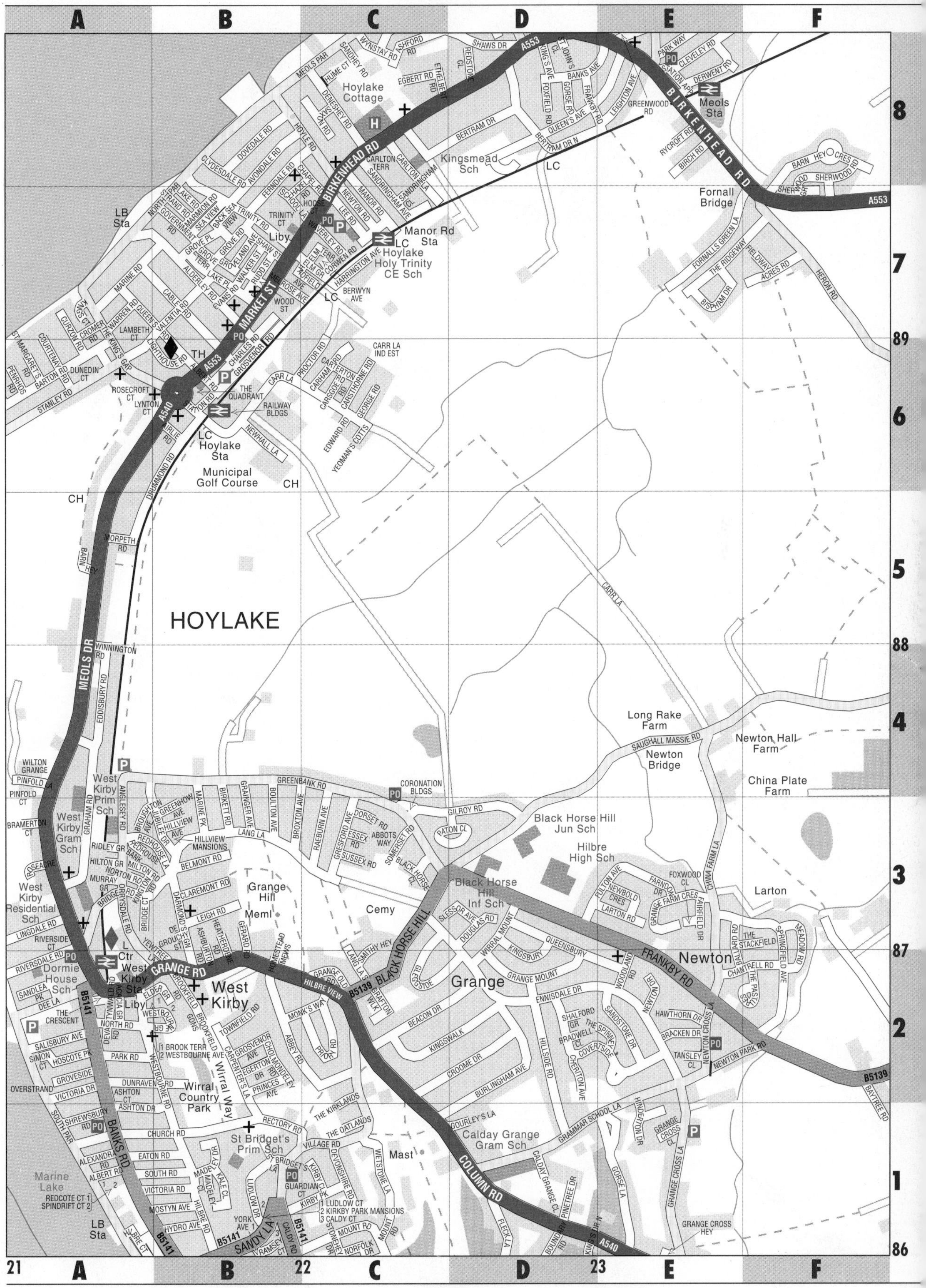
A
B
C
D
E
F
8
7
89
6
5
88
4
3
87
2
1
86
21
22
23
HOYLAKE
Hoylake Cottage
Kingsmead Sch
Meols Sta
Fornall Bridge
LB Sta
Manor Rd Sta
Hoylake Holy Trinity CE Sch
Liby
TH
Hoylake Sta
Municipal Golf Course
CH
LC
CARR LA IND EST
THE QUADRANT
RAILWAY BLDGS
Long Rake Farm
Newton Bridge
Newton Hall Farm
China Plate Farm
CORONATION BLDGS
Black Horse Hill Jun Sch
Hilbre High Sch
Black Horse Hill Inf Sch
Larton
Newton
Grange
Grange Hill Meml
Cemy
West Kirby Prim Sch
West Kirby Gram Sch
West Kirby Residential Sch
Dormie House Sch
L Ctr
West Kirby Sta
West Kirby
Wirral Country Park
Wirral Way
St Bridget's Prim Sch
Calday Grange Gram Sch
Mast
Marine Lake
A553
A540
A553
B5139
B5141
BIRKENHEAD RD
MARKET ST
MEOLS DR
GRANGE RD
HILBRE VIEW
BLACK HORSE HILL
FRANKBY RD
COLUMN RD
BANKS RD
SANDY LA
CARR LA
SAUGHALL MASSIE RD
1 BROOK TERR
2 WESTBOURNE AVE
1 LUDLOW CT
2 KIRKBY PARK MANSIONS
3 CALDY CT
REDCOTE CT 1
SPINDRIFT CT 2

75
64

63
49

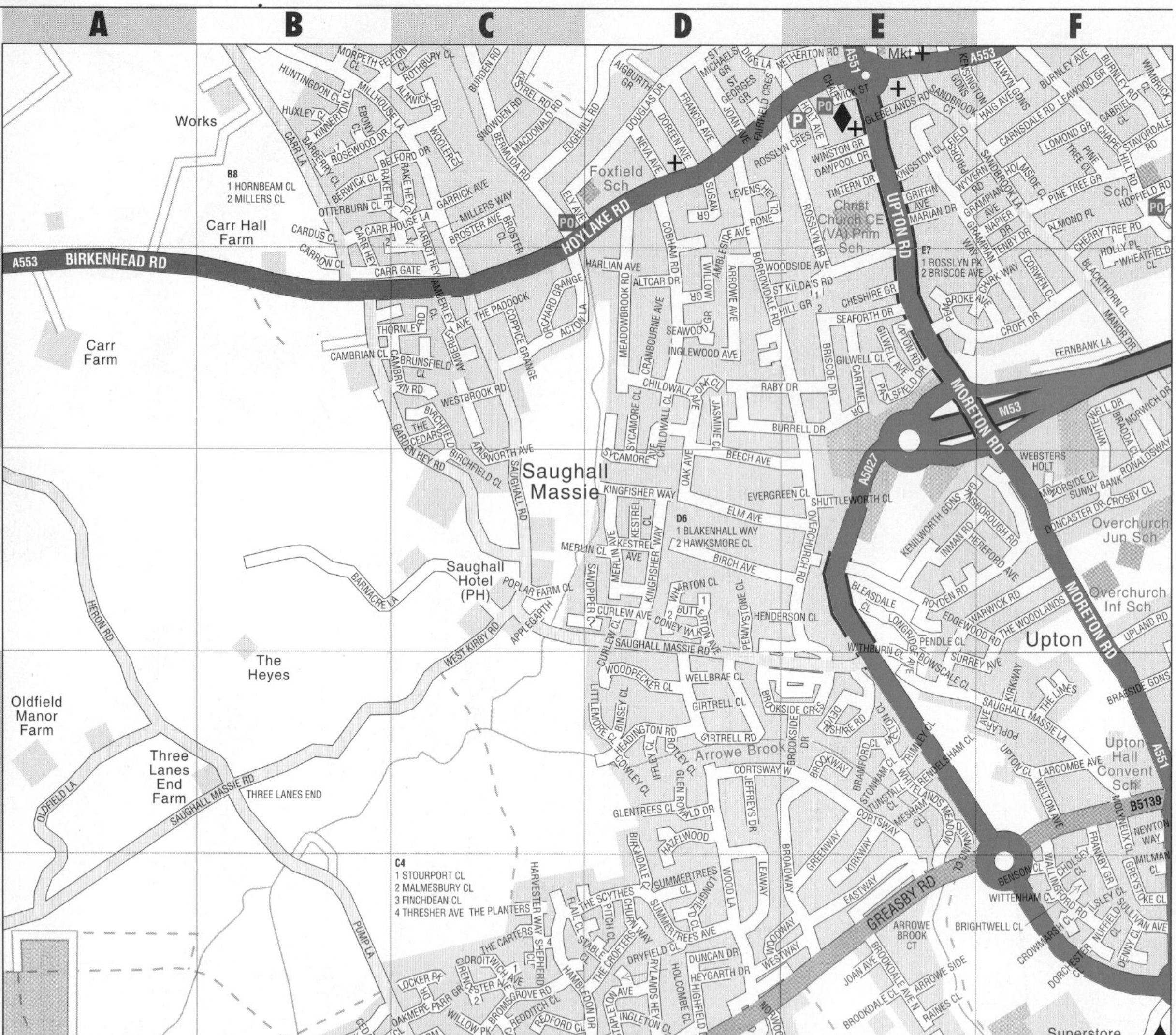
A B C D E F
8 7 89 6 5 88 4 3 87 2 1 86
24 25 26
A553 BIRKENHEAD RD
HOYLAKE RD
UPTON RD
MORETON RD
M53
A5027
A551
B5139
B5140
GREASBY RD
FRANKBY RD
SAUGHALL MASSIE RD
HILLBARK RD
MONTGOMERY HILL
ARROWE BROOK LA
ARROWE BROOK RD
ARROWE PARK RD
Works
Carr Hall Farm
Carr Farm
B8
1 HORNBEAM CL
2 MILLERS CL
Foxfield Sch
Christ Church CE (VA) Prim Sch
E7
1 ROSSLYN PK
2 BRISCOE AVE
Mkt
Sch
Saughall Massie
D6
1 BLAKENHALL WAY
2 HAWKSMORE CL
Saughall Hotel (PH)
The Heyes
Oldfield Manor Farm
Three Lanes End Farm
THREE LANES END
Arrowe Brook
WEBSTERS HOLT
Overchurch Jun Sch
Overchurch Inf Sch
Upton
Upton Hall Convent Sch
C4
1 STOURPORT CL
2 MALMESBURY CL
3 FINCHDEAN CL
4 THRESHER AVE THE PLANTERS
C3
1 DAYS MEADOW
2 REDCROFT
Greasby Brook
Brookdale Prim Sch
Superstore
Liby
THE WIRRAL BSNS PK
Factory
Manor House Farm
Royden Hall
Frankby
Greasby
Arrowe Brook Farm
Arrowe Bridge
Playing Fields
Gorse Covert
Greasby Inf Sch
Greasby Copse
Our Lady of Pity RC Prim Sch
Greasby Jun Sch
Cemy
The Farmers Arms (PH)
Arrowebrook Farm
FB
Nicholson's Plantation

F8
1 BERTHA GDNS
2 MIRIAM PL
3 VULCAN ST
4 GILLBROOK SQ
5 LANSDOWNE PL
6 LANSDOWNE CT
7 GOSCHEN ST

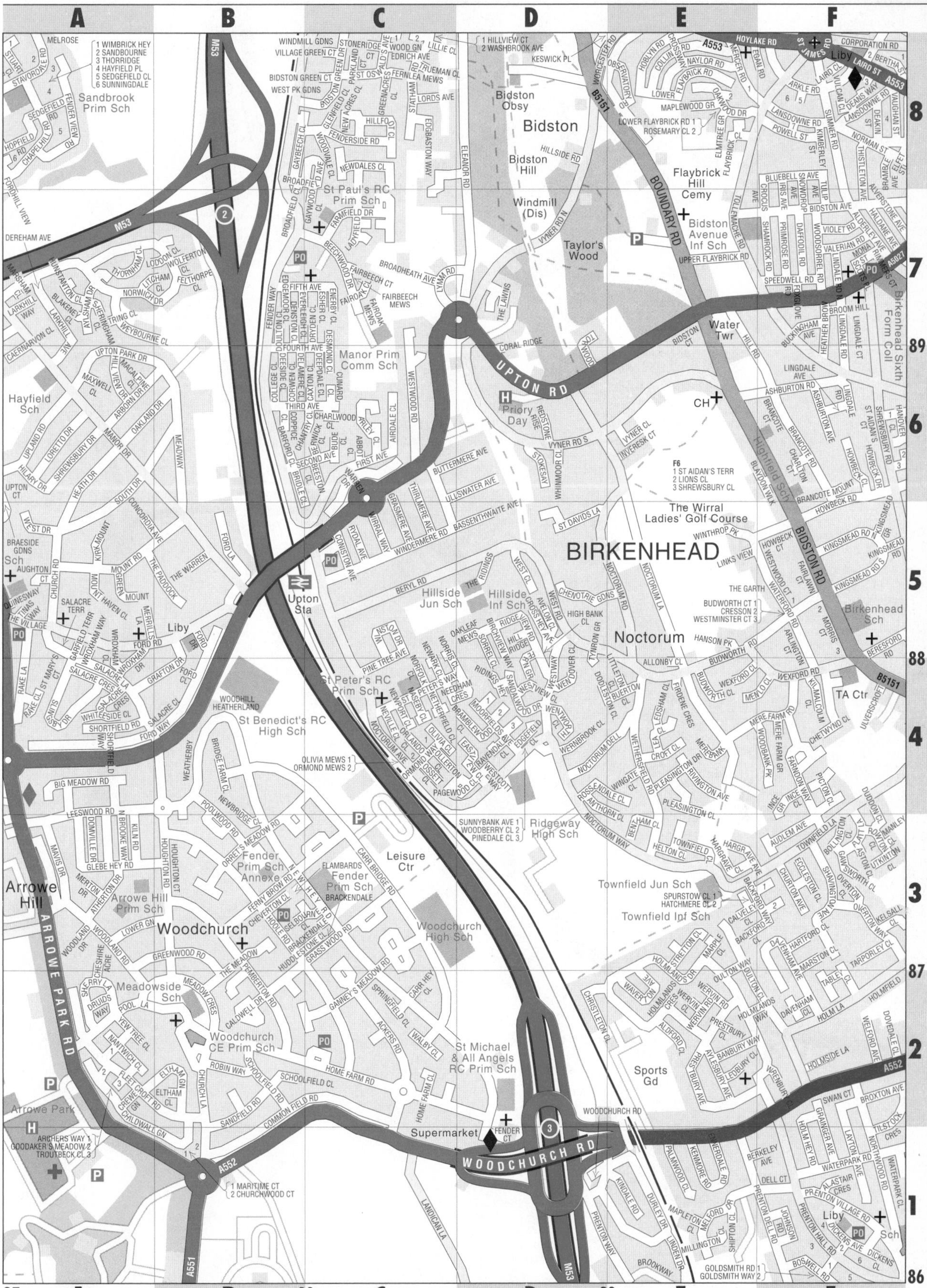

C5
1 RAVENSCROFT RD
2 BARTON ST
3 CLAYTON PL
4 MARITIME PK
5 QUARRYBANK ST
6 WILKINSON ST
7 MIDLAND ST
8 CARLISLE MEWS
9 CARLISLE CL
10 CLARENDON WLK
11 BELMONT GR
12 CARNFORTH CL
13 TURNER ST

65

C5
14 MOUNT GROVE PL
15 BRIMSTAGE ST
D5
1 THE WOODLANDS
2 WHALLEY RD
3 RAWCLIFFE RD

51

D6
1 CONWAY CT
2 BENTINCK CT
3 EXMOUTH GDNS
4 VINCENT ST
5 HORATIO ST
6 ST JOHN'S PAVEMENT
7 MILTON PAVEMENT
8 COVENTRY ST
9 CONWAY PL
E6
1 CAMDEN PL
2 CLWYD ST
3 BURLINGTON ST
4 BANK ST
5 ALMA ST
6 HINSON ST
7 THOMAS ST
8 GRANGE RD E
9 BACK OLIVER ST
10 BOROUGH PL
11 CLIFTON CRES
12 GRANGE RD
13 ST WERBURGH'S SQ
14 PRINCESS PAVEMENT
15 KENDAL ST
16 WALTON ST

1 LAURENCE DEACON CT
2 CHARLES ST
3 BROOKLANDS
4 ROBERT ST
5 ST ANNE ST
6 ST ANNE'S CL
7 KEIGHTLEY ST

1 LINCOLN GDNS
2 CONNAUGHT CL
3 DUNDONALD ST
4 METHUEN ST
5 COLWYN ST
6 FALKLAND ST
7 NORMAN ST

1 GERTRUDE ST
2 CAMPERDOWN ST
3 CROSS ST
4 MONK ST
5 MARKET PL

1 BLACKPOOL ST
2 THOMAS ST
3 VINCENT NAUGHTON CT
4 VENTURE CT
5 HELENA ST

1 REDMOND ST
2 WESTBURY ST
3 KINGSDOWN ST
4 RIPON ST
5 SEYMOUR CT
6 HILLSIDE CT
7 SIDNEY GDNS
8 NORBURY GDNS

1 BEACONSFIELD CL
2 COBDEN AVE
3 COBDEN PL
4 GRENVILLE RD
5 GLADSTONE RD
6 LIVINGSTONE RD
7 LYDBROOK CL

65

78

F1
1 WORDSWORTH AVE
2 KIPLING AVE
3 TENNYSON AVE
4 THE BEECHES

E8
1 ROSCOE PL
2 OLDHAM ST
3 BACK RENSHAW ST
4 LEECE ST
5 BALTIMORE ST
6 GRIFFITHS ST
7 LITTLE HARDMAN ST
8 ST LUKE'S PL

52

F8
1 SOUTH HUNTER ST
2 BACK BEDFORD ST
3 SUGNALL ST
4 UPPER HOPE PL
5 PHILHARMONIC CT
6 BEDFORD CL
7 BEDFORD WLK
8 HOPE WAY
9 BACK CATHARINE ST
10 ST BRIDE ST
11 BACK ST BRIDE ST
12 LITTLE ST BRIDE ST
13 SIR HOWARD ST
14 SIR HOWARD WAY
15 SANDON ST

68

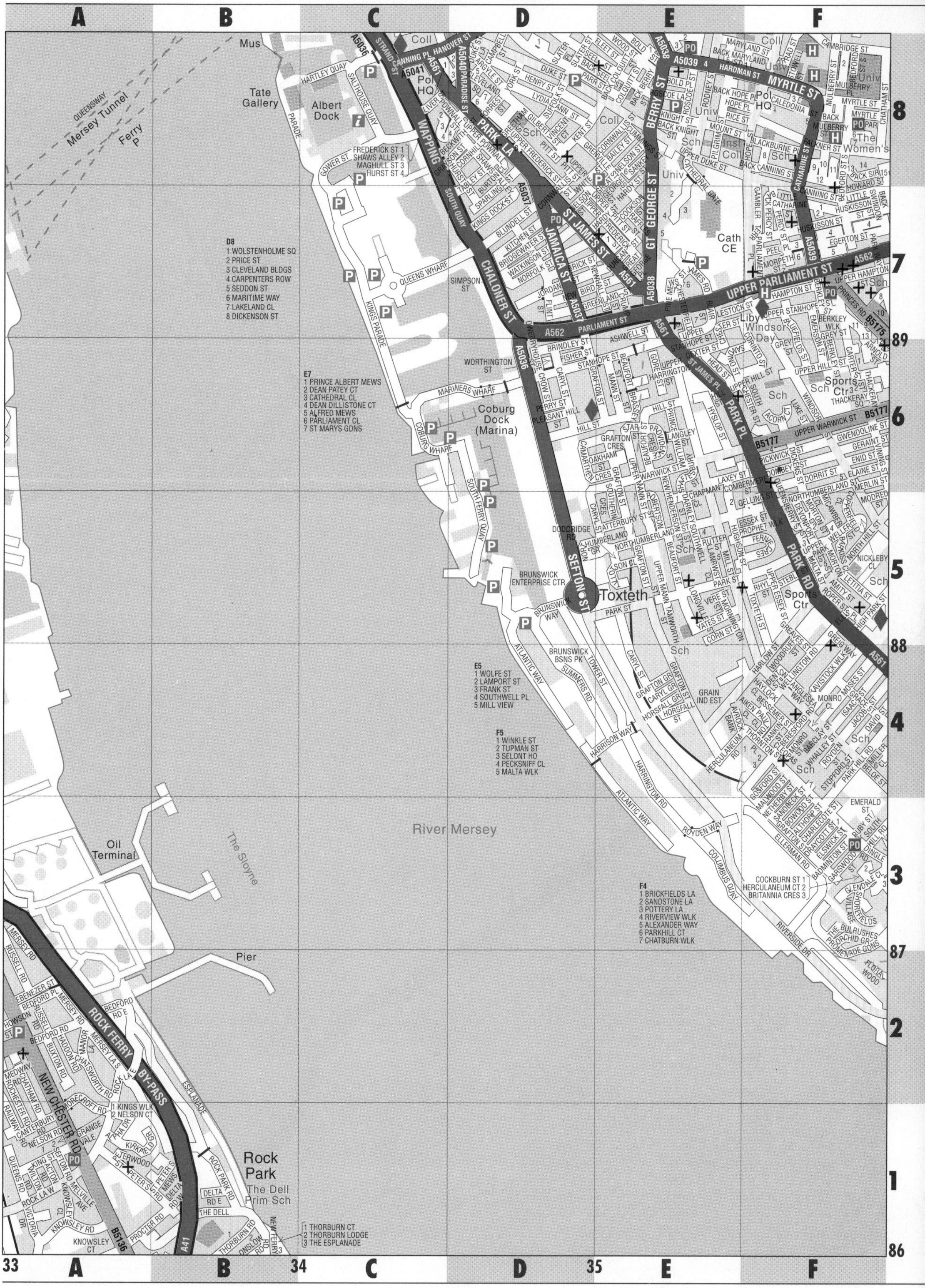

79

68

F6
1 TENNYSON WLK
2 THACKERAY PL
3 MAKEPEACE WLK
4 RADLEY'S CT
5 WINDSOR CT

F7
1 LITTLE CANNING ST
2 BACK LITTLE CANNING ST
3 BACK HUSKISSON ST
4 BACK EGERTON ST N
5 BACK EGERTON ST S
6 BIRLEY CT
7 MAHAN CT
8 SELBORNE ST
9 ALEXANDRA TERR
10 PRINCES AVE
11 BACK GIBSON ST
12 UPPER HILL ST
13 GIBSON ST

A6
1 ARNOLD CL
2 CELTIC ST
A7
1 SELBORNE CL
2 ADELE THOMPSON DR
3 HATHERLEY CL

B6
1 PRINCES GATE E
2 PRINCES GATE W
B7
1 BUTTERMERE ST
2 STEVE BIKO CL
3 RIVER AVON ST

67

4 MAITLAND ST
5 BACK WINDSOR VIEW
C7
1 RIVER AVON ST
C8
1 HEATHCOTE CL
2 WAINWRIGHT CL

53

C8
3 LIGHTWOOD DR
4 WILFER CL
5 LIGHTWOOD ST
6 LINDLEY CL
7 BARNET CL
8 CLAYPOLE CL
9 HAWDON CT

F5
1 BLENHEIM RD
2 DOVEDALE RD
3 INGLETON RD
4 BELHAVEN RD
5 ZETLAND RD
6 STANTON RD

7 BECKENHAM AVE
8 NORBURY AVE
9 NEWBOROUGH AVE
10 ARLINGTON AVE
F8
1 MAFEKING CL
2 BACK SANDOWN LA
3 VICTORIA AVE

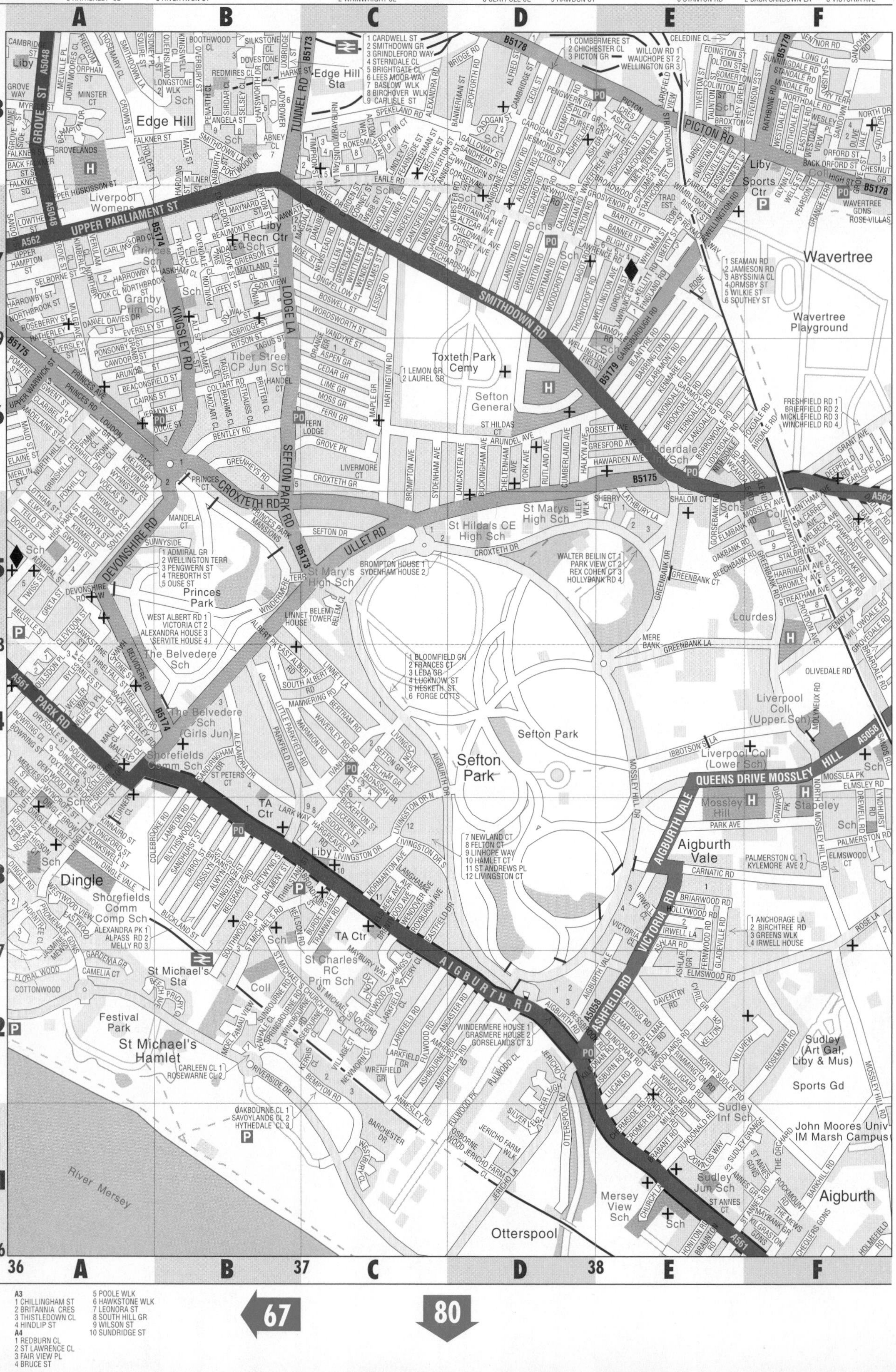

A3
1 CHILLINGHAM ST
2 BRITANNIA CRES
3 THISTLEDOWN CL
4 HINDLIP ST
A4
1 REDBURN CL
2 ST LAWRENCE CL
3 FAIR VIEW PL
4 BRUCE ST

5 POOLE WLK
6 HAWKSTONE WLK
7 LEONORA ST
8 SOUTH HILL GR
9 WILSON ST
10 SUNDRIDGE ST

67

80

A5
1 CRAMOND AVE
2 DUDDINGSTON AVE
3 WESTGATE RD
4 CRONTON RD
5 SMITHDOWN PL
6 SUNSDALE RD

54
70

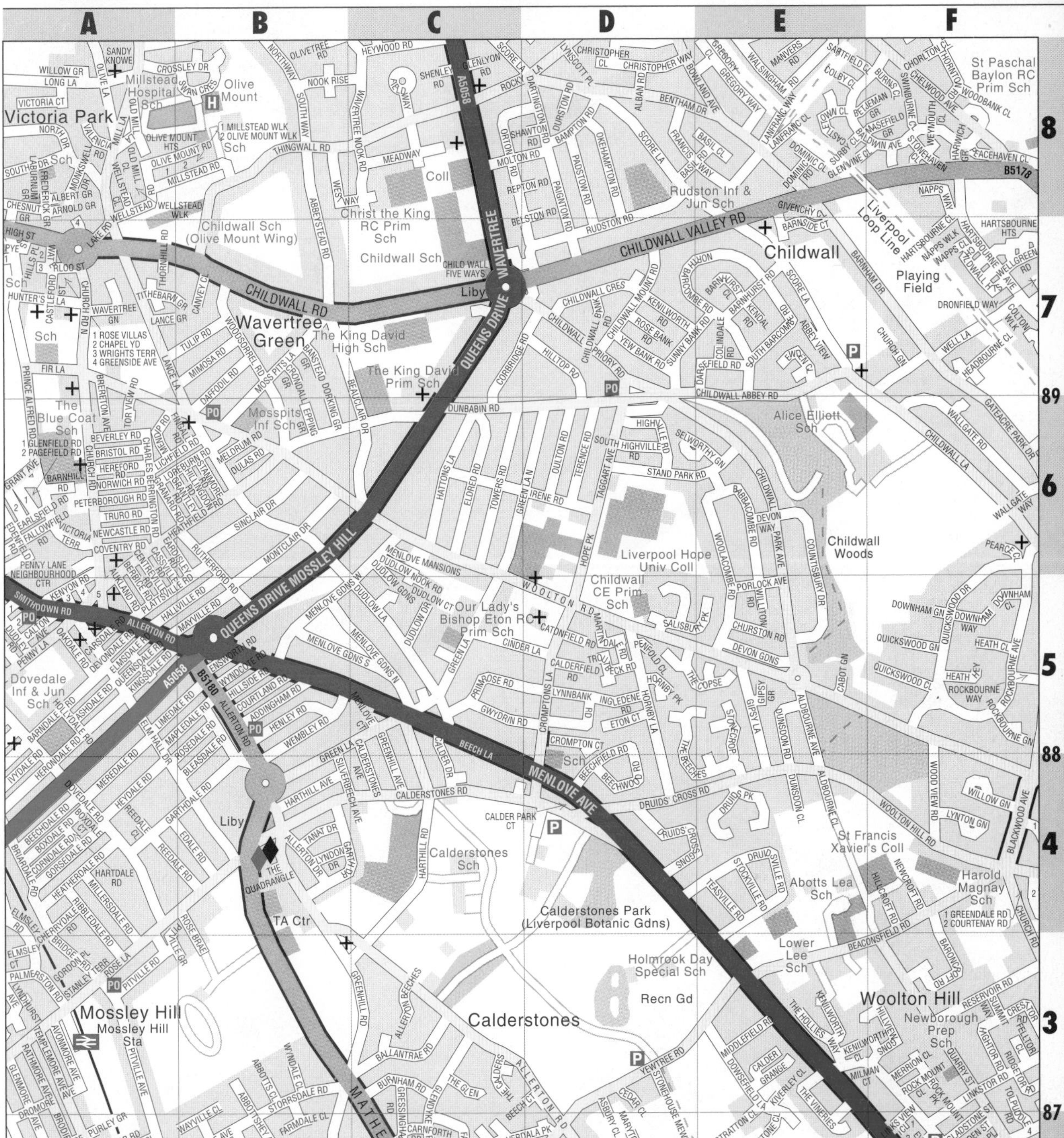

81
70

69
55

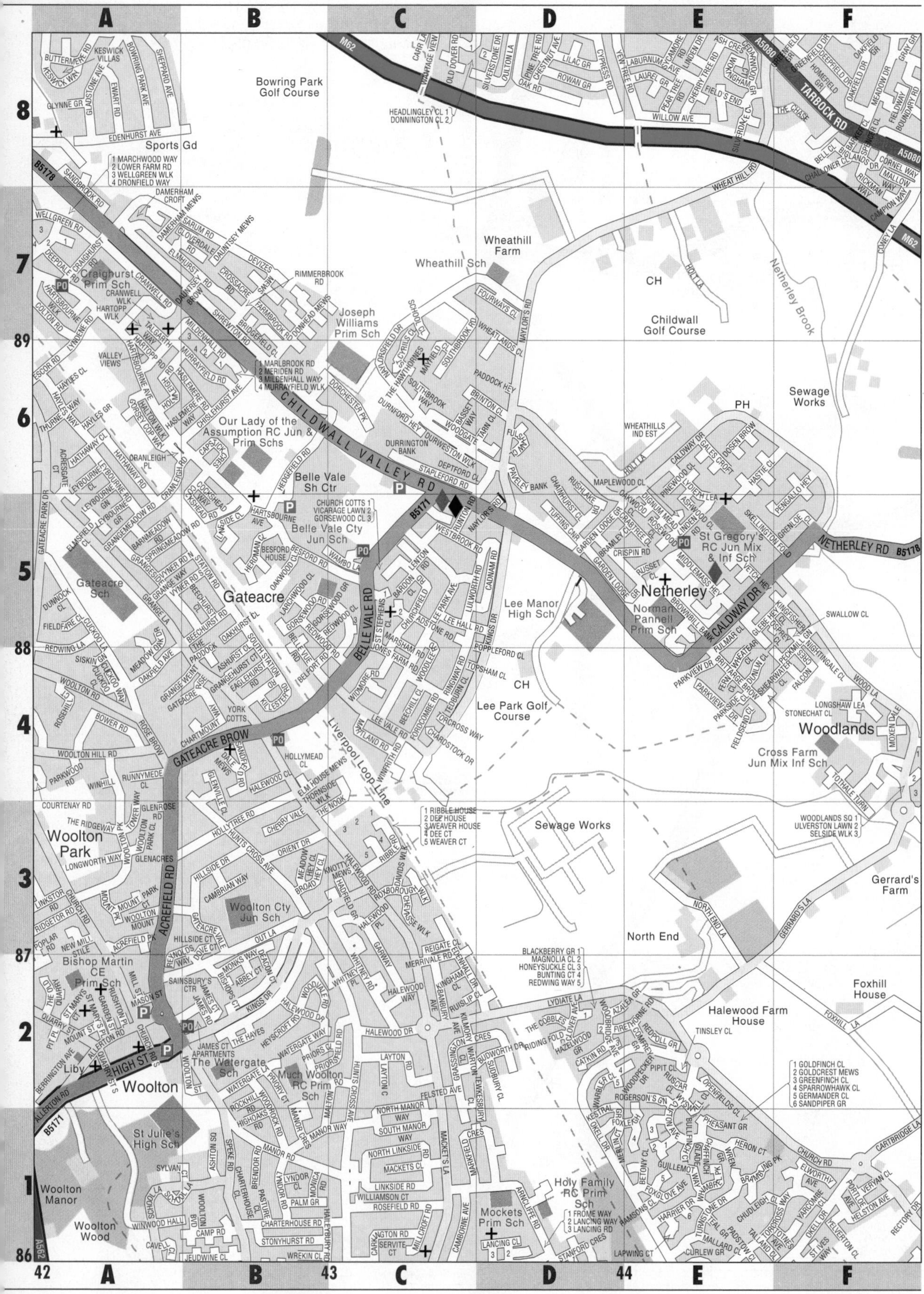
A
B
C
D
E
F
8
7
89
6
5
88
4
3
87
2
1
86
42
43
44
Bowring Park Golf Course
Sports Gd
M62
A5080
TARBOCK RD
B5178
CHILDWALL VALLEY RD
Wheathill Farm
Wheathill Sch
CH
Childwall Golf Course
Netherley Brook
Sewage Works
PH
Joseph Williams Prim Sch
Craighurst Prim Sch
Our Lady of the Assumption RC Jun & Prim Schs
Belle Vale Sh Ctr
Belle Vale Cty Jun Sch
B5171
BELLE VALE RD
Gateacre
Gateacre Sch
WHEATHILLS IND EST
St Gregory's RC Jun Mix & Inf Sch
Netherley
Norman Pannell Prim Sch
NETHERLEY RD
CALDWAY DR
Lee Manor High Sch
Lee Park Golf Course
Woodlands
Cross Farm Jun Mix Inf Sch
GATEACRE BROW
Liverpool Loop Line
Sewage Works
Woolton Park
Gerrard's Farm
ACREFIELD RD
Woolton Cty Jun Sch
North End
Bishop Martin CE Prim Sch
Foxhill House
Halewood Farm House
HIGH ST
Woolton
The Watergate Sch
Much Woolton RC Prim Sch
St Julie's High Sch
Woolton Manor
Woolton Wood
Mockets Prim Sch
Holy Family RC Prim Sch
Liby
1 MARCHWOOD WAY
2 LOWER FARM RD
3 WELLGREEN WLK
4 DRONFIELD WAY
1 MARLBROOK RD
2 MERIDEN RD
3 MILDENHALL WAY
4 MURRAYFIELD WLK
HEADLINGLEY CL 1
DONNINGTON CL 2
CHURCH COTTS 1
VICARAGE LAWN 2
GORSEWOOD CL 3
1 RIBBLE HOUSE
2 DEE HOUSE
3 WEAVER HOUSE
4 DEE CT
5 WEAVER CT
WOODLANDS SQ 1
ULVERSTON LAWN 2
SELSIDE WLK 3
BLACKBERRY GR 1
MAGNOLIA CL 2
HONEYSUCKLE CL 3
BUNTING CT 4
REDWING WAY 5
1 GOLDFINCH CL
2 GOLDCREST MEWS
3 GREENFINCH CL
4 SPARROWHAWK CL
5 GERMANDER CL
6 SANDPIPER GR
1 FROME WAY
2 LANCING WAY
3 LANCING RD

69
82

56
72

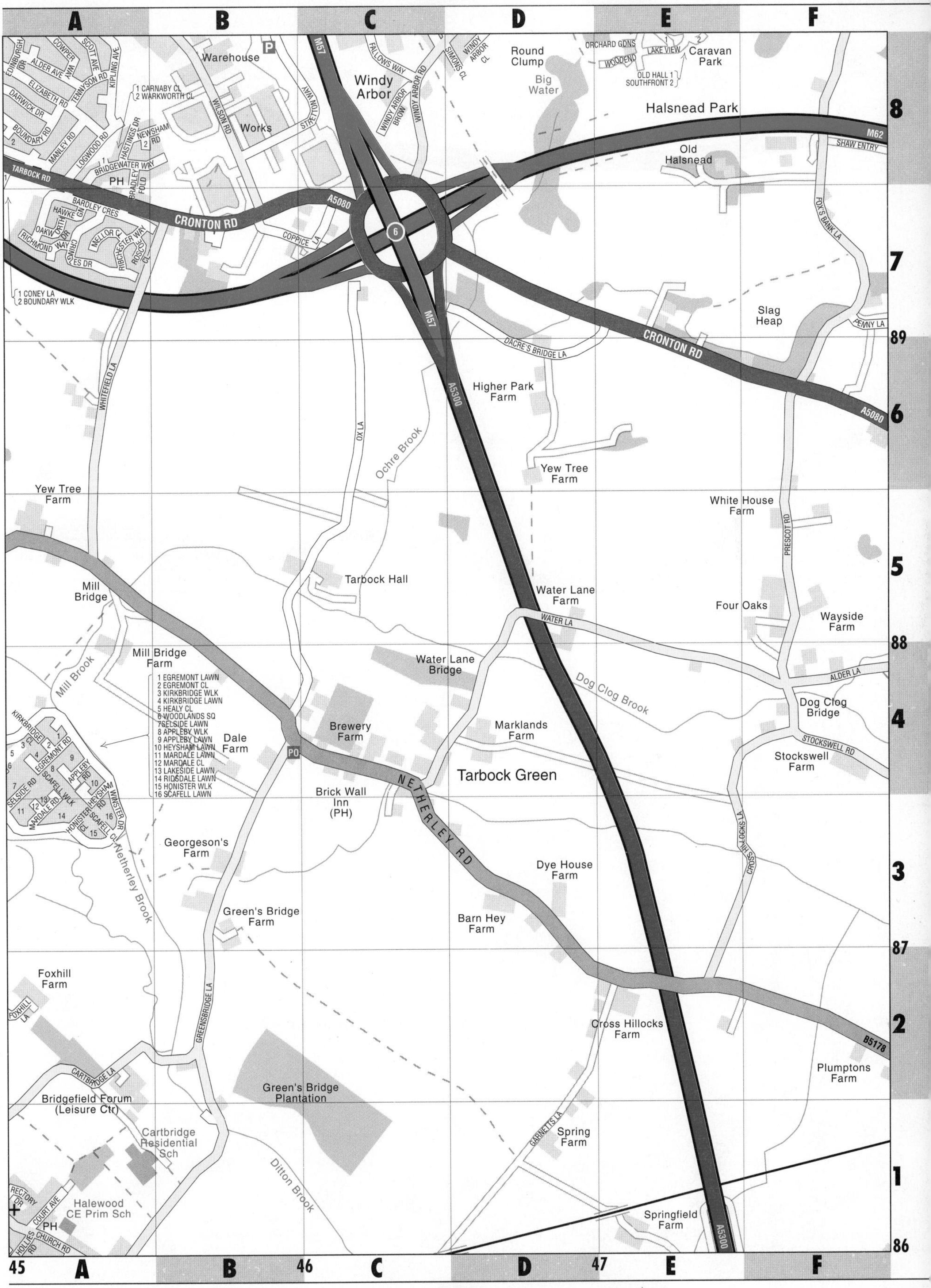
A
B
C
D
E
F
Warehouse
Works
Windy Arbor
Round Clump
Big Water
Caravan Park
Halsnead Park
Old Halsnead
ORCHARD GDNS
WOODEND
LAKE VIEW
OLD HALL 1
SOUTHFRONT 2
M62
SHAW ENTRY
M57
A5080
CRONTON RD
TARBOCK RD
1 CARNABY CL
2 WARKWORTH CL
NEWSHAM RD
HASTINGS DR
BRIDGEWATER WAY
BRADLEY FOLD
BARDLEY CRES
WILSON RD
STRETTON WAY
FALLOWS WAY
WINDY ARBOR RD
WINDY ARBOR BROW
SIMONS CL
WINDY ARBOR CL
COPPICE LA
EDINBURGH DR
ALDER AVE
COWPER AVE
SCOTT AVE
KIPLING AVE
TENNYSON RD
ELIZABETH RD
DARWICK DR
BOUNDARY RD
MANLEY RD
LOGWOOD RD
HAWKE GN
OAKWORTH DR
RICHMOND WAY
MELLOR CL
RIBCHESTER WAY
ROSCOE CL
1 CONEY LA
2 BOUNDARY WLK
PH
FOX'S BANK LA
Slag Heap
PENNY LA
DACRE'S BRIDGE LA
Higher Park Farm
A5300
A5080
OX LA
Ochre Brook
Yew Tree Farm
WHITEFIELD LA
Yew Tree Farm
White House Farm
PRESCOT RD
Tarbock Hall
Mill Bridge
Water Lane Farm
WATER LA
Four Oaks
Wayside Farm
Mill Bridge Farm
Mill Brook
Water Lane Bridge
Dog Clog Brook
ALDER LA
Dog Clog Bridge
1 EGREMONT LAWN
2 EGREMONT CL
3 KIRKBRIDGE WLK
4 KIRKBRIDGE LAWN
5 HEALY CL
6 WOODLANDS SQ
7 SELSIDE LAWN
8 APPLEBY WLK
9 APPLEBY LAWN
10 HEYSHAM LAWN
11 MARDALE LAWN
12 MARDALE CL
13 LAKESIDE LAWN
14 RIDSDALE LAWN
15 HONISTER WLK
16 SCAFELL LAWN
Brewery Farm
Marklands Farm
STOCKSWELL RD
Stockswell Farm
Dale Farm
PO
Tarbock Green
KIRKBRIDGE CL
EGREMONT RD
SELSIDE RD
SCAFELL WLK
APPLEBY RD
HEYSHAM RD
MARDALE RD
HONISTER CL
SCAFELL CL
WINSTER DR
Brick Wall Inn (PH)
NETHERLEY RD
Georgeson's Farm
Netherley Brook
CROSS HILLOCKS LA
Dye House Farm
Green's Bridge Farm
Barn Hey Farm
Foxhill Farm
FOXHILL LA
GREENSBRIDGE LA
Cross Hillocks Farm
B5178
Plumptons Farm
CARTBRIDGE LA
Bridgefield Forum (Leisure Ctr)
Green's Bridge Plantation
Cartbridge Residential Sch
GARNETTS LA
Spring Farm
Ditton Brook
RECTORY DR
COURT AVE
Halewood CE Prim Sch
PH
HOLLIES RD
CHURCH RD
Springfield Farm
8
89
7
6
88
5
4
3
87
2
1
86
45
46
47

83
72

71 57

A B C D E F
8 7 6 5 4 3 2 1
89 88 87 86
48 49 50
Mill Wood
M62
WARRINGTON RD
A57
7
WARRINGTON RD A57
Sandhill Farm
WATKINSON WAY A557
NORLAND'S LA
A569
CRONTON LA
HALL LA
Higher Shaw Farm
SHAW ENTRY
Rough Head
Fox's Bank Brook
Cronton Wood
PENNY LA
Penny Lane Farm
Town End
Picnic Area
Pex Hill
Norland's House
A5080
TUE LA
Nursery
Cronton Farm
Smaller Gorse Farm
Cronton C of E Prim Sch
Holy Family RC Prim Sch
Hotel
CRONTON LA A5080
CRONTON RD
Caxton Lodge
Cronton
Widnes Coll
Black Horse Hotel
ALDER LA
SANDY LA
CHAPEL LA
LODGE LA
Rose Farm
Holly Farm
Upton
Ppg Sta
Stock's Well House
STOCKSWELL RD
OLD UPTON LA
ROCK LA
Linacre House
Upton Cty Inf Sch
All Saints CE Jun Sch
HOUGH GREEN RD
The Four Topped Oak (PH)
QUEENSBURY WAY
St Basil RC Prim Sch
PRESCOT RD
Rugby Football Ground
WIDNES
Ball o' Ditton
Hough Green
Hough Green Sta
Our Lady of Perpetual Succour RC Inf Sch
Saints Peter & Paul RC High Sch
B5178 NETHERLEY RD
The Bankfield Sch
Golf Course
Ditton C of E Prim Sch
LIVERPOOL RD
B5178
LEIGH AVE
CH
Our Lady of Perpetual Succour Inf Sch
Ditton Cty Prim Sch
Ashley Sch
Chestnut Lodge Sch
ROYAL AVE

58
74

A1
1 CLAYTON CRES
2 HENDERSON RD
3 SQUIRES AVE
4 BRUNNER RD
5 MOND RD

C1
1 PARR ST
2 RUNNYMEDE CT
3 CLIFFE ST
4 HENRY ST
5 RUNNYMEDE GDNS

74

73
59

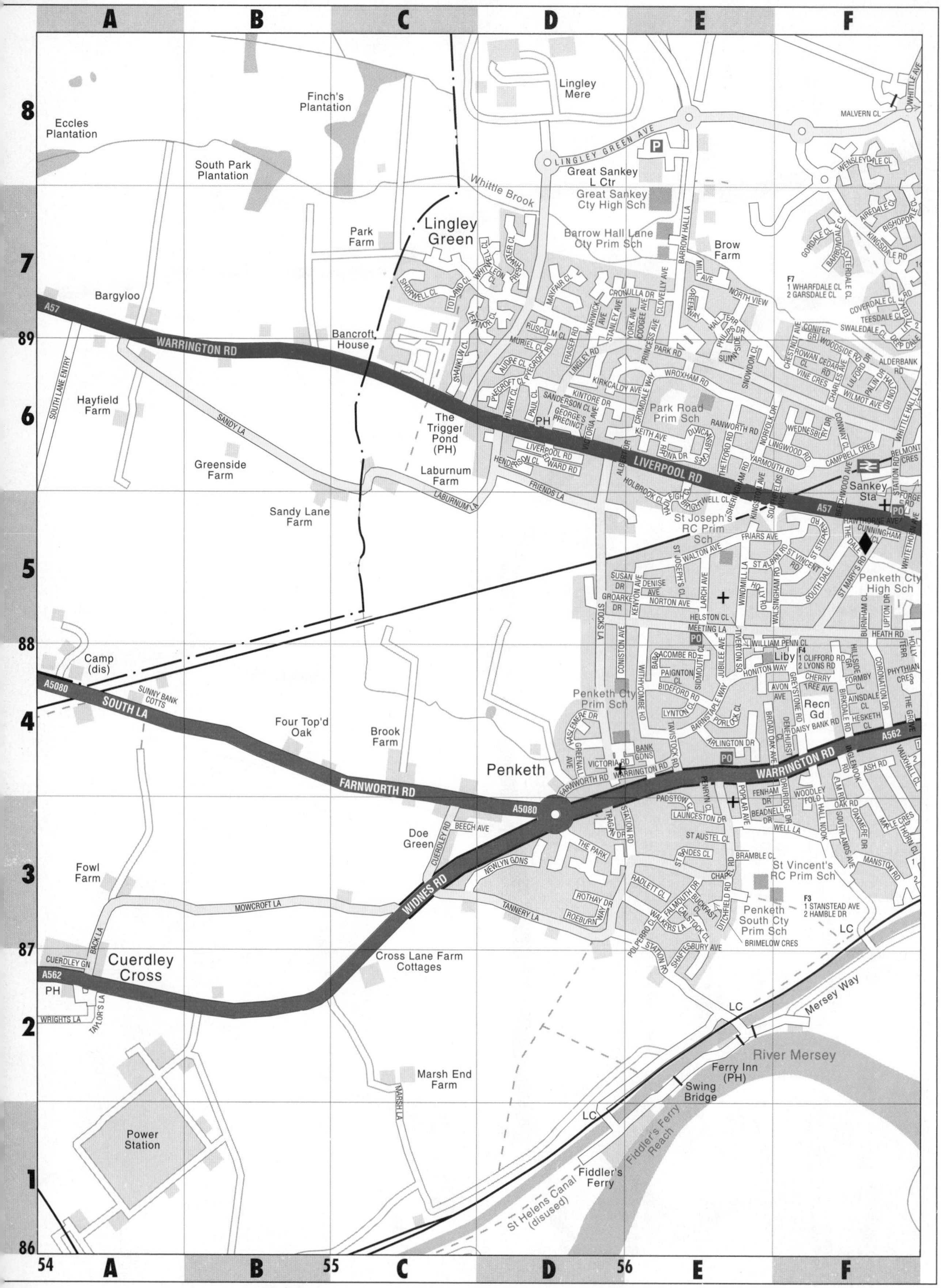
Lingley Mere
Finch's Plantation
Eccles Plantation
South Park Plantation
Great Sankey L Ctr
Great Sankey Cty High Sch
Whittle Brook
Lingley Green
Park Farm
Barrow Hall Lane Cty Prim Sch
Brow Farm
Bargyloo
A57
WARRINGTON RD
Bancroft House
Hayfield Farm
The Trigger Pond (PH)
Park Road Prim Sch
LIVERPOOL RD
Greenside Farm
Laburnum Farm
Sankey Sta
Sandy Lane Farm
St Joseph's RC Prim Sch
Penketh Cty High Sch
Camp (dis)
A5080
SOUTH LA
Liby
Four Top'd Oak
Brook Farm
Penketh Cty Prim Sch
Recn Gd
Penketh
FARNWORTH RD
A562
Doe Green
Fowl Farm
WIDNES RD
St Vincent's RC Prim Sch
Penketh South Cty Prim Sch
Cross Lane Farm Cottages
Cuerdley Cross
Mersey Way
River Mersey
Ferry Inn (PH)
Swing Bridge
Marsh End Farm
Power Station
Fiddler's Ferry
Fiddler's Ferry Reach
St Helens Canal (disused)

63
76

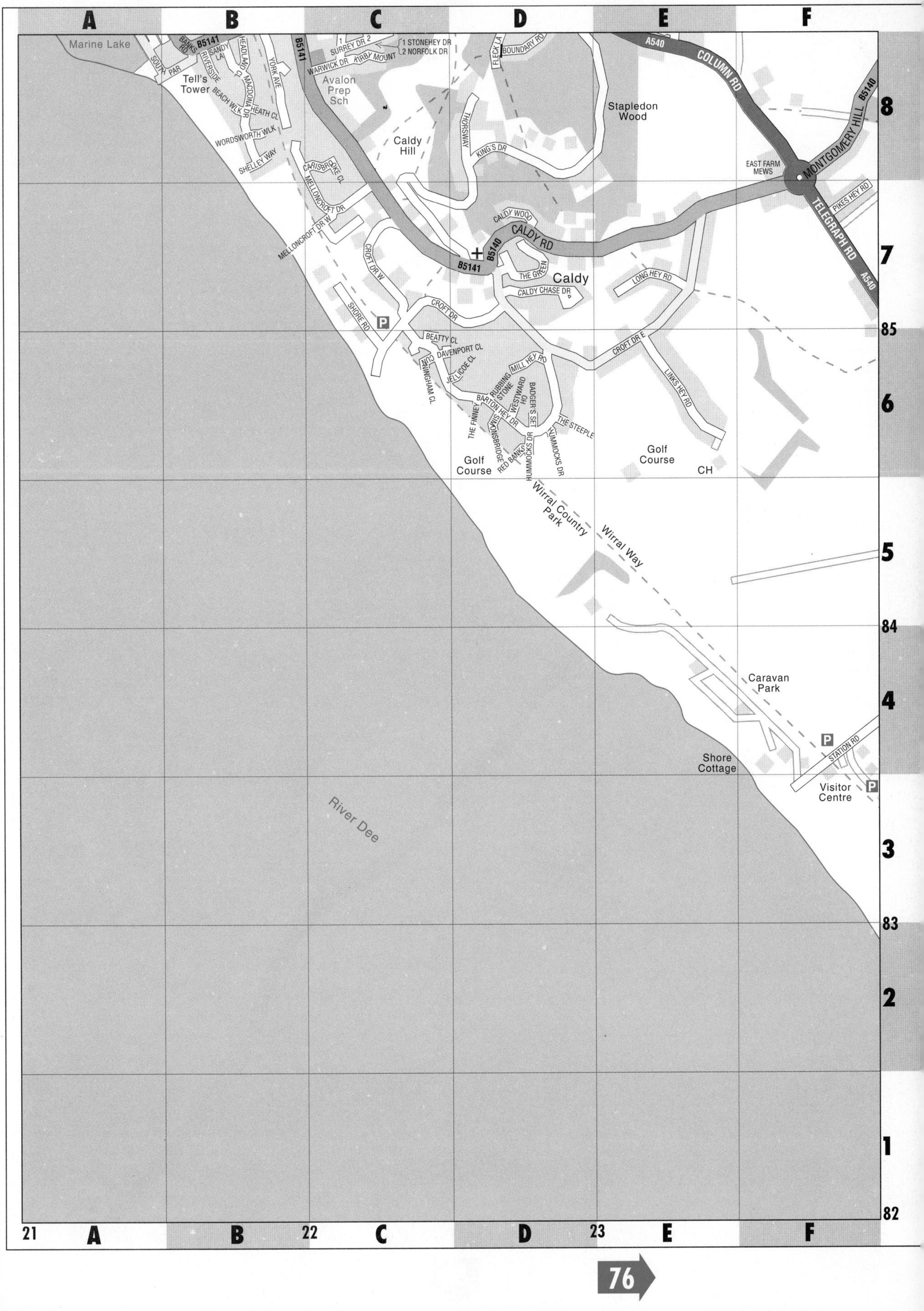
A
B
C
D
E
F
Marine Lake
BANKS RD
B5141
SOUTH PAR
SANDY LA
RIVERSIDE
HEADLAND CL
MACDONA DR
YORK AVE
Tell's Tower
BEACH WLK
HEATH CL
WORDSWORTH WLK
SHELLEY WAY
B5141
1 SURREY DR 2
1 STONEHEY DR
2 NORFOLK DR
WARWICK DR
KIRBY MOUNT
Avalon Prep Sch
FLECK LA
BOUNDARY RD
A540
COLUMN RD
Stapledon Wood
Caldy Hill
THORSWAY
KING'S DR
CARISBROOKE CL
MELLONCROFT DR
MELLONCROFT DR W
CALDY WOOD
CALDY RD
B5140
B5141
CROFT DR W
THE GREEN
Caldy
CALDY CHASE DR
LONG HEY RD
SHORE RD
CROFT DR
CROFT DR E
BEATTY CL
DAVENPORT CL
JELLICOE CL
CUNNINGHAM CL
RUBBING STONE
MILL HEY RD
BARTON HEY DR
WESTWARD HO
BADGER'S SET
THE FINNEY
THE STEEPLE
LINKS HEY RD
HUMMOCKS DR
RED BANKS
Golf Course
Golf Course
CH
Wirral Country Park
Wirral Way
EAST FARM MEWS
MONTGOMERY HILL
B5140
PIKES HEY RD
TELEGRAPH RD
A540
Caravan Park
Shore Cottage
STATION RD
Visitor Centre
River Dee
8
7
85
6
5
84
4
3
83
2
1
82
21
22
23

76

75
64

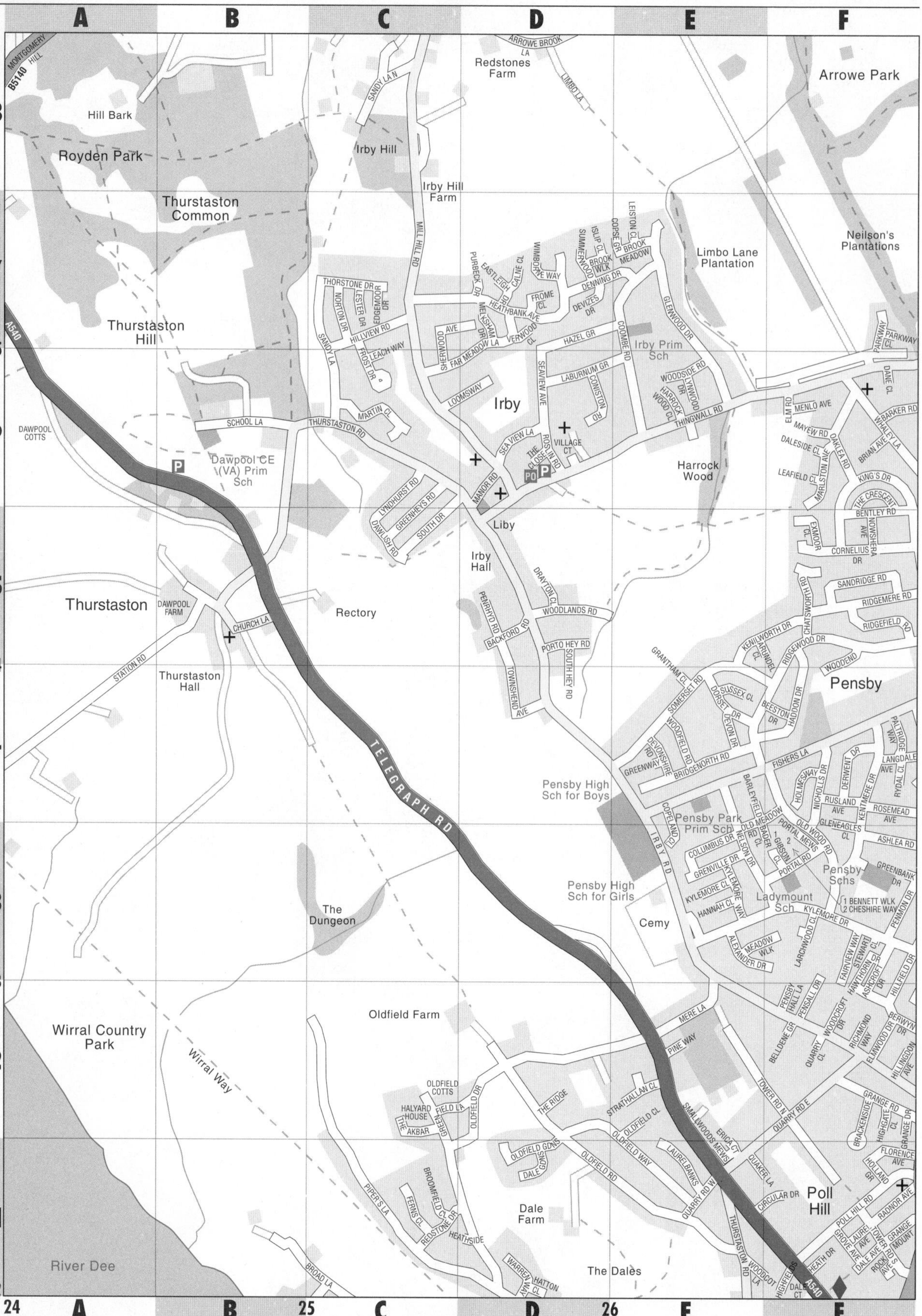
A
B
C
D
E
F
8
7
85
6
5
84
4
3
83
2
1
82
24
25
26
B5140
MONTGOMERY HILL
Hill Bark
Royden Park
Thurstaston Common
Thurstaston Hill
A540
DAWPOOL COTTS
Dawpool CE (VA) Prim Sch
P
Thurstaston
DAWPOOL FARM
CHURCH LA
STATION RD
Thurstaston Hall
Rectory
SCHOOL LA
THURSTASTON RD
Redstones Farm
ARROWE BROOK LA
LIMBO LA
SANDY LA N
Irby Hill
Irby Hill Farm
MILL HILL RD
THORSTONE DR
NORTON DR
LESTER DR
EDGEMOOR DR
HILLVIEW RD
SANDY LA
FROST DR
LEACH WAY
MARTIN CL
LYNDHURST RD
GREENHEYS RD
DAWLISH RD
SOUTH DR
MANOR RD
Liby
Irby Hall
PENRHYD RD
BACKFORD RD
TOWNSHEND AVE
DRAYTON CL
WOODLANDS RD
PORTO HEY RD
SOUTH HEY RD
Irby
PURBECK DR
EASTLEIGH RD
CALNE CL
WIMBORNE WAY
FROME CL
HEATHBANK AVE
MELKSHAM DR
VERWOOD CL
SHERWOOD AVE
FAR MEADOW LA
LOOMSWAY
SEAVIEW AVE
SEA VIEW LA
THE CLOSE
ROSLIN RD
VILLAGE CT
PO
DEVIZES DR
DENNING DR
SUMMERWOOD
ISLIP CL
BROOK WLK
COPSE GR
LEISTON CL
BROOK MEADOW
HAZEL GR
LABURNUM GR
CONISTON RD
COOMBE RD
Irby Prim Sch
GLENWOOD DR
WOODSIDE RD
LYNWOOD DR
HARROCK WOOD CL
THINGWALL RD
Harrock Wood
Limbo Lane Plantation
Arrowe Park
Neilson's Plantations
PARKWAY
PARKWAY CL
DANE CL
ELM RD
MENLO AVE
MAYEW RD
DALESIDE CL
LEAFIELD CL
MARLSTON AVE
OAKLEA RD
BRIAN AVE
WHALLEY LA
BARKER RD
KING'S DR
THE CRESCENT
BENTLEY RD
NOWSHERA AVE
EXMOOR CL
CORNELIUS DR
SANDRIDGE RD
RIDGEMERE RD
RIDGEFIELD RD
CHATSWORTH RD
KENILWORTH DR
ARUNDEL CL
RIDGEWOOD DR
WOODEND
Pensby
GRANTHAM CL
SOMERSET RD
SUSSEX CL
DORSET DR
DEVON DR
BEESTON DR
HADDON DR
WOODFIELD RD
DEVONSHIRE RD
GREENWAY
BRIDGENORTH RD
FISHERS LA
HOLMESWAY
NICHOLLS DR
DERWENT DR
PALTRIDGE WAY
LANGDALE AVE
RYDAL CL
KENTMERE DR
RUSLAND AVE
ROSEMEAD AVE
GLENEAGLES CL
ASHLEA RD
Pensby High Sch for Boys
Pensby Park Prim Sch
COPELAND CL
IRBY RD
BARLEYFIELD
OLD MEADOW
BADER CL
NELSON DR
COLUMBUS DR
GRENVILLE DR
KYLEMORE WAY
KYLEMORE CL
HANNAH CL
GIBSON CL
PORTAL MEWS
PORTAL RD
OLD WOOD RD
Pensby Schs
GREENBANK DR
1 BENNETT WLK
2 CHESHIRE WAY
PEMMON DR
Ladymount Sch
KYLEMORE DR
Pensby High Sch for Girls
Cemy
MEADOW WLK
ALEXANDER DR
LARCHWOOD CL
FAIRVIEW WAY
STEWART CL
HAWTHORN CL
ASHCROFT DR
HILLFIELD DR
PENSBY HALL LA
PENSALL DR
WOODCROFT DR
RICHMOND WAY
BERWYN DR
BELLDENE GR
QUARRY CL
ELMWOOD DR
HILLINGDON AVE
TOWER RD N
QUARRY RD E
BRACKENSIDE
HIGHGATE CL
GRANGE RD
GRANGE DR
FLORENCE AVE
HOLLAND GR
Poll Hill
POLL HILL RD
RADNOR AVE
GROVE AVE
LAUREL AVE
DALE AVE
TOWER RD S
ROCK AVE
GRANGE MOUNT
HEATH DR
DALE CT
HIGHFIELDS
TELEGRAPH RD
The Dungeon
Oldfield Farm
Wirral Country Park
Wirral Way
River Dee
MERE LA
PINE WAY
STRATHALLAN CL
OLDFIELD CL
OLDFIELD WAY
SMALLWOODS MEWS
ERICA CT
QUAKER LA
CIRCULAR DR
LAURELBANKS
QUARRY RD W
THURSTASTON RD
WOODCOT LA
THE RIDGE
OLDFIELD COTTS
HALYARD HOUSE
THE AKBAR
GREENFIELD LA
OLDFIELD DR
OLDFIELD GDNS
DALE GDNS
OLDFIELD RD
Dale Farm
PIPER'S LA
BROOMFIELD CL
FERNS CL
REDSTONE DR
HEATHSIDE
BROAD LA
WARREN WAY
HATTON CL
The Dales

75
85

65
78

A
B
C
D
E
F
Arrowe Park
CH
Crem
Cemy
Home Farm
Landican
LANDICAN LA
NORTH CHESHIRE TRADING EST
BROOKWAY
BADGER WAY
PARKVALE AVE
PRENTON WAY
M53
BYRON CL
GARRICK RD
PRENTON DELL RD
Prenton Golf Course
Golf Course
ARROWE PARK RD
A551
Old Hall Farm
LANDICAN RD
RICHMOND WAY
B5138
THINGWALL RD E
HAZELDENE WAY
The Farm
Cow Hey Covert
LANDICAN LA
Thingwall Prim Sch
Stanley Sch
TORRINGTON DR
TORRINGTON GDNS
HAZELDENE AVE
BEAUMARIS DR
BEVERLEY GDNS
HEYWOOD CL
HEYWOOD BVD
THINGWALL DR
MILL RD
CLEMERE DR
HOWARDS RD
NURSE RD
TURMAR AVE
BERWYN AVE
PENRHYN AVE
AMBLESIDE CL
PH
Stanley Wood
ANDERSON CL
WHALEY LA
HEATHFIELD HOUSE
QUARRY LA
SPARKS LA
THE LEAS
Liby
LOWER THINGWALL LA
REGENTS CL
AXHOLME RD
BARNSDALE AVE
BENTY FARM GR
AINSDALE CL
WIMBOURNE AVE
SEVEN ACRES LA
AXHOLME CL
Murrayfield
Prenton Brook
CORNELIUS DR
LYNDHURST CL
Thingwall
ANTONS RD
PENSBY CL
CESTRIAN DR
NORTHRIDGE RD
HESWALL MOUNT
RIDGEMERE RD
RYLAND PK
GWENDOLINE CL
Cross Hill
HOLMWOOD AVE
HOLMWOOD DR
STATION RD
RIDGEWOOD DR
SOUTHRIDGE RD
DE VIEW CL
SUNNINGDALE DR
PRIVATE DR
OVERDALE AVE
THORNCROFT DR
LOW WOOD GR
WOODLANDS DR
DALE END RD
New Hay Covert
FISHERS LA
BEECH AVE
MARLFIELD LA
GILLS LA
LAURELHURST AVE
1 SHEARMAN CL
2 SHEARMAN RD
3 CHRISTOPHERS CL
PENSBY RD
FELLDER WAY
Tree Tops
STORETON LA
ELM CL
MARKSWAY
OAKS LA
Ley Farm
ROSEMEAD AVE
BELMONT DR
ASHLEA RD
BARNSTON RD
PH
Beech Farm
Bank Farm
Barnston
GREENBANK DR
KINGSLEY CL
HILLFIELD DR
LYNDHURST AVE
Manor Farm
PINE VIEW
KYLEMORE DR
BERWYN DR
NAPPS WAY
DOWNHAM RD N
Carnsdale Farm
Greenhayes Cottages
IRBY RD
RAVENSWOOD RD
OAKLANDS TERR
OAKLANDS DR
Heswall Cty Prim Sch
Whitehouse Farm
Fairfield
The Brooklet
HEATHER RD
SANDY LA
SHREWSBURY RD
WHITFIELD LA
HESWALL
BRUNSTATH CL
WHITEHOUSE LA
A5137
CONSTANTINE AVE
HESKETH DR
DOWNHAM RD S
GORSEHILL RD
MILTON CRES
Whitfield Common
BUFFS LA
MILNER RD
PINE RD
FIELDWAY
PEAR TREE CL
MEADOWCROFT
BROOKLET RD
BARCOMBE RD
NORTHWAY
Dunster House
BRIMSTAGE RD
MANOR RD
FOREST RD
EPPING CT
MAPLE TREE GR
ACRE LA
8
7
85
6
5
84
4
3
83
2
1
82
27
28
29

86
78

77
66

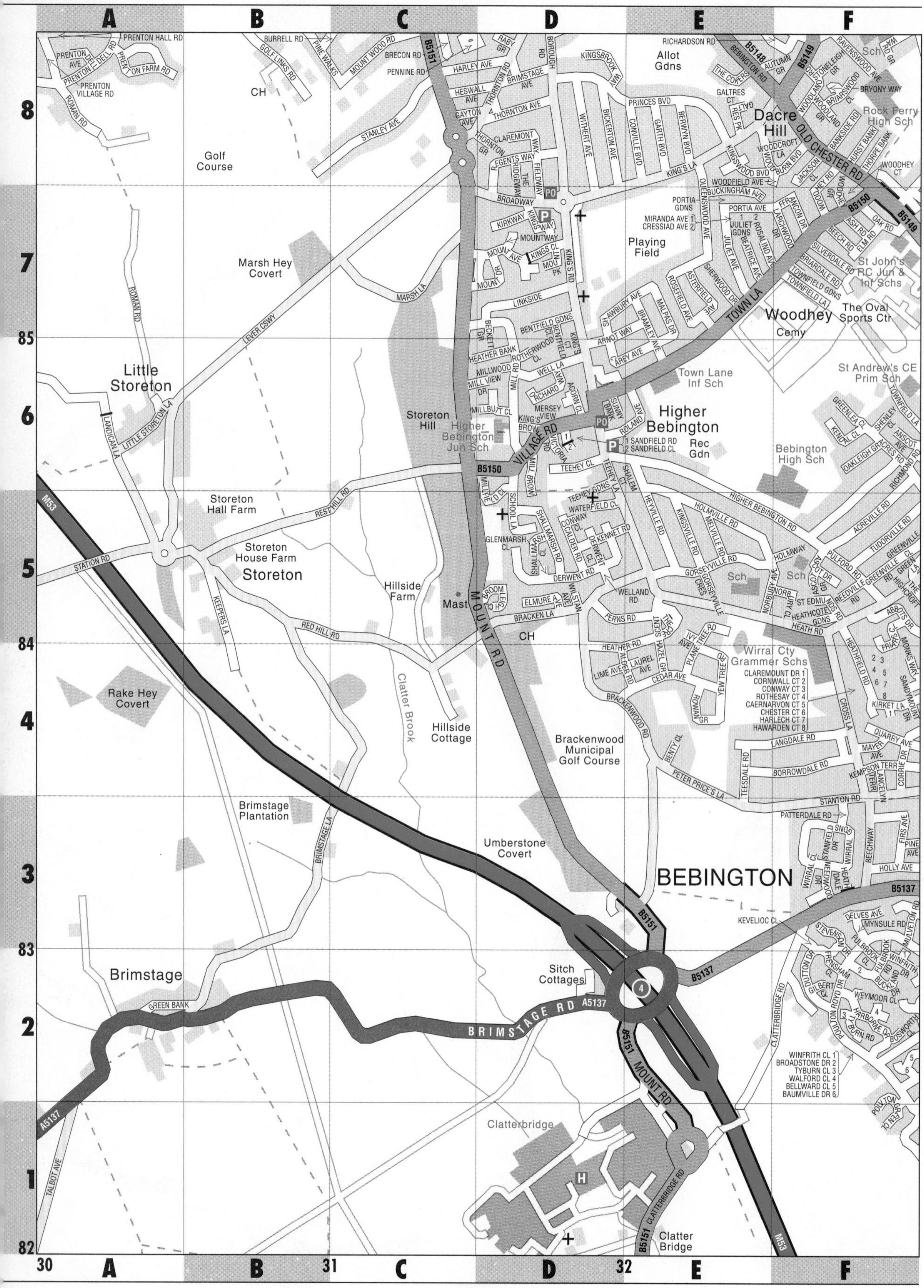
A
B
C
D
E
F
8
7
85
6
5
84
4
3
83
2
1
82
30
31
32
PRENTON HALL RD
PRENTON AVE
PRENTON DELL RD
PRENTON FARM RD
PRENTON VILLAGE RD
ROMAN RD
BURRELL RD
GOLF LINKS RD
PINE WALKS
MOUNT WOOD RD
BRECON RD
PENNINE RD
B5151
HARLEY AVE
RABY GR
HESWALL AVE
THORNTON RD
BRIMSTAGE AVE
BOROUGH RD
KINGSBROOK WAY
RICHARDSON RD
Allot Gdns
B5148
B5149
BEBINGTON RD
AUTUMN GR
THE COPPERS
RAVENSWOOD AVE
Sch
BRYONY WAY
CH
GAYTON AVE
THORNTON AVE
STANLEY AVE
PRINCES BVD
GALTRES CT
Dacre Hill
Rock Ferry High Sch
Golf Course
CLAREMONT WAY
THORNTON GR
REGENTS WAY
WITHERT AVE
BICKERTON AVE
CONVILLE BVD
GARTH BVD
BERWYN BVD
KING'S LA
OLD CHESTER RD
WOODHEY CT
WOODFIELD AVE
BUCKINGHAM AVE
BROADWAY
PO
PORTIA GDNS
PORTIA AVE
MIRANDA AVE 1
CRESSIAD AVE 2
B5150
KIRKWAY
MOUNTWAY
KINGS CL
Marsh Hey Covert
Playing Field
St John's RC Jun & Inf Schs
MARSH LA
LINKSIDE
TOWN LA
TOWNFIELD LA
Woodhey
Cemy
The Oval Sports Ctr
LEVER CSWY
ROMAN RD
BENTFIELD GDNS
ARNOT WAY
BRAMLEY AVE
HEATHER BANK
ROTHERWOOD CL
Town Lane Inf Sch
St Andrew's CE Prim Sch
Little Storeton
MILLWOOD
MILL VIEW
WELL LA
Higher Bebington
Storeton Hill
Higher Bebington Jun Sch
LANDICAN LA
LITTLE STORETON LA
VILLAGE RD
1 SANDFIELD RD
2 SANDFIELD CL
Rec Gdn
Bebington High Sch
TEEHEY CL
M53
Storeton Hall Farm
REST HILL RD
TEEHEY GDNS
WATERFIELD CL
HIGHER BEBINGTON RD
HOLMVILLE RD
ACREVILLE RD
STATION RD
Storeton House Farm
Storeton
SCHOOL LA
GLENMARSH CL
CONWAY CL
KENNET RD
HEYVILLE RD
KINGSVILLE RD
MELVILLE RD
HOLMWAY
PULFORD RD
DERWENT RD
GORSEYVILLE RD
Sch
Hillside Farm
Mast
MOUNT RD
ELMURE AVE
WELLAND RD
BRACKEN LA
FERNS RD
HEATH RD
KEEPERS LA
RED HILL RD
CH
HEATHER RD
LIME AVE
LAUREL AVE
CEDAR AVE
Wirral Cty Grammer Schs
CLAREMOUNT DR 1
CORNWALL CT 2
CONWAY CT 3
ROTHESAY CT 4
CAERNARVON CT 5
CHESTER CT 6
HARLECH CT 7
HAWARDEN CT 8
Rake Hey Covert
Clatter Brook
Hillside Cottage
BRACKENWOOD RD
Brackenwood Municipal Golf Course
LANGDALE RD
BORROWDALE RD
KIRKET LA
CROSS LA
QUARRY AVE
PETER PRICE'S LA
TEESDALE RD
STANTON RD
PATTERDALE RD
Brimstage Plantation
Umberstone Covert
BRIMSTAGE LA
BEBINGTON
HOLLY AVE
B5137
KEVELIOC CL
DELVES AVE
MYNSULE RD
Brimstage
Sitch Cottages
GREEN BANK
A5137
BRIMSTAGE RD
4
CLATTERBRIDGE RD
WEYMOOR CL
WINFRITH CL 1
BROADSTONE DR 2
TYBURN CL 3
WALFORD CL 4
BELLWARD CL 5
BAUMVILLE DR 6
TALBOT AVE
Clatterbridge
H
Clatter Bridge

77
87

67
80

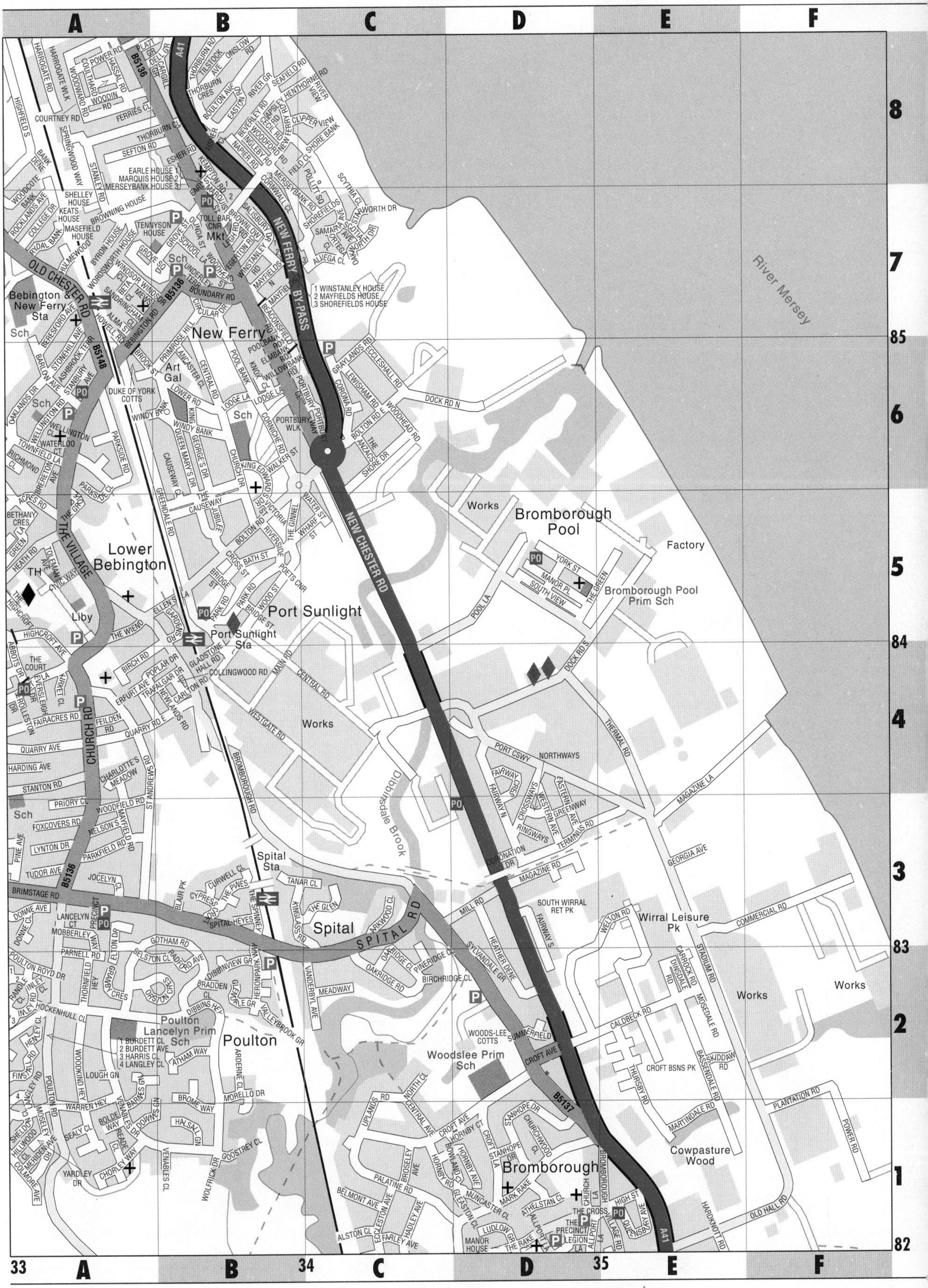
A
B
C
D
E
F
8
7
85
6
5
84
4
3
83
2
1
82
33
34
35
New Ferry
NEW FERRY BY-PASS
NEW CHESTER RD
A41
B5136
B5148
B5137
OLD CHESTER RD
Bebington & New Ferry Sta
Art Gal
Lower Bebington
THE VILLAGE
CHURCH RD
Port Sunlight
Port Sunlight Sta
Works
Bromborough Pool
Bromborough Pool Prim Sch
Factory
River Mersey
DOCK RD N
DOCK RD S
THERMAL RD
MAGAZINE LA
GEORGIA AVE
COMMERCIAL RD
PORT CSWY
NORTHWAYS
Dibbinsdale Brook
Spital Sta
Spital
SPITAL RD
BRIMSTAGE RD
BROMBOROUGH RD
SOUTH WIRRAL RET PK
Wirral Leisure Pk
STADIUM RD
CROFT BSNS PK
Poulton
Poulton Lancelyn Prim Sch
Woodslee Prim Sch
Bromborough
Cowpasture Wood
PLANTATION RD
POWER RD
OLD HALL RD
HARDKNOTT RD
HIGH ST
Liby
TH
Sch
Mkt
1 WINSTANLEY HOUSE
2 MAYFIELDS HOUSE
3 SHOREFIELDS HOUSE
1 BURDETT CL
2 BURDETT AVE
3 HARRIS CL
4 LANGLEY CL

88
80

79
68

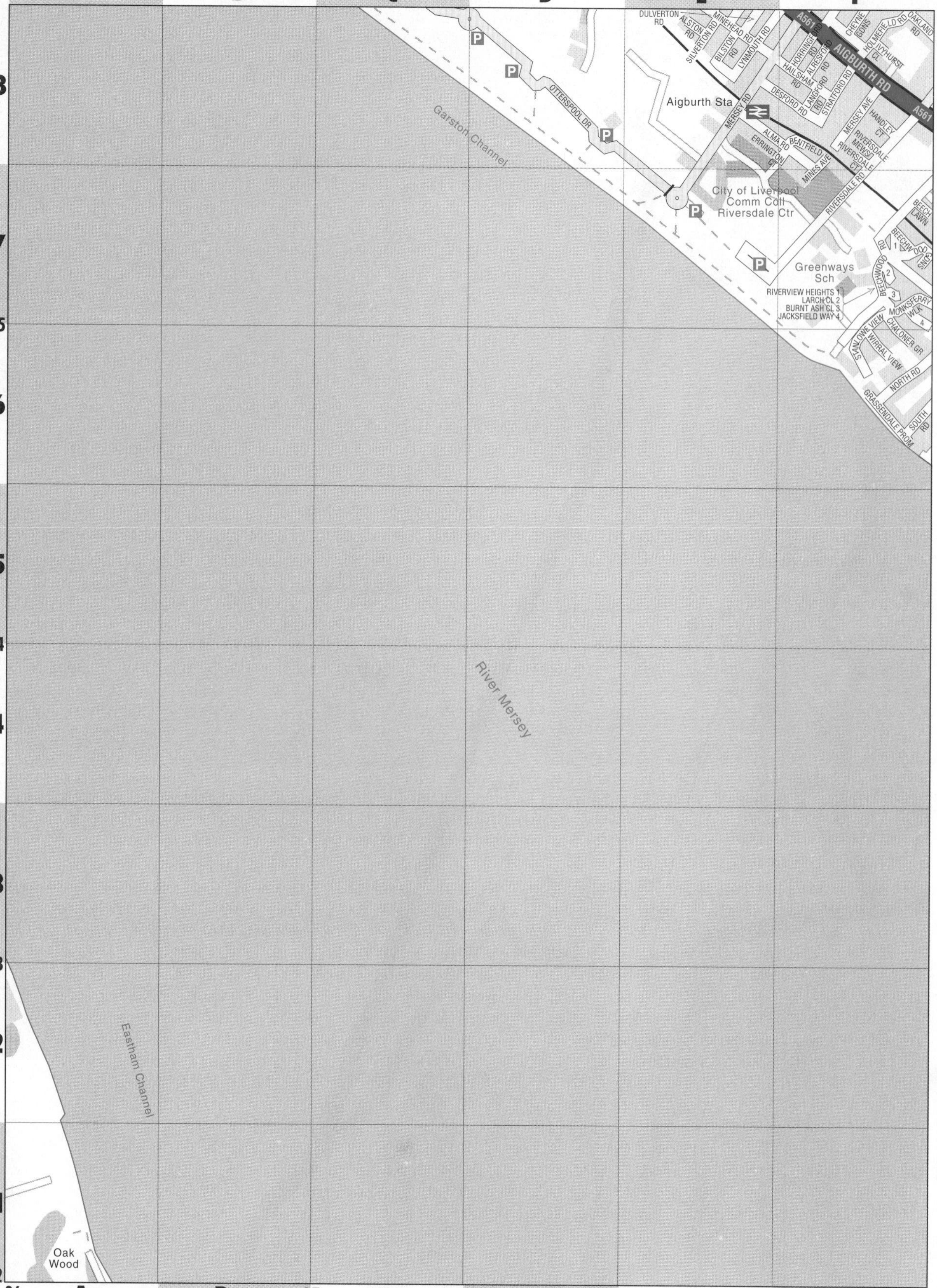
A
B
C
D
E
F
8
7
85
6
5
84
4
3
83
2
1
82
36
37
38
DULVERTON RD
ALSTON RD
MINEHEAD RD
SILVERTON RD
BILSTON RD
LYNMOUTH RD
HORRINGER RD
ALRESFORD RD
HAILSHAM RD
LANGFORD RD
STRATFORD RD
A561
AIGBURTH RD
CHEYNE GDNS
HOLMEFIELD RD
OAKLAND RD
IVYHURST CL
Aigburth Sta
MERSEY RD
DESFORD RD
MERSEY AVE
HANDLEY CT
OTTERSPOOL DR
ALMA RD
BENTFIELD
ERRINGTON CT
MINES AVE
RIVERSDALE MEWS
RIVERSDALE CT
RIVERSDALE RD
Garston Channel
City of Liverpool Comm Coll Riversdale Ctr
BEECH LAWN
BEECHWOOD RD
Greenways Sch
RIVERVIEW HEIGHTS 1
LARCH CL 2
BURNT ASH CL 3
JACKSFIELD WAY 4
MONKSFERRY WLK
STANLOWE VIEW
CHALONER GR
WIRRAL VIEW
NORTH RD
GRASSENDALE PROM
SOUTH RD
River Mersey
Eastham Channel
Oak Wood

79
89

69
82

A
B
C
D
E
F
Allerton
Grassendale
New Heys Community Comp Sch
Simpson Gd
Clarke Gdns
Springfield Crem
St Austin's RC Prim Sch
Gilmour South Bank Inf Sch
Nursery
Springwood Prim Sch
Springwood Recn Gd
Allerton Cemy
Long Lane Recn Gd
Gilmour Sch
Cressington Sta
Liby
Allerton Sta
Wood End Park
Garston Sta
Garston CE Prim Sch
Cressington Park
Sch
Mkt
Sir Alfred Jones Mem
St John Almond High Sch
Speke Sidings
Garston
Wks
MERSEY COTTS
Holy Trinity RC Prim Sch
RAVENSIDE IND PK
Bank's Road Prim Sch
Ind Est
WEAVER IND EST
Liverpool Airport
River Mersey
Mersey Way
Speke Hall
Light Gantry
AIGBURTH RD
ST MARY'S RD
GARSTON WAY
SPEKE RD
WOOLTON RD
MATHER AVE
B5180
B5171
A561
1 PRIOR FARM CL
2 LAWRENCE CL
3 DUGDALE CL
4 GRASSENDALE CT
1 BOWFIELD RD
2 PRIZETT RD
1 CHAPEL RD
2 ISLAND PL
3 GRANVILLE RD
5 BEECHWOOD GR
6 BEECHWOOD CL
9 SHREWSBURY PL
10 BELMONT PL
11 QUEEN'S CL
MERSEY VIEW 4
JACKSON ST 5
MERCER ST 6
WOODGER ST 7
QUEEN ST 8
1 OTWAY ST
2 SHAKESPEARE ST
3 RAGLAN ST
4 BLAKE CT
5 RAGLAN WLK
CARONIA ST 6
UMBRIA ST 7
ETRURIA ST 8
CARPATHIA ST 9
ULTONIA ST 10
8
7
85
6
5
84
4
3
83
2
1
82
39
40
41

82

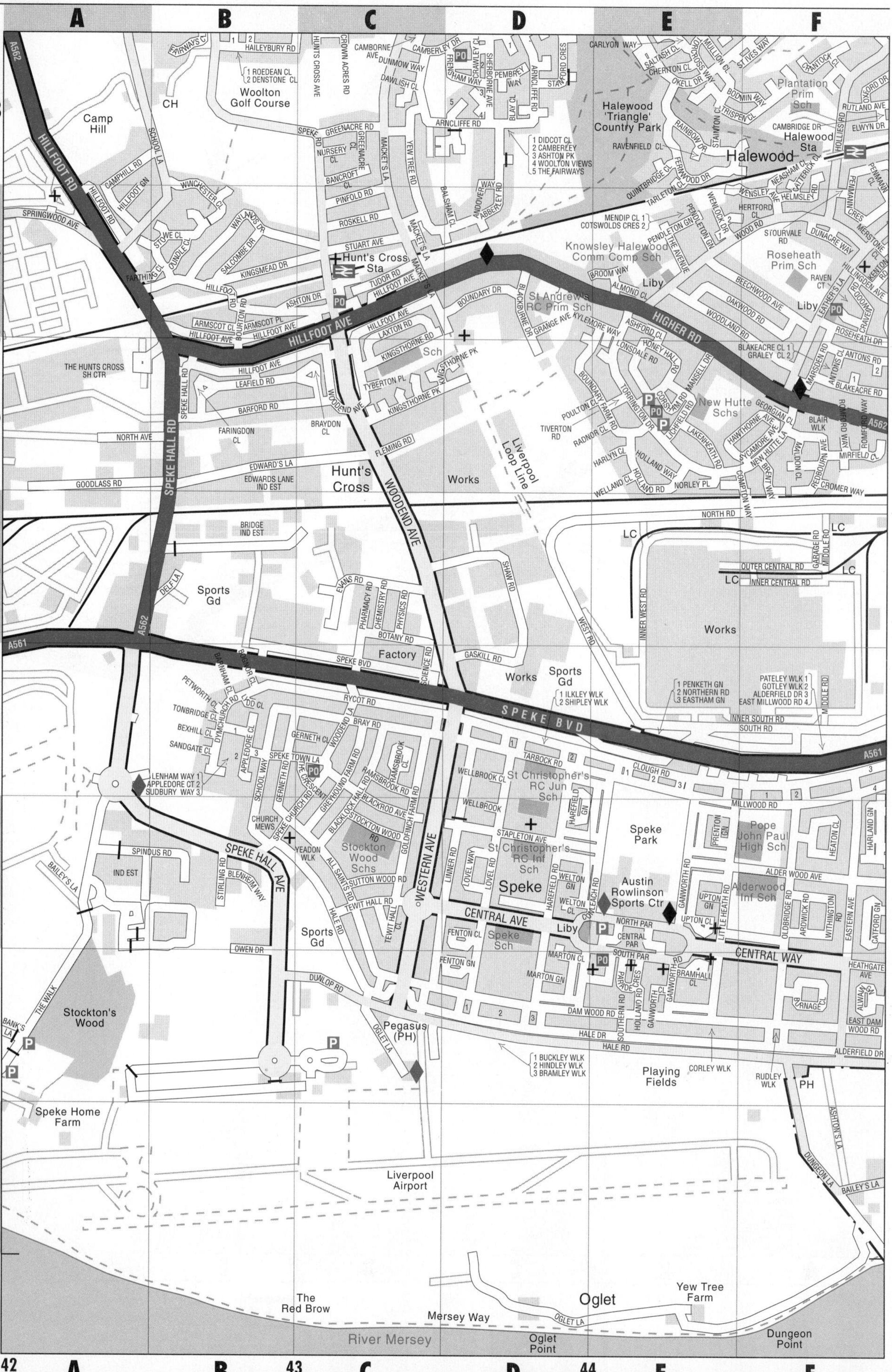
A
B
C
D
E
F
8
7
85
6
5
84
4
3
83
2
1
82
42
43
44
A562
HILLFOOT RD
Camp Hill
CH
Woolton Golf Course
FAIRWAYS CL
HAILEYBURY RD
1 ROEDEAN CL
2 DENSTONE CL
HUNTS CROSS AVE
CROWN ACRES RD
CAMBORNE AVE
DUNMOW WAY
DAWLISH CL
CAMBERLEY DR
FRENSHAM WAY
CRAWLEY CL
SHERBORNE AVE
PEMBREY WAY
BLAY CL
ARNCLIFFE RD
STAMFORD CRES
1 DIDCOT CL
2 CAMBERLEY
3 ASHTON PK
4 WOOLTON VIEWS
5 THE FAIRWAYS
SCHOOL LA
CAMPHILL RD
HILLFOOT GN
WINCHESTER CL
SPRINGWOOD AVE
STOWE CL
OUNDLE CL
WAYLANDS DR
SALCOMBE DR
KINGSMEAD DR
FARTHING CL
SPEKE RD
GREENACRE RD
NURSERY CL
GREENACRE CL
BANCROFT CL
PINFOLD RD
ROSKELL RD
STUART AVE
MACKET'S LA
YEW TREE RD
BALSHAM CL
ANDOVER WAY
ABBERLEY RD
Hunt's Cross Sta
TUDOR RD
HILLFOOT AVE
ASHTON DR
ARMSCOT CL
ARMSCOT PL
BOURTON RD
HILLFOOT AVE
PO
HILLFOOT AVE
LAXTON RD
KINGSTHORNE RD
Sch
KINGSTHORNE PK
TYBERTON PL
BOUNDARY DR
BLACKBURNE DR
GRANGE AVE
St Andrew's RC Prim Sch
THE HUNTS CROSS SH CTR
SPEKE HALL RD
LEAFIELD RD
BARFORD RD
FARINGDON CL
BRAYDON CL
WOODEND AVE
NORTH AVE
FLEMING RD
EDWARD'S LA
Hunt's Cross
GOODLASS RD
EDWARDS LANE IND EST
Works
Liverpool Loop Line
CARLYON WAY
SALTASH CL
CHERITON CL
POLCROSS WAY
MULLION CL
ST IVES WAY
OKELL DR
BODMIN WAY
TRISPEN CL
Plantation Prim Sch
CHANTOCK CL
OXFORD DR
RUTLAND AVE
CAMBRIDGE DR
ELWYN DR
Halewood 'Triangle' Country Park
RAVENFIELD CL
RAINBOW DR
STAINTON CL
Halewood Sta
Halewood
HOLLIES RD
NEASHAM CL
CATTERICK CL
QUINTBRIDGE CL
FERNWOOD DR
TARLETON CL
WENSLEY AVE
HELMSLEY RD
HERTFORD CL
PENMANN CL
PENMANN CRES
MENDIP CL 1
COTSWOLDS CRES 2
PENDLETON GN
PENDLETON DR
WENLOCK DR
WOOD RD
STOURVALE RD
DUNACRE WAY
MERSTONE CL
Knowsley Halewood Comm Comp Sch
THE AVENUE
Roseheath Prim Sch
KENTON CL
HILLINGDEN AVE
BROOM WAY
ALMOND CL
Liby
RAVEN CT
BEECHWOOD AVE
OAKWOOD RD
WOODLAND RD
HIGHER RD
Liby
PO
ROSEHEATH DR
KYLEMORE WAY
ASHFORD CL
HONEY HALL RD
LONSDALE RD
MANSELL DR
BLAKEACRE CL 1
GRALEY CL 2
ANTONS CL
ANTONS RD
BLAKEACRE RD
MARSDEN RD
BOUNDARY FARM RD
TORRINGTON DR
CORSHAM RD
LICHFIELD RD
New Hutte Schs
GEORGIAN CL
POULTON CL
TIVERTON RD
RADNOR CL
BLAIR WLK
A562
LAKENHEATH RD
HAWTHORNE AVE
SYCAMORE AVE
NEW HUTTE LA
ROMFORD WAY
MIRFIELD CL
HARLYN CL
HOLLAND WAY
HOLLAND RD
MALDON CL
REDBOURN AVE
WELLAND CL
WELLAND RD
NORLEY PL
COMPTON WAY
BRENT WAY
CROMER WAY
NORTH RD
BRIDGE IND EST
SHAW RD
LC
LC
LC
LC
OUTER CENTRAL RD
INNER CENTRAL RD
GARAGE RD
MIDDLE RD
DELF LA
Sports Gd
EVANS RD
PHARMACY RD
CHEMISTRY RD
PHYSICS RD
WEST RD
INNER WEST RD
Works
A561
BOTANY RD
Factory
GASKILL RD
SPEKE BVD
SCIENCE RD
Works
Sports Gd
1 ILKLEY WLK
2 SHIPLEY WLK
1 PENKETH GN
2 NORTHERN RD
3 EASTHAM GN
PATELEY WLK 1
GOTLEY WLK 2
ALDERFIELD DR 3
EAST MILLWOOD RD 4
MIDDLE RD
INNER SOUTH RD
SOUTH RD
SPEKE BVD
A561
BARNHAM CL
BOGNOR CL
PETWORTH CL
TONBRIDGE CL
LYDD CL
BEXHILL CL
SANDGATE CL
DYMCHURCH RD
APPLEDORE CL
RYCOT RD
BRAY RD
GERNETH CL
WOODEND LA
SPEKE TOWN LA
RAMSBROOK CL
LENHAM WAY 1
APPLEDORE CT 2
SUDBURY WAY 3
SCHOOL WAY
GERNETH RD
THE CRESCENT
GREYHOUND FARM RD
RAMSBROOK RD
BLACKLOCK HALL RD
BLACKROD AVE
GOLDFINCH FARM RD
CHURCH MEWS
SPEKE CHURCH RD
STOCKTON WOOD RD
Stockton Wood Schs
YEADON WLK
ALL SAINTS RD
SUTTON WOOD RD
TEWIT HALL RD
HALE RD
TARBOCK RD
WELLBROOK CL
WELLBROOK
St Christopher's RC Jun Sch
HAREFIELD GN
CLOUGH RD
MILLWOOD RD
STAPLETON AVE
St Christopher's RC Inf Sch
LOVEL WAY
LOVEL RD
LINNER RD
Speke
HAREFIELD RD
WELTON GN
WELTON CL
Speke Park
PRENTON GN
Pope John Paul High Sch
HEATON CL
HARLAND GN
ALDER WOOD AVE
GANWORTH RD
UPTON GN
Alderwood Inf Sch
OLDBRIDGE RD
ARDWICK RD
WITHINGTON RD
EASTERN AVE
CATFORD GN
Austin Rowlinson Sports Ctr
COWLEACH RD
NORTH PAR
UPTON CL
LITTLE HEATH RD
SPINDUS RD
IND EST
STIRLING RD
BLENHEIM WAY
SPEKE HALL AVE
BAILEY'S LA
WESTERN AVE
CENTRAL AVE
Liby
FENTON CL
Speke Sch
CENTRAL PAR
SOUTH PAR
CENTRAL WAY
HEATHGATE AVE
Sports Gd
OWEN DR
MARTON CL
FENTON GN
MARTON GN
PO
PARADE CRES
BRAMHALL CL
ALWAIN GN
BURNAGE CL
DUNLOP RD
DAM WOOD RD
SOUTHERN RD
HOLLAND RD
GANWORTH
EAST DAM WOOD RD
Stockton's Wood
THE WALK
BANK'S LA
P
Pegasus (PH)
OGLET LA
HALE DR
HALE RD
ALDERFIELD DR
1 BUCKLEY WLK
2 HINDLEY WLK
3 BRAMLEY WLK
Playing Fields
CORLEY WLK
RUDLEY WLK
PH
ASHTON'S LA
Speke Home Farm
Liverpool Airport
DUNGEON LA
BAILEY'S LA
The Red Brow
Mersey Way
Oglet
OGLET LA
Yew Tree Farm
River Mersey
Oglet Point
Dungeon Point

71
84

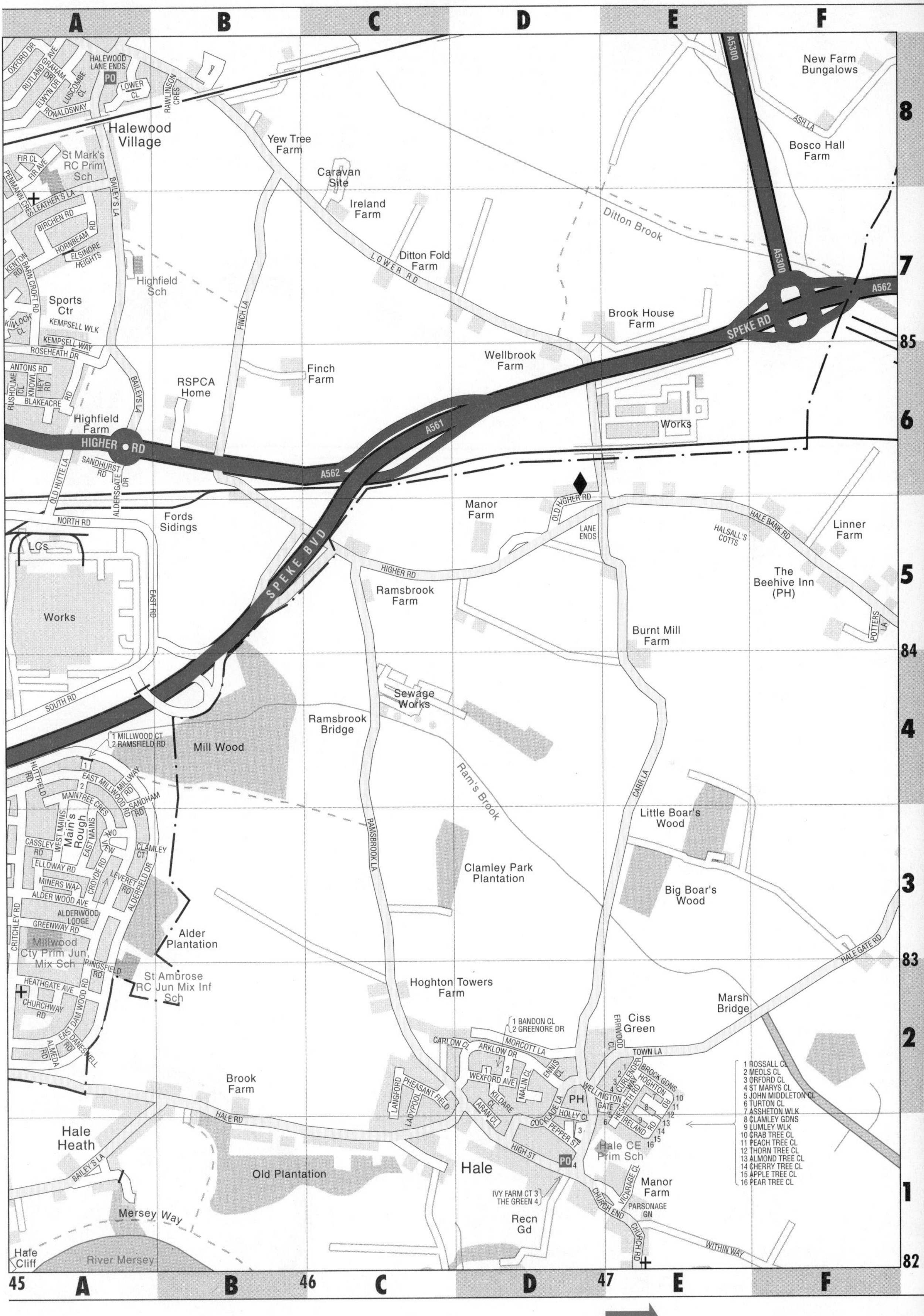
A
B
C
D
E
F
Halewood Village
Yew Tree Farm
Caravan Site
Ireland Farm
New Farm Bungalows
Bosco Hall Farm
ASH LA
A5300
St Mark's RC Prim Sch
FIR CL
FIR AVE
LEATHER'S LA
BIRCHEN RD
HORNBEAM RD
ELSINORE HEIGHTS
BAILEY'S LA
HALEWOOD LANE ENDS
PO
LOWER CL
RAWLINSON CRES
OXFORD DR
RUTLAND AVE
GRAHAM DR
ELWYN DR
LUSCOMBE CL
RONALDSWAY
Ditton Brook
Ditton Fold Farm
LOWER RD
Highfield Sch
Sports Ctr
KENTON RD
BARN CROFT RD
KINLOCH CL
KEMPSELL WLK
KEMPSELL WAY
ROSEHEATH DR
ANTONS RD
BLAKEACRE RD
Brook House Farm
SPEKE RD
A562
Wellbrook Farm
Finch Farm
FINCH LA
RSPCA Home
Highfield Farm
HIGHER RD
SANDHURST RD
ALDERSGATE DR
OLD HUTTE LA
A561
A562
Works
Manor Farm
OLD HIGHER RD
LANE ENDS
HALE BANK RD
HALSALL'S COTTS
Linner Farm
The Beehive Inn (PH)
POTTERS LA
Fords Sidings
NORTH RD
LCs
Works
EAST RD
SPEKE BLVD
HIGHER RD
Ramsbrook Farm
Burnt Mill Farm
SOUTH RD
Sewage Works
Ramsbrook Bridge
1 MILLWOOD CT
2 RAMSFIELD RD
Mill Wood
Ram's Brook
CARR LA
Little Boar's Wood
Big Boar's Wood
Clamley Park Plantation
RAMSBROOK LA
HUTTFIELD RD
EAST MILLWOOD RD
MILLWAY
MAINTREE CRES
SANDHAM
Main's Rough
WEST MAINS
EAST MAINS
CASSLEY RD
ELLOWAY RD
MINERS WAY
CROYDE RD
ALDER WOOD AVE
ALDERWOOD LODGE
GREENWAY RD
LEVERET RD
CLAMLEY CT
ALDERFIELD DR
CRITCHLEY RD
Millwood Cty Prim Jun Mix Sch
Alder Plantation
St Ambrose RC Jun Mix Inf Sch
RINGSFIELD RD
HEATHGATE AVE
CHURCHWAY RD
EAST DAM WOOD RD
ALMEDA RD
EAST DANESWELL
Hoghton Towers Farm
HALE GATE RD
Marsh Bridge
Ciss Green
1 BANDON CL
2 GREENORE DR
CARLOW CL
MORCOTT LA
ARKLOW DR
WEXFORD AVE
ENNIS CL
MALIN CL
KILDARE CL
ARAN CL
LANGFORD
PHEASANT FIELD
LADYPOOL
ERRWOOD CL
TOWN LA
BROCK GDNS
HOGHTON RD
CURLENDER WAY
WELLINGTON GATE
HESKETH RD
IRELAND RD
PH
COCKLADE LA
HOLLY CL
PEPPER ST
HIGH ST
PO
Hale CE Prim Sch
1 ROSSALL CL
2 MEOLS CL
3 ORFORD CL
4 ST MARYS CL
5 JOHN MIDDLETON CL
6 TURTON CL
7 ASSHETON WLK
8 CLAMLEY GDNS
9 LUMLEY WLK
10 CRAB TREE CL
11 PEACH TREE CL
12 THORN TREE CL
13 ALMOND TREE CL
14 CHERRY TREE CL
15 APPLE TREE CL
16 PEAR TREE CL
Brook Farm
HALE RD
Hale Heath
BAILEY'S LA
Old Plantation
Hale
IVY FARM CT 3
THE GREEN 4
VICARAGE CL
Manor Farm
CHURCH END
PARSONAGE GN
CHURCH RD
WITHIN WAY
Recn Gd
Mersey Way
Hale Cliff
River Mersey
8
7
85
6
5
84
4
3
83
2
1
82
45
46
47

84

83

C8
1 LEVENS WAY
2 RIDSDALE
3 LONSDALE CL
4 LEIGH GREEN CL
5 APPLEBY WLK
6 AYCLIFFE WLK

72

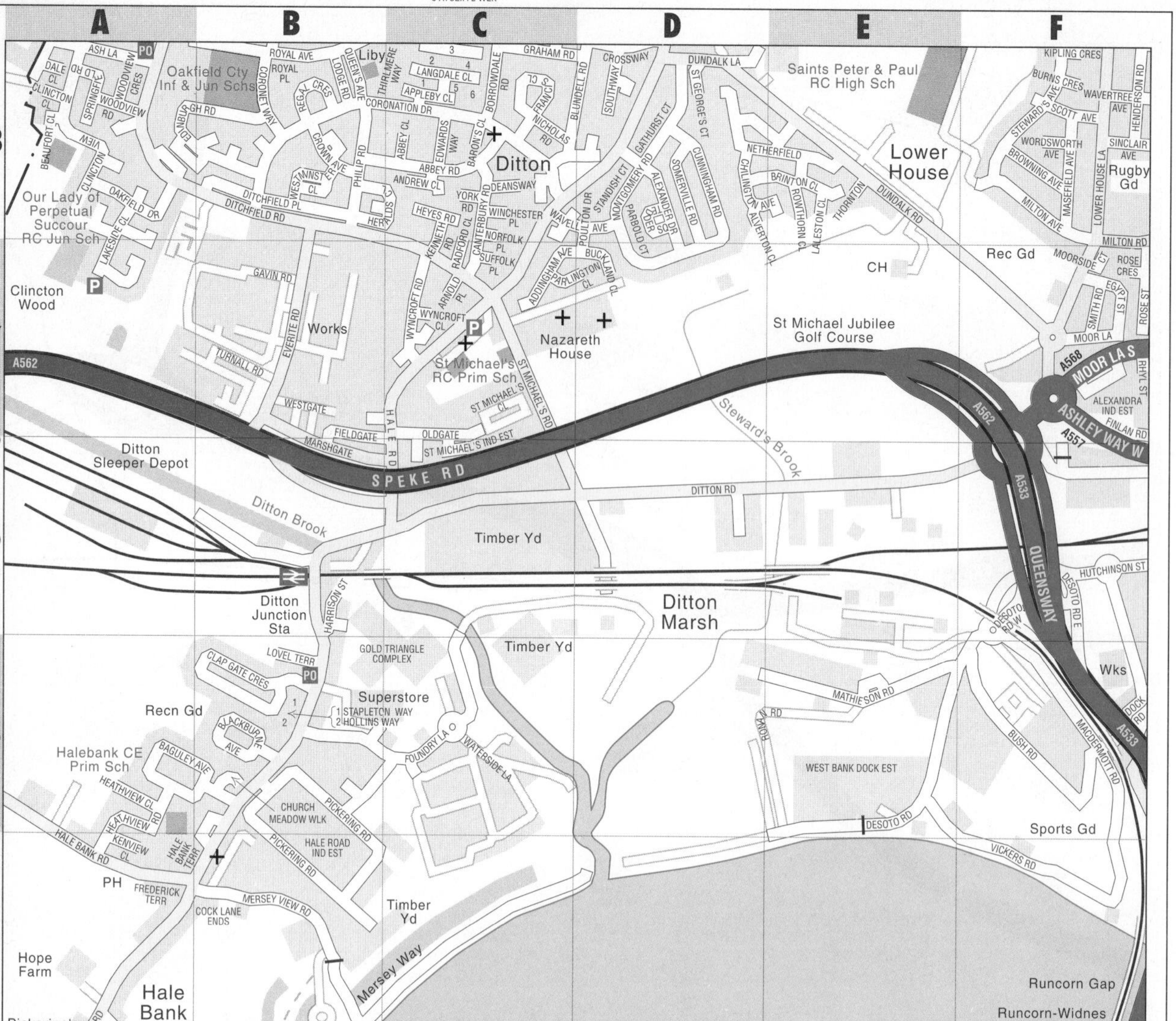

83

F1
1 PICOW ST
2 HAVERGAL ST
3 CURZON ST
4 LIGHTBURN ST
5 STANLEY VILLAS
6 SOUTHLANDS MEWS

76
86

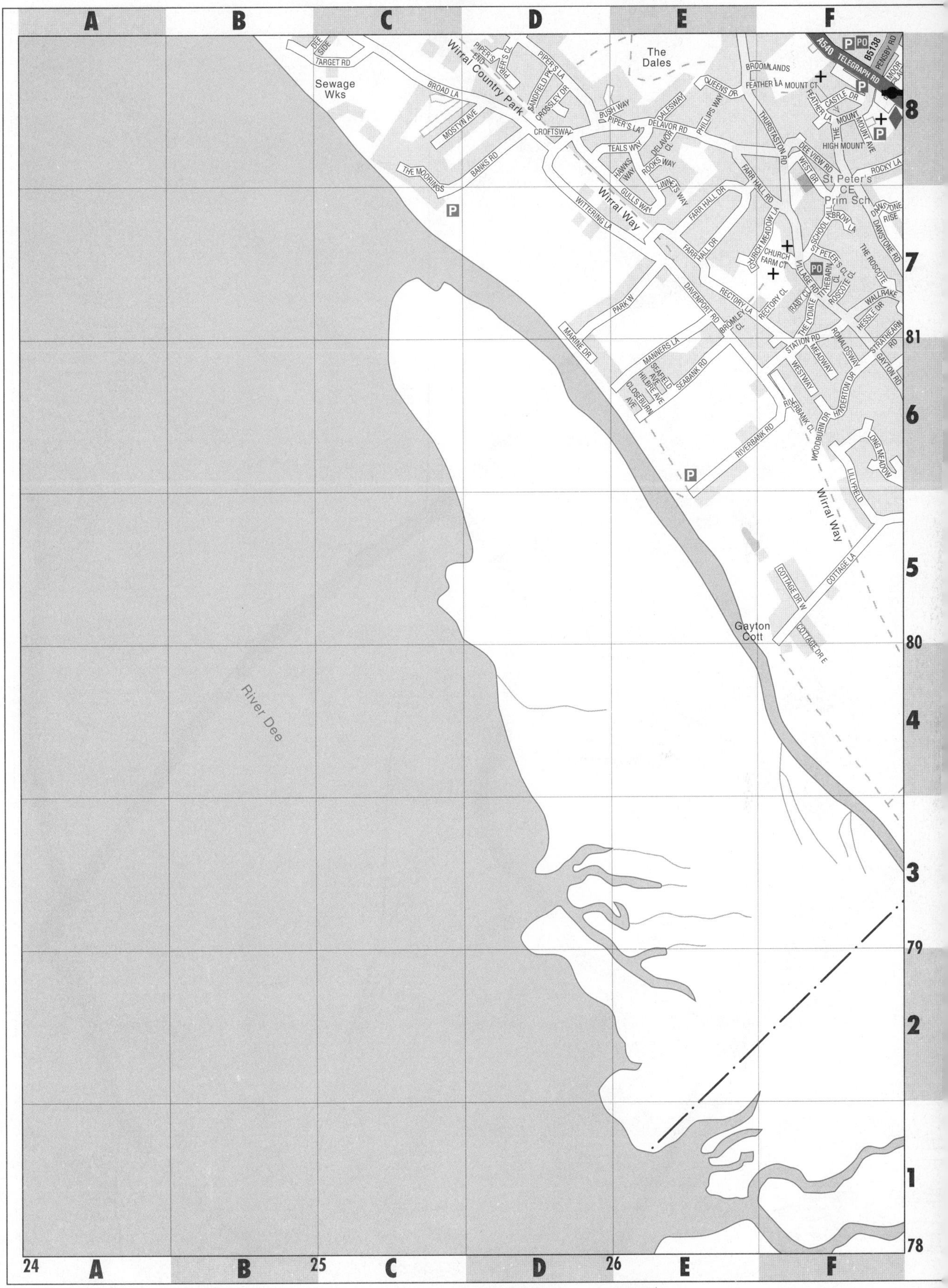
A
B
C
D
E
F
DEE SIDE
TARGET RD
Sewage Wks
Wirral Country Park
PIPER'S END
PIPER'S CL
PIPER'S LA
SANDFIELD PK
CROSSLEY DR
The Dales
BROAD LA
MOSTYN AVE
CROFTSWAY
THE MOORINGS
BANKS RD
BUSH WAY
PIPER'S LA
DALESWAY
DELAVOR RD
DELAVOR CL
TEALS WAY
HAWKS WAY
ROOKS WAY
LINNETS WAY
GULLS WAY
QUEENS DR
PHILLIPS WAY
BROOMLANDS
FEATHER LA
MOUNT CT
THURSTASTON RD
A540 TELEGRAPH RD
B5138
PENSBY RD
MOOR LA
CASTLE DR
FEATHER LA
THE MOUNT
MOUNT AVE
HIGH MOUNT
DEE VIEW RD
WEST GR
ROCKY LA
St Peter's CE Prim Sch
FARR HALL RD
FARR HALL DR
WITTERING LA
Wirral Way
CHURCH MEADOW LA
CHURCH FARM CT
SCHOOL HILL
BROW LA
DAWSTONE RISE
DAWSTONE RD
THE ROSCOTE
ST PETER'S CL
VILLAGE RD
TITHEBARN CL
ROSCOTE CL
RECTORY CL
RECTORY LA
RABY CL
THE LYDIATE
WALLRAKE
HESSLE DR
STRATHEARN RD
PARK W
DAVENPORT RD
BROMLEY CL
MARINE DR
MANNERS LA
SEAFIELD AVE
HILBRE AVE
CLOSEBURN AVE
SEABANK RD
STATION RD
MEADWAY
RONALDSWAY
WESTWAY
GAYTON RD
HADERTON DR
RIVERBANK CL
RIVERBANK RD
WOODBURN DR
LONG MEADOW
LILLYFIELD
Wirral Way
COTTAGE LA
COTTAGE DR W
COTTAGE DR E
Gayton Cott
River Dee
8
81
7
6
5
80
4
3
79
2
1
78
24
25
26

86

85
77

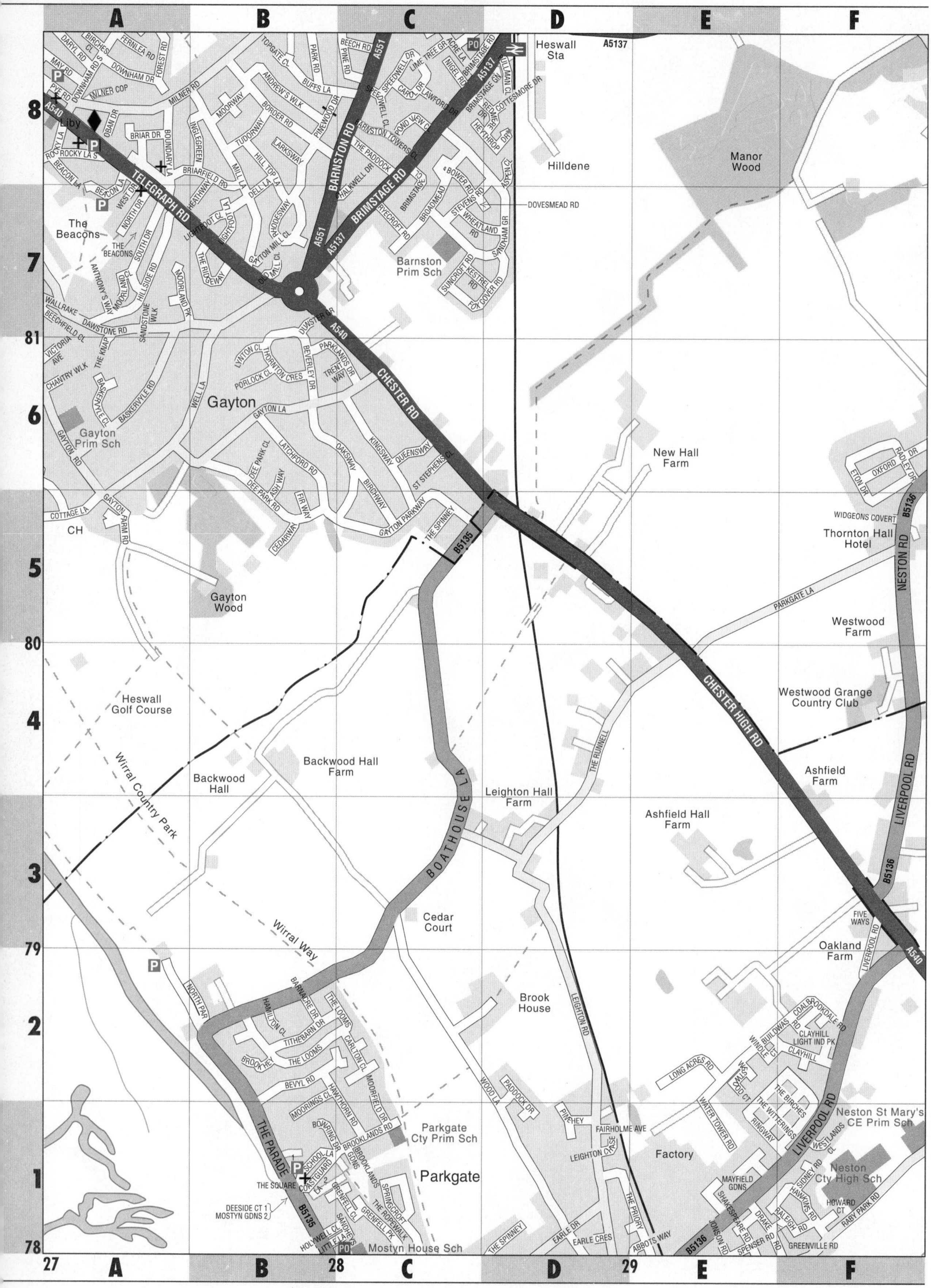
A
B
C
D
E
F
8
7
81
6
5
80
4
3
79
2
1
78
27
28
29
Heswall Sta
A5137
Manor Wood
Hilldene
DOVESMEAD RD
The Beacons
THE BEACONS
Barnston Prim Sch
Gayton
Gayton Prim Sch
New Hall Farm
WIDGEONS COVERT
Thornton Hall Hotel
CH
Gayton Wood
Westwood Farm
Heswall Golf Course
Westwood Grange Country Club
Wirral Country Park
Backwood Hall Farm
Backwood Hall
Leighton Hall Farm
Ashfield Farm
Ashfield Hall Farm
Cedar Court
Wirral Way
FIVE WAYS
Oakland Farm
Brook House
Parkgate Cty Prim Sch
Parkgate
Factory
Neston St Mary's CE Prim Sch
Neston Cty High Sch
Mostyn House Sch
Liby
TELEGRAPH RD
A540
A551
A5137
BARNSTON RD
BRIMSTAGE RD
CHESTER RD
CHESTER HIGH RD
B5135
B5136
BOATHOUSE LA
THE PARADE
LIVERPOOL RD
NESTON RD
LEIGHTON RD
WOOD LA
PARKGATE LA
THE RUNNELL
GAYTON LA
GAYTON RD
GAYTON FARM RD
GAYTON PARKWAY
COTTAGE LA
WELL LA
MILNER RD
MILL LA
DAWSTONE RD
KINGSWAY
QUEENSWAY
OAKSWAY
BIRCHWAY
ST STEPHENS CL
THE SPINNEY
DEESIDE CT 1
MOSTYN GDNS 2
THE SQUARE
NORTH PAR
CLAYHILL LIGHT IND PK
RABY PARK RD
GREENVILLE RD
FAIRHOLME AVE
LEIGHTON CHASE
EARLE DR
EARLE CRES
THE PRIORY
ABBOTS WAY
LONG ACRES RD
WATER TOWER RD
MAYFIELD GDNS
HOWARD CT

85

78
88

A
B
C
D
E
F
Clatterbridge
Thornton Manor
Wirral Manor House
Clatter Brook
M53
New Rocklands
Grange Farm
ROCKLANDS LA
CLATTERBRIDGE RD
B5151
MANOR RD
THORNTON COMMON RD
B5136
GRANGE DR
Willow Farm
The Foxes
Hesketh Grange
ST GEORGE'S WAY
Thornton Hough
SMITHY HILL
PH
PO
Thornton Hough Prim Sch
THORNTON HOUSE
CHURCH RD
1 THE BUNGALOWS
2 D'ARCY COTTS
THE FOLDS
RABY MERE RD
Lodge Farm
NESTON RD
OXFORD DR
Raby Vale
Raby Hall Farm
Thornton Farm
FOUR LANES END
RABY HALL RD
RABY RD
Hillyard Farm
HARGRAVE LA
Raby
Wheatsheaf Inn (PH)
THE GREEN
THE CROSSWAY
WILLASTON RD
Yew Tree House
Willowbrow Farm
Hargrave Hall Farm
WILLOW LA
WILLOWBROW RD
Hargrave Cottages
BENTY HEATH LA
Raby House Farm
Cherry Farm
Upland's Farm
UPPER RABY RD
Leawood
The Red Farm
CHESTER HIGH RD
SCHOOL LA
RABY PARK RD
Hinderton Hall
BIRKENHEAD RD
MILL LA
The Old Mill
Roselea
QUARRY RD
Mill Lane Farm
The Lydiate
WHITEGATES CL
WHITEGATES CRES
MEADOW LA
LYDIATE LA
HINDERTON RD
HINDERTON LA
QUARRY LA
B5134
A540
HANNS HALL RD
B5133
8
7
81
6
5
80
4
3
79
2
1
78
30
31
32

88

87
79

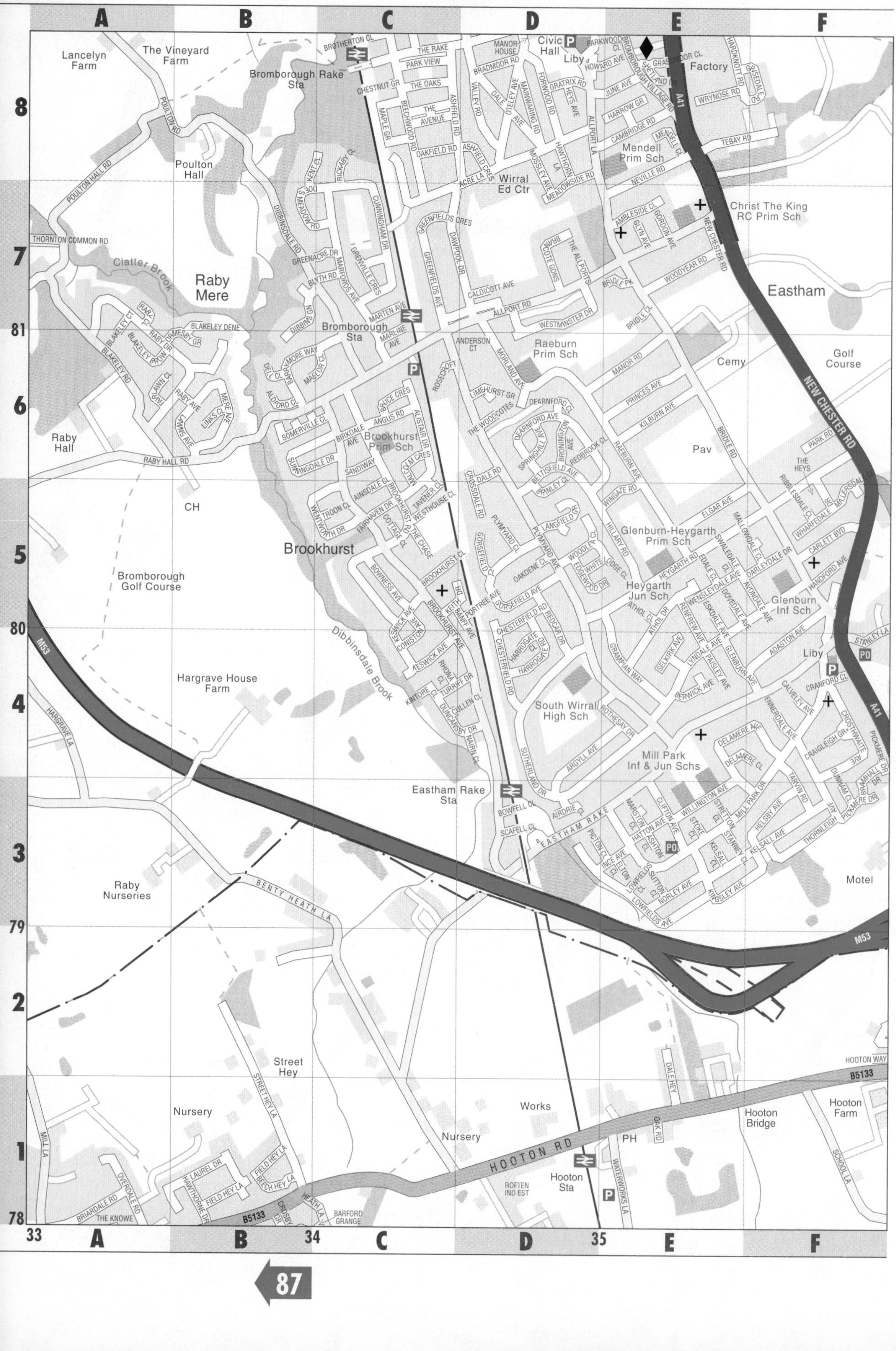
Lancelyn Farm
The Vineyard Farm
Bromborough Rake Sta
Poulton Hall
Raby Mere
Clatter Brook
Raby Hall
CH
Bromborough Golf Course
Brookhurst
Bromborough Sta
Brookhurst Prim Sch
Dibbinsdale Brook
Hargrave House Farm
Raby Nurseries
Street Hey
Nursery
Works
Hooton Sta
ROFTEN IND EST
BARFORD GRANGE
HOOTON RD
B5133
M53
A41
NEW CHESTER RD
Civic Hall
Liby
Factory
Mendell Prim Sch
Wirral Ed Ctr
Christ The King RC Prim Sch
Eastham
Raeburn Prim Sch
Cemy
Golf Course
Pav
Glenburn-Heygarth Prim Sch
Heygarth Jun Sch
Glenburn Inf Sch
South Wirral High Sch
Mill Park Inf & Jun Schs
Eastham Rake Sta
EASTHAM RAKE
BENTY HEATH LA
Motel
PO
PH
Hooton Bridge
Hooton Farm
HOOTON WAY
33
34
35
78
79
80
81

80

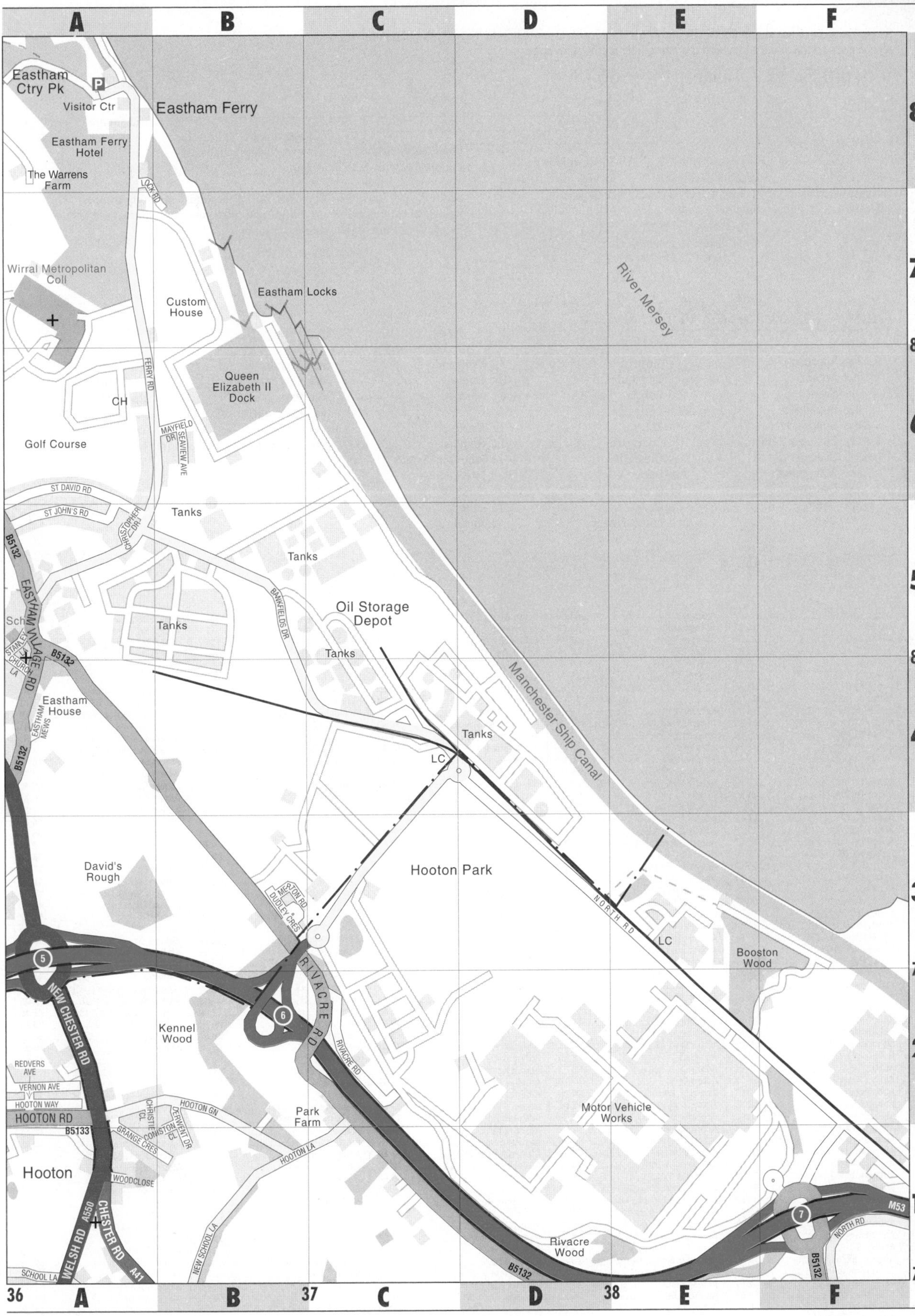
A
B
C
D
E
F
8
7
81
6
5
80
4
3
79
2
1
78
36
37
38
Eastham Ctry Pk
P
Visitor Ctr
Eastham Ferry
Eastham Ferry Hotel
The Warrens Farm
LOCK RD
Wirral Metropolitan Coll
Custom House
Eastham Locks
River Mersey
Queen Elizabeth II Dock
FERRY RD
CH
MAYFIELD DR
SEAVIEW AVE
Golf Course
ST DAVID RD
ST JOHN'S RD
CHRISTOPHER DR
Tanks
Tanks
B5132
EASTHAM VILLAGE RD
Sch
Tanks
BANKFIELDS DR
Oil Storage Depot
Tanks
STANLEY LA
CHURCH LA
B5132
Eastham House
EASTHAM MEWS
Manchester Ship Canal
Tanks
LC
B5132
David's Rough
Hooton Park
MERTON RD
DUDLEY CRES
NORTH RD
LC
Booston Wood
5
NEW CHESTER RD
RIVACRE RD
6
Kennel Wood
RIVACRE RD
REDVERS AVE
VERNON AVE
HOOTON WAY
HOOTON RD
B5133
CHRISTIE CL
CONISTON CL
DERWENT DR
GRANGE CRES
HOOTON GN
Park Farm
HOOTON LA
Motor Vehicle Works
Hooton
WOODCLOSE
A550
CHESTER RD
WELSH RD
NEW SCHOOL LA
SCHOOL LA
A41
Rivacre Wood
B5132
7
M53
NORTH RD
B5132
36
A
B
37
C
D
38
E
F

Index

Street names are listed alphabetically and show the locality, the Postcode District, the page number and a reference to the square in which the name falls on the map page

Vincent St. [4] Birkenhead L41 ....**66** D6

Full street name This may have been abbreviated on the map

Location Number If present, this indicates the street's position on a congested area of the map instead of the name

Town, village or locality in which the street falls.

Postcode District for the street name

Page number of the map on which the street name appears

Grid square in which the centre of the street falls

Schools, hospitals, sports centres, railway stations, shopping centres, industrial estates, public amenities and other places of interest are also listed. These are highlighted in magenta

Abbreviations used in the index

App	Approach	Cl	Close	Espl	Esplanade	Orch	Orchard	Sq	Square
Arc	Arcade	Comm	Common	Est	Estate	Par	Parade	Strs	Stairs
Ave	Avenue	Cnr	Corner	Gdns	Gardens	Pk	Park	Stps	Steps
Bvd	Boulevard	Cotts	Cottages	Gn	Green	Pas	Passage	St	Street, Saint
Bldgs	Buildings	Ct	Court	Gr	Grove	Pl	Place	Terr	Terrace
Bsns Pk	Business Park	Ctyd	Courtyard	Hts	Heights	Prec	Precinct	Trad Est	Trading Estate
Bsns Ctr	Business Centre	Cres	Crescent	Ind Est	Industrial Estate	Prom	Promenade	Wlk	Walk
Bglws	Bungalows	Dr	Drive	Intc	Interchange	Ret Pk	Retail Park	W	West
Cswy	Causeway	Dro	Drove	Junc	Junction	Rd	Road	Yd	Yard
Ctr	Centre	E	East	La	Lane	Rdbt	Roundabout		
Cir	Circus	Emb	Embankment	N	North	S	South		

Cawfield Ave. WA8 72 D1
Cawthorne Ave. L32 40 E8
Cawthorne Cl. L32 40 E8
Cawthorne Wlk. L32 40 E8
Caxton Cl. Birkenhead L43 65 C6
Caxton Cl. Widnes WA8 72 C3
Caxton Rd. L35 57 E1
Cazneau St. L3 52 D3
Cearns Rd. L43 66 A5
Cecil Dr. WA10 43 A4
Cecil Rd. Bebington L62 79 B8
Cecil Rd. Birkenhead L42 66 B2
Cecil Rd. Seaforth L21 37 F6
Cecil Rd. Wallasey L44 51 B4
Cecil St. Liverpool L15 68 D8
Cecil St. St Helens WA9 58 F7
Cedar Ave. Bebington L63 78 E4
Cedar Ave. Golborne WA3 47 F7
Cedar Ave. Widnes WA8 73 B2
Cedar Cl. Liverpool L18 69 D3
Cedar Cl. Prescot L35 56 E4
Cedar Cres. Huyton-w-R L36 55 D1
Cedar Cres. Newton-le-W WA12 46 D2
Cedar Cres. Ormskirk L39 13 D4
Cedar Dr. Formby L37 9 C1
Cedar Gr. Crosby L22 26 D2
Cedar Gr. Garswood WN4 34 D5
Cedar Gr. Haydock WA11 45 E7
Cedar Gr. Liverpool L8 68 C6
Cedar Gr. Maghull L31 28 D6
Cedar Gr. Orrell WN5 25 F6
Cedar Gr. Skelmersdale WN8 15 E1
Cedar Rd. Liverpool L9 39 B6
Cedar Rd. Prescot L35 56 D3
Cedar Rd. Warrington WA5 74 F6
Cedar St. Birkenhead L41 66 D5
Cedar St. Bootle L20 38 C4
Cedar St. Newton-le-W WA12 46 C2
Cedar St. Southport PR8 4 D4
Cedar St. St Helens WA10 43 D2
Cedar Towers. L33 29 F3
Cedardale Rd. L9 39 A4
Cedars The. Birkenhead L46 64 C7
Cedars The. Liverpool L12 40 F3
Cedarway. L60 86 B5
Cedarwood Cl. L49 64 B4
Cedarwood Ct. L36 70 E8
Celebration Dr. L6 53 C5
Celedine Cl. L15 68 E8
Celia St. L20 38 D1
Celt St. L6 53 C4
Celtic Rd. L47 48 E1
Celtic St. 2 L8 68 A6
Cemetery Rd. PR8 4 C4
Central Ave. Bebington L62 79 C8
Central Ave. Liverpool L24 82 D3
Central Ave. Prescot L34 56 C5
Central Ave. Southport PR8 7 F8
Central Ave. St Helens L34 & L35 57 A7
Central Dr. Haydock WA11 45 B6
Central Dr. Liverpool L12 54 B5
Central Dr. Rainford WA11 31 F7
Central Par. L24 82 E3
Central Park Ave. L44 51 C4
Central Rd. Bebington L62 79 B6
Central Rd. Bebington L62 79 C4
Central Sq. L31 20 D2
Central St. WA10 44 A4
Central Sta. L1 52 D1
Central Trad Est. L20 38 C7
Central Way. Liverpool L24 82 F2
Central Way. Newton-le-W WA12 46 E2
Centre Way. Huyton-w-R L36 55 E2
Centreville Rd. L15 & L18 69 A6
Centurion Cl. L47 48 E1
Centurion Dr. L47 48 E1
Century Rd. L23 26 D4
Ceres St. L20 38 C1
Cestrian Dr. L61 77 A5
Chadlow Rd. L32 40 F7
Chadwell Rd. L33 29 F4
Chadwick Rd. WA11 44 C7
Chadwick St. Birkenhead L46 64 E8
Chadwick St. Liverpool L3 52 B3
Chaffinch Cl. L12 40 F1
Chaffinch Glade. L26 70 E1
Chain La. WA11 44 E6
Chain Lane Sh Prec. WA11 44 D7
Chainhurst Cl. L27 70 D5
Chalfont Rd. L18 69 D1
Chalfont Way. L14 & L28 55 B7
Chalgrave Cl. WA8 73 F3
Chalkwell Dr. L60 86 C7
Challis St. L41 & L43 50 E1
Challoner Cl. L36 70 F8
Chalon Way. WA10 & WA9 44 A3
Chalon Way Ind Est. WA9 44 A2
Chalon Way W. St Helens WA10 44 A3
Chaloner Gr. L19 80 F6
Chaloner St. L1 & L72 67 D7
Chamberlain St. Birkenhead L41 66 F4
Chamberlain St. St Helens WA10 43 D3
Chamberlain St. Wallasey L44 51 A2
Chambres Rd. PR8 4 D5
Chambres Rd N. PR8 4 D6
Chancel St. L4 52 E7
Chancery La. WA9 44 E3
Chandley Cl. PR8 7 A5
Chandos St. 7 L7 53 B1
Changford Gn. L33 30 A3
Changford Rd. L33 30 A3
Channel Rd. L23 26 B3
Channel Reach. L23 26 B3
Channel The. L45 50 E8
Channell Rd. L6 53 C3
Chantrell Rd. L48 63 F2
Chantry Cl. L43 65 C6
Chantry Wlk. Ashton-in-M WN4 34 F5
Chantry Wlk. Heswall L60 86 A6
Chapel Ave. L9 39 A5
Chapel Gdns. L5 52 D5
Chapel La. Burtonwood WA5 59 F6
Chapel La. Formby L37 9 F3
Chapel La. Kirkby L31 29 A4
Chapel La. Litherland L30 27 F5
Chapel La. Litherland L30 28 A5
Chapel La. Rainhill L35 & WA9 57 F2
Chapel La. St Helens WA10 43 B4
Chapel La. Widnes WA8 72 D4
Chapel Mews. L39 13 F4
Chapel Pl. Ashton-in-M WN4 35 B3
Chapel Pl. Liverpool L19 81 C6
Chapel Rd. Hoylake L47 63 C8
Chapel Rd. 3 Liverpool L6 53 C6
Chapel Rd. Liverpool L19 81 C6
Chapel Rd. Warrington WA5 74 E3
Chapel St. Ashton-in-M WN4 35 B3
Chapel St. Haydock WA11 45 E6
Chapel St. Liverpool L2 & L3 52 C2
Chapel St. Newton-le-W WA12 46 B3
Chapel St. Ormskirk L39 13 F4
Chapel St. 9 Prescot L34 56 D6
Chapel St. Southport PR8 4 B7
Chapel St. St Helens WA10 43 F5
Chapel Street Sta. PR8 4 B7
Chapel Terr. L20 38 B3
Chapel Yd. L15 69 A7
Chapelhill Rd. L46 64 F8
Chapelhouse Wlk. L37 10 A3
Chapman Cl. Liverpool L8 67 E5
Chapman Cl. Widnes WA8 72 D4
Chardstock Dr. L25 & L27 70 C4
Charing Cross. L41 66 D6
Charlecombe St. L42 66 D4
Charlecote St. L8 67 F3
Charles Ave. Southport PR8 7 E6
Charles Ave. Warrington WA5 74 F6
Charles Berrington Rd. L15 69 A6
Charles Rd. L47 63 B6
Charles St. Birkenhead L41 66 D7
Charles St. Golborne WA3 36 A1
Charles St. St Helens WA10 44 A4
Charles Wlk. L14 54 F3
Charlesbye Ave. L39 & L40 14 B6
Charlesbye Cl. L40 14 B6
Charlesville. L43 66 B5
Charlesville Ct. L43 66 B5
Charlesworth Cl. L31 20 B5
Charley Wood Rd. L33 30 C1
Charlotte Rd. L44 51 D5
Charlotte Way. 14 L1 52 D1
Charlotte's Meadow. L63 79 A4
Charlton Ct. L43 65 F6
Charlton Pl. L13 54 A1
Charlton Rd. L13 54 A1
Charlwood Ave. L36 55 E1
Charlwood Cl. L43 65 C6
Charmalue Ave. L23 26 F4
Charmouth Cl. 2 L12 40 E3
Charnley's La. PR9 2 E7
Charnock Ave. WA12 45 F3
Charnock Rd. L9 39 D3
Charnwood Rd. L36 55 B3
Charnwood St. WA9 44 E4
Charter House. L44 51 D4
Charterhouse Cl. L25 70 B1
Charterhouse Dr. L10 28 E2
Charterhouse Rd. L25 70 B1
Chartmount Way. L25 70 B4
Chartwell Rd. PR8 7 B6
Chase Cl. PR8 3 F4
Chase Heys. PR9 2 A1
Chase The. Bebington L63 88 C5
Chase The. Liverpool L36 70 F8
Chase Way. L3 & L5 52 E4
Chatburn Ave. WA3 36 C1
Chatburn Wlk. 7 L8 67 F4
Chater Cl. L35 57 A5
Chatham Cl. L21 37 F7
Chatham Pl. L7 53 B1
Chatham Rd. L42 67 A2
Chatham St. L69 & L7 67 F8
Chatsworth Ave. Bootle L9 38 F5
Chatsworth Ave. Wallasey L44 51 C4
Chatsworth Cl. WN4 34 F4
Chatsworth Cty Prim Mix & Inf Sch. L7 68 B8
Chatsworth Dr. Liverpool L7 68 B8
Chatsworth Dr. Widnes WA8 72 C3
Chatsworth Rd. Birkenhead L42 67 A2
Chatsworth Rd. Heswall L61 76 F5
Chatsworth Rd. Rainhill L35 57 B4
Chatsworth Rd. Southport PR8 7 B6
Chatsworth St. L7 53 B1
Chatterton Rd. L12 & L14 54 C4
Chaucer Dr. L12 40 F2
Chaucer Rd. WA10 43 D6
Chaucer St. Bootle L20 38 A4
Chaucer St. Liverpool L3 52 D3
Cheadle Ave. L13 53 F4
Cheapside. Formby L37 10 A2
Cheapside. Liverpool L1 & L2 52 C2
Cheapside Alley. 13 L2 52 C2
Cheddar Cl. L25 69 F2
Cheddar Gr. Burtonwood WA5 59 F7
Cheddar Gr. Kirkby L32 40 E7
Chedworth Dr. WA8 72 C4
Chedworth Rd. L14 54 E4
Cheldon Rd. L11 40 C2
Chelford Ave. WA3 47 D8
Chellowdene. L23 27 A6
Chelmarsh Ave. WN4 35 C3
Chelsea Ct. L12 54 E8
Chelsea Lea. L9 38 F6
Chelsea Rd. Bootle L21 38 B6
Chelsea Rd. Liverpool L9 39 A6
Cheltenham Ave. L17 & L8 68 D6
Cheltenham Cl. L10 28 E1
Cheltenham Cres. L36 55 D1
Cheltenham Dr. Newton-le-W WA12 46 C5
Cheltenham Dr. Orrell WN5 25 D2
Cheltenham Rd. L45 50 E6
Cheltenham Way. PR8 4 F3
Chelwood Ave. Liverpool L14 & L16 54 E1
Chemical St. WA12 46 B3
Chemistry Rd. L24 82 C5
Chenotrie Gdns. L43 65 D5
Chepstow Ave. L44 51 C4
Chepstow Cl. WA5 60 E2
Chepstow St. L4 38 F1
Chequer Cl. WN8 24 F5
Chequer La. WN8 24 F6
Chequers Gdns. L19 68 F1
Cheriton Ave. L48 63 D2
Cheriton Cl. L26 82 E8
Chermside Rd. L17 68 E1
Cherry Ave. L4 39 B1
Cherry Cl. Liverpool L4 39 B1
Cherry Cl. Newton-le-W WA12 45 F4
Cherry Gn. L39 13 B1
Cherry La. Liverpool L4 39 B1
Cherry La. Liverpool L13 & L4 53 D8
Cherry Rd. PR8 7 D2
Cherry Sq. L44 51 B4
Cherry Tree Ave. WA5 74 F4
Cherry Tree Cl. Hale L24 83 E1
Cherry Tree Cl. Haydock WA11 45 A5
Cherry Tree Cl. Prescot L35 56 D3
Cherry Tree Dr. WA9 45 A2
Cherry Tree La. Ormskirk L39 13 B1
Cherry Tree La. St Helens WA11 33 A2
Cherry Tree Rd. Birkenhead L46 64 F8
Cherry Tree Rd. Golborne WA3 47 F8
Cherry Tree Rd. Liverpool L36 70 E8
Cherry Vale. L25 70 B3
Cherrybank. L44 51 B2
Cherrycroft. WN8 24 E6
Cherrydale Rd. L18 69 A4
Cherryfield Cres. L32 29 E2
Cherryfield Dr. L32 29 E2
Cherryfield Hts. L32 40 F7
Cherryfield Prim Sch. L32 40 E7
Cherrysutton. WA8 72 B3
Cheryl Dr. WA8 73 D1
Cheshire Acre. L49 65 A2
Cheshire Ave. L10 40 B7
Cheshire Cl. WA12 46 E3
Cheshire Gdns. WA10 43 E2
Cheshire Gr. L46 64 E7
Cheshire Way. L61 76 F3
Chesnut Gr. Birkenhead L41 & L42 66 D4
Chesnut Gr. Bootle L20 38 B4
Chesnut Gr. Liverpool L15 69 A8
Chester Ave. Golborne WA3 47 D8
Chester Ave. Litherland L30 27 F1
Chester Ave. Southport PR9 4 F8
Chester Cl. L23 27 B4
Chester Ct. L63 78 F4
Chester Dr. WN4 35 D2
Chester High Rd. Heswall L64 86 E4
Chester High Rd. Neston L64 87 A1
Chester La. WA9 58 B4
Chester Rd. Bebington L66 89 A1
Chester Rd. Heswall L60 & L64 86 C6
Chester Rd. Huyton-w-R L36 56 A4
Chester Rd. Liverpool L6 53 D5
Chester Rd. Southport PR9 4 F8
Chester Row. WA12 60 D8
Chester St. Birkenhead L41 66 F6
Chester St. Liverpool L8 67 E7
Chester St. Prescot L34 56 D6
Chester St. Wallasey L44 51 A3
Chester St. Widnes WA8 73 B1
Chester Wlk. L36 56 A4
Chesterfield Cl. PR8 7 C4
Chesterfield Dr. L33 29 E5
Chesterfield High Sch. Crosby L23 27 A4
Chesterfield High Sch (Annexe). Crosby L22 26 F1
Chesterfield Rd. Bebington L62 88 D4
Chesterfield Rd. Crosby L23 27 A4
Chesterfield Rd. Southport PR8 7 C5
Chesterfield St. L8 67 E7
Chesterton St. L19 81 C4
Chestnut Ave. Crosby L23 26 F6
Chestnut Ave. Liverpool L36 70 D8
Chestnut Ave. St Helens WA11 44 F5
Chestnut Ave. Warrington WA5 74 F6
Chestnut Ave. Widnes WA8 73 B2
Chestnut Cl. Birkenhead L49 64 C2
Chestnut Cl. Prescot L35 56 E4
Chestnut Ct. WA8 72 D1
Chestnut Gr. Ashton-in-M WN4 35 D4
Chestnut Gr. Bebington L62 88 C8
Chestnut Gr. Bootle L20 38 B5
Chestnut Gr. Golborne WA3 47 F8
Chestnut Gr. St Helens WA11 44 D7
Chestnut House. L20 38 B4
Chestnut Lodge Sch. WA8 72 E1
Chestnut Rd. Liverpool L9 39 C3
Chestnut Rd. Seaforth L21 37 F8
Chestnut St. Liverpool L7 52 F1
Chestnut St. Southport PR8 4 C5
Chestnut Way. L37 9 C1
Chetham Ct. WA2 61 A3
Chetwode Ave. WN4 35 B1
Chetwood Ave. L23 26 F5
Chetwood Dr. WA8 72 F4
Chetwynd Cl. L43 65 F4
Chetwynd Rd. L43 66 A5
Chetwynd St. L17 68 B3
Chevasse Wlk. L25 70 C3
Cheverton Cl. L49 65 B3
Chevin Rd. L9 39 A5
Cheviot Ave. St Helens WA9 44 F3
Cheviot Ave. Warrington WA2 61 A3
Cheviot Cl. L42 66 D1
Cheviot La. L33 29 F6
Cheviot Rd. Birkenhead L42 66 D1
Cheviot Rd. Liverpool L7 53 E2
Cheyne Cl. L23 26 A3
Cheyne Gdns. L19 80 F8
Cheyne Wlk. WA9 57 F6
Chichester Cl. L15 68 D8
Chidden Cl. L49 64 C3
Chigwell Cl. L12 40 E3
Chilcott Rd. L13 & L14 54 C3
Child Wall Five Ways. L15 69 C7
Childers St. 1 L13 54 A3
Childwall Abbey Rd. L16 69 E7
Childwall Ave. Birkenhead L46 & L49 64 D7
Childwall Ave. Liverpool L15 68 D7
Childwall Bank Rd. L16 69 D7
Childwall CE Prim Sch. L18 69 D5
Childwall Cl. L46 64 D7
Childwall Cres. L16 69 D7
Childwall Gn. L49 65 A2
Childwall Golf Course. L27 70 E7
Childwall Hts. L25 69 F7
Childwall La. Huyton-w-R L14 & L36 55 A2
Childwall La. Liverpool L16 & L25 69 F6
Childwall Mount Rd. L16 69 D7
Childwall Park Ave. L16 & L18 69 E6
Childwall Priory Rd. L15 & L16 69 D7
Childwall Rd. L15 69 B7
Childwall Sch. L15 69 C7
Childwall Sch (Annexe). L15 69 B8
Childwall Sch (Olive Mount Wing). L15 69 B8
Childwall Valley Rd. Liverpool L16 & L25 & L27 70 C6
Chilington Ave. WA8 84 D8
Chillerton Rd. L12 54 D8
Chillingham St. 1 L8 68 A3
Chiltern Ave. WA2 61 A3
Chiltern Cl. Ashton-in-M WN4 35 C2
Chiltern Cl. Kirkby L32 29 C4
Chiltern Cl. Liverpool L12 40 F2
Chiltern Cres. WA2 61 A3
Chiltern Dr. L32 29 C4
Chiltern Pl. WA2 61 A3
Chiltern Rd. Birkenhead L42 66 C1
Chiltern Rd. Southport PR8 7 B6
Chiltern Rd. St Helens WA9 45 A3
Chiltern Rd. Warrington WA2 61 A3
Chilwell Cl. WA8 72 D4
Chimes Rd. WN4 34 F6
China Farm La. L48 63 E3
Chindit Cl. L37 9 D2
Chippenham Ave. L49 64 C3
Chipping Ave. PR8 7 A5
Chirk Way. L46 64 F7
Chirkdale St. Bootle L4 38 E1
Chirkdale St. 2 Liverpool L4 52 E8
Chisenhale St. L3 52 C4
Chisledon Cl. WA11 45 D7
Chislehurst Ave. L25 70 B6
Chisnall Ave. WA10 43 C4
Chiswell St. L7 53 C2
Cholmondeley Rd. L48 63 B2
Cholsey Cl. Birkenhead L49 64 F4
Chorley Cl. Banks PR9 2 F5
Chorley Rd. L34 56 B6
Chorley St. WA10 43 F4
Chorley Way. L63 79 A1
Chorley's La. WA8 73 E3
Chorlton Cl. L16 69 F8
Chorlton Gr. L45 50 D5
Chris Ward Cl. 1 L7 53 C1
Christ Church CE Prim Sch. Birkenhead L41 66 C5
Christ Church CE Prim Sch. Bootle L20 38 D4
Christ Church CE Prim Sch. Ormskirk L39 13 C3
Christ Church CE (VA) Prim Sch. L46 64 E8
Christ The King RC Prim Sch. Bebington L62 88 E7
Christ the King RC Prim Sch. Liverpool L15 69 C8
Christ The King Sch. PR8 4 B2
Christchurch Rd. L43 66 B4
Christian St. L3 52 E3
Christiana Hartley Maternity Hospl. PR8 4 D5
Christie Cl. L66 89 A2
Christie St. WA8 73 D1
Christleton Cl. L43 65 D2
Christmas St. L20 38 D1
Christopher Cl. L16 69 D8
Christopher Dr. L62 89 A5
Christopher St. L4 52 F8
Christopher Taylor House. L31 28 D8
Christopher Way. L16 69 D8
Christophers Cl. L61 77 A4
Christowe Wlk. L11 40 C5
Chudleigh Cl. L26 70 E1
Chudleigh Rd. L13 53 F3
Church Alley. L1 52 D1
Church Ave. Bickershaw WN2 36 F8
Church Ave. Liverpool L9 39 B7
Church Cl. Formby L37 10 A3
Church Cl. Southport PR9 5 A8
Church Cl. Wallasey L44 51 D4
Church Close Ct. L37 10 A3
Church Cotts. L25 70 C5
Church Cres. 9 L44 51 E2
Church Dr. Bebington L62 79 B6
Church Dr. Newton-le-W WA12 46 C1
Church Dr. Orrell WN5 25 D5
Church Dr Prim Sch. L62 79 B6
Church End. L24 83 D1
Church Farm Ct. L60 85 F7
Church Fields. L39 13 E5
Church Gdns. Bootle L20 38 B3
Church Gdns. Wallasey L44 51 D4
Church Gn. Formby L37 9 C2
Church Gn. Kirkby L32 29 E3
Church Gn. Liverpool L16 69 F7
Church Gr. L21 37 F6
Church Gr. Seaforth L21 37 F6
Church Hill. L44 50 F5
Church Hill Rd. L39 13 D6
Church La. Aughton L39 21 A7
Church La. Bebington L62 79 D1
Church La. Bebington L62 89 A4
Church La. Birkenhead L49 65 B2
Church La. Bootle L4 38 F2
Church La. Golborne WA3 47 D7
Church La. Kirkby L34 41 C4
Church La. Liverpool L17 68 E1
Church La. Maghull L39 20 A8
Church La. St Helens WA10 43 A4
Church La. Thurstaston L61 76 B5
Church La. Wallasey L44 51 D4
Church Meadow La. L60 85 F7
Church Meadow Wlk. WA8 84 B5
Church Mews. L24 82 B3
Church Mount. 2 L7 53 B1
Church Rd. Bebington L63 79 A4
Church Rd. Bickerstaffe L39 22 E6
Church Rd. Birkenhead L49 65 A5
Church Rd. Birkenhead L42 66 D3
Church Rd. Bootle L21 38 C8
Church Rd. Bootle L20 38 D6
Church Rd. Crosby L23 26 E4
Church Rd. Formby L37 10 A5
Church Rd. Hale L24 83 E1
Church Rd. Haydock WA11 45 E7
Church Rd. Huyton-w-R L36 55 C3
Church Rd. Litherland L21 & L30 & L22 27 D1
Church Rd. Liverpool L4 39 A1
Church Rd. Liverpool L13 53 F3
Church Rd. Liverpool L15 & L18 69 A6
Church Rd. Liverpool L25 70 A3
Church Rd. Liverpool L26 70 F1
Church Rd. Liverpool L19 81 C5
Church Rd. Maghull L31 28 D7
Church Rd. Raby L63 87 B6
Church Rd. Rainford WA11 32 A5
Church Rd. Seaforth L22 37 E8
Church Rd. Skelmersdale WN8 15 F1
Church Rd. Southport PR9 2 F6
Church Rd. Wallasey L44 51 E2
Church Rd. West Kirby L48 63 B1
Church Rd N. L15 69 A7
Church Rd S. L25 70 A2
Church Rd W. L4 38 F2
Church Sq. 10 WA10 44 A3
Church St. Birkenhead L41 66 F6
Church St. Bootle L20 38 A3
Church St. Golborne WA3 36 B1
Church St. Liverpool L1 52 D1
Church St. Newton-le-W WA12 46 E4
Church St. Ormskirk L39 13 E5
Church St. Orrell WN8 25 C7
Church St. Orrell WN5 25 E5
Church St. Prescot L34 56 D6
Church St. Southport PR9 4 C7
Church St. St Helens WA10 44 A3
Church St. Wallasey L44 51 D4
Church Terr. L42 66 D3
Church View. Aughton L39 21 A7
Church View. Bootle L20 38 B3
Church View. Liverpool L12 54 B7
Church View Ct. L39 13 E5
Church Way. Formby L37 9 C2
Church Way. Kirkby L32 29 E3
Church Way. Litherland L30 27 D5
Church Wlk. Bootle L20 38 B3
Church Wlk. Winwick WA2 61 A6
Church Wlks. L39 13 E5
Churchdown Cl. L14 54 F4
Churchdown Gr. L14 54 E4
Churchdown Rd. L14 54 E4
Churchfield Rd. L25 70 C5
Churchfields. Southport PR8 3 F3
Churchfields. 5 St Helens WA9 58 C4
Churchfields. Widnes WA8 73 B5
Churchgate. Southport PR9 1 F1
Churchgate Mews. PR9 2 A1
Churchill Ave. PR9 1 F2
Churchill Gr. L44 51 C5
Churchill House. 6 L21 37 F7
Churchill Ind Est. L9 39 C8
Churchill Way. L1 & L3 52 D2
Churchlands. 13 L44 51 E2
Churchmeadow Cl. L44 51 D4
Churchtown Ct. PR9 2 A2
Churchtown Prim Sch. PR9 2 B2
Churchview Rd. L41 66 B8
Churchway Rd. L24 83 A2
Churchwood Cl. L62 79 D1
Churchwood Ct. L49 65 B1
Churn Way. L49 64 D4
Churnet St. L4 52 E8
Churston Rd. L16 69 E5
Churton Ave. L43 65 F3
Churton Ct. 22 L6 53 A3

Ordnance Survey STREET ATLASES ORDER FORM

NEW COLOUR EDITIONS

	HARDBACK	SPIRAL	POCKET	
	Quantity @ £10.99 each	Quantity @ £8.99 each	Quantity @ £4.99 each	£ Total
BERKSHIRE	0 540 06170 0	0 540 06172 7	0 540 06173 5	➤
	Quantity @ £10.99 each	Quantity @ £8.99 each	Quantity @ £3.99 each	£ Total
MERSEYSIDE	0 540 06480 7	0 540 06481 5	0 540 06482 3	➤
	Quantity @ £12.99 each	Quantity @ £8.99 each	Quantity @ £4.99 each	£ Total
SURREY	0 540 06435 1	0 540 06436 X	0 540 06438 6	➤
	Quantity @ £12.99 each	Quantity @ £9.99 each	Quantity @ £4.99 each	£ Total
DURHAM	0 540 06365 7	0 540 06366 5	0 540 06367 3	➤
GREATER MANCHESTER	0 540 06485 8	0 540 06486 6	0 540 06487 4	➤
HERTFORDSHIRE	0 540 06174 3	0 540 06175 1	0 540 06176 X	➤
TYNE AND WEAR	0 540 06370 3	0 540 06371 1	0 540 06372 X	➤
SOUTH YORKSHIRE	0 540 06330 4	0 540 06331 2	0 540 06332 0	➤
WEST YORKSHIRE	0 540 06329 0	0 540 06327 4	0 540 06328 2	➤
	Quantity @ £14.99 each	Quantity @ £9.99 each	Quantity @ £4.99 each	£ Total
LANCASHIRE	0 540 06440 8	0 540 06441 6	0 540 06443 2	➤

BLACK AND WHITE EDITIONS

	HARDBACK	SOFTBACK	POCKET	
	Quantity @ £12.99 each	Quantity @ £9.99 each	Quantity @ £4.99 each	£ Total
BRISTOL AND AVON	0 540 06140 9	0 540 06141 7	0 540 06142 5	➤
CARDIFF	0 540 06186 7	0 540 06187 5	0 540 06207 3	➤
CHESHIRE	0 540 06143 3	0 540 06144 1	0 540 06145 X	➤
DERBYSHIRE	0 540 06137 9	0 540 06138 7	0 540 06139 5	➤
EDINBURGH	0 540 06180 8	0 540 06181 6	0 540 06182 4	➤
GLASGOW	0 540 06183 2	0 540 06184 0	0 540 06185 9	➤
STAFFORDSHIRE	0 540 06134 4	0 540 06135 2	0 540 06136 0	➤

See more titles overleaf

Ordnance Survey STREET ATLASES ORDER FORM

BLACK AND WHITE EDITIONS

	HARDBACK Quantity @ £12.99 each	SOFTBACK Quantity @ £8.99 each	POCKET Quantity @ £4.99 each	£ Total
EAST ESSEX	0 540 05848 3	0 540 05866 1	0 540 05850 5	
WEST ESSEX	0 540 05849 1	0 540 05867 X	0 540 05851 3	
NORTH HAMPSHIRE	0 540 05852 1	0 540 05853 X	0 540 05854 8	
SOUTH HAMPSHIRE	0 540 05855 6	0 540 05856 4	0 540 05857 2	
EAST KENT	0 540 06026 7	0 540 06027 5	0 540 06028 3	
NOTTINGHAMSHIRE	0 540 05858 0	0 540 05859 9	0 540 05860 2	
OXFORDSHIRE	0 540 05986 2	0 540 05987 0	0 540 05988 9	
EAST SUSSEX	0 540 05875 0	0 540 05874 2	0 540 05873 4	
	Quantity @ £12.99 each	Quantity @ £9.99 each	Quantity @ £4.99 each	£ Total
BUCKINGHAMSHIRE	0 540 05989 7	0 540 05990 0	0 540 05991 9	
WEST KENT	0 540 06029 1	0 540 06031 3	0 540 06030 5	
WEST SUSSEX	0 540 05876 9	0 540 05877 7	0 540 05878 5	

BLACK AND WHITE EDITIONS

	HARDBACK Quantity @ £10.99 each	SOFTBACK Quantity @ £8.99 each	POCKET Quantity @ £4.99 each	£ Total
WARWICKSHIRE	0 540 05642 1	—	—	

Name...

Address...

....

....Postcode

◆ Free postage and packing

◆ All available titles will normally be dispatched within 5 working days of receipt of order but please allow up to 28 days for delivery

☐ Please tick this box if you do not wish your name to be used by other carefully selected organisations that may wish to send you information about other products and services

Registered Office: Michelin House, 81 Fulham Road, London SW3 6RB.
Registered in England number: 1974080

I enclose a cheque / postal order, for a **total** of

made payable to *Reed Book Services*, or please debit my

☐ Access ☐ American Express ☐ Visa

account by

Account no ☐☐☐☐ ☐☐☐☐ ☐☐☐☐ ☐☐☐☐

Expiry date ☐☐ ☐☐

Signature...

Post to:
Reed Books Direct, 43 Stapledon Road, Orton Southgate, Peterborough PE2 6TD